Indian Mujahideen

Indian Mujahideen

Brij Lal, IPS (Retd.)

Published by
PRABHAT PRAKASHAN PVT. LTD.
4/19 Asaf Ali Road,
New Delhi-110 002 (INDIA)
e-mail: prabhatbooks@gmail.com

ISBN 978-93-5521-847-6
INDIAN MUJAHIDEEN
by Shri Brij Lal

Edition
First, 2023

Price
₹ 700.00 (Rupees Seven Hundred only)

Printed at
R-Tech Offset Printers, Delhi

Dedication

This book is dedicated to the soldiers and officers who were a part of the Indian Army, paramilitary forces and state police forces and laid down their lives in battle against terror and extremism. This book is an attempt to keep alive the memories of their sacrifices.

संख्या-G-337/om-2/2022

योगी आदित्यनाथ

लोक भवन,
लखनऊ - 226001

दिनांक : 31 जुलाई 2022

प्राक्कथन

राज्य सभा सांसद एवं भारतीय पुलिस सेवा के पूर्व अधिकारी श्री बृजलाल जी ने अपनी लगन, परिश्रम व प्रतिबद्धता के साथ साढ़े 37 वर्षों तक पुलिस सेवा की। अपने सेवा काल के अनुभवों, अर्जित साक्ष्यों और अध्ययनों के आधार पर उन्होंने इस पुस्तक को एक दस्तावेज के रूप में संकलित किया है।

यह पुस्तक 1980 के दशक से लेकर इस सदी के पहले दशक तक की प्रमुख आतंकवादी घटनाओं से संबंधित महत्वपूर्ण जानकारियों से सम्पन्न है। इसलिए यह पुस्तक आतंकवादी संगठनों के तंत्र एवं गतिविधियों को समझने के उद्देश्य सामान्य जन के लिए महत्वपूर्ण है। पुलिस अधिकारियों और पुलिस संगठन के लिए भी यह साक्ष्यों की दृष्टि से संग्रहणीय हो सकती है।

इस पुस्तक के लिए बृजलाल जी को हार्दिक बधाई एवं शुभकामनाएं।

(योगी आदित्यनाथ)

दूरभाष : 0522-2236181 / 2239296 फैक्स - 0522-2239234 ईमेल - cmup@nic.in

Introduction

India was divided because of the obduracy of Jinnah and in August 1947, India was partitioned and a separate country called Pakistan came into existence. The demand for creation of a separate Islamic country for Muslims by dividing India was being raised since 1940. This demand was embodied in the 'Lahore Resolution' of the Muslim League. A three-day convention was organised by the Muslim League in Lahore on 22-24 March, 1940 where a formal demand was raised for creation of a separate nation by dividing India. The Congress Party did not take this demand seriously and senior leaders of the Party kept saying that creation of Pakistan was not possible. **However, in 1946 elections to the Constituent Assembly were held and nearly 90 per cent Muslims of the then undivided India voted in favour of Muslim League, thereby strengthening Jinnah's claim of creating Pakistan.**

Babasaheb Dr. Bhimrao Ambedkar believed that the Partition of India into two countries on religious lines was not practically possible, and such a Partition would be more harmful for humanity than the nation as it would lead to large-scale violence, which actually happened at the time of Partition. Babasaheb Dr. Bhimrao Ambedkar believed that Hindus and Sikhs living in the newly-created Pakistan should come to India and Muslims in India should go to Pakistan, an Islamic country created on religious lines.

Nearly 2 million people were killed in the violence that erupted due to Partition and about 10 million people were forced to leave their homes and became refugees.

Their rehabilitation took decades. India and Pakistan came into existence in the aftermath of the Partition but the cycle of violence continued to roll. The worst hit in this violence were Hindus, Sikhs and people of other non-Muslim minority groups in Pakistan.

On 8 April, 1950, an agreement was signed between India's Prime Minister Jawahar Lal Nehru and Pakistan's Prime Minister Liaquat Ali Khan. It came to be known as the 'Delhi Agreement' and it laid down that India and Pakistan will ensure the safety and security of minorities in their respective countries. India followed the Delhi Agreement and in addition to ensuring the security of Muslims in India, it also provided them equal opportunities for religious, social, cultural, economic and political freedom, thus protecting their interests. Since that time, the Congress Party chose the path of appeasement of Muslims for its own political interests and this continued unabated at the cost of neglecting the interests of the majority community, i.e. the Hindus.

On the other hand, in Pakistan, Hindus, Sikhs, Christians were subjected to mass slaughter, molestation and rape, arson and plunder, besides a campaign to forcibly convert them to Islam. **At the time of Partition, the population of Hindus and Sikhs in (the then) West Pakistan was about 24 per cent of the total population, but as per the Census of 2017, the population of Hindus had dwindled to only about 2 per cent. In East Pakistan (now Bangladesh), Hindus numbered about 28 per cent of the population whereas in 2020, their number had dropped to 8 per cent. A large number of Hindus, Sikhs and other religious minorities from Pakistan and Bangladesh fled to India, but those who stayed back were either slaughtered or forcibly converted to Islam, something that continues to this day.**

As against the situation in Pakistan and Bangladesh, the

Muslims living in India did not face any obstacle whatsoever in their progress and could lead a life of dignity like other Indians.

In less than three decades after India's independence, some Muslim fundamentalists in India started weaving a web of conspiracy to convert India from *Darul Harb* to *Darul Islam*. Pakistan was divided in 1971 and Bangladesh came into existence as a separate country. After its devastating defeat at the hands of India in the Bangladesh war of independence in 1971, Pakistan in anger initiated a conspiracy to break up India. Pakistan knows very well that it cannot ever win a direct war with India and thus it planned to inflict thousands of wounds on India without military action.

It was under this policy that on 25 April, 1977, an organisation called SIMI (Students' Islamic Movement of India) was constituted in Aligarh, Uttar Pradesh. The objective of 'SIMI' was clear – 'convert India into an Islamic land – *Gajwa-e-Hind* – and establish Darul Islam.' In order to break up India, the Khalistan movement was supported and terrorists were provided training with deadly weapons and ammunition. However, the Pakistani plot to carve Khalistan out of Punjab failed. After this failure, Pakistan devoted all its energy to getting Kashmir separated from India. At the same, terrorist activities were triggered in many other parts of India. Burning in a fire of vengeance, Pakistan has been wanting to create such a chasm between Hindus and Muslims in India that communal harmony gets disturbed. Pakistan has also been very active in extending support to Naxalites and re-igniting the Khalistan movement, apparently in the hope of defeating India in a conventional war. In order to weaken India by instigating terrorist activities through Muslim *jihadists,* who indulge in sabotage and riots, Pakistan aims to strike at the pace of development that is taking place in India and divide it again.

Over the years, Pakistan has continued to strengthen SIMI. The anti-Indian activities of this organisation continued unabated and previous regimes, including that of the Congress, took no action because of their politics of appeasement. The Government headed by former Prime Minister Atal Bihari Vajpayee, for the first-time banned SIMI on 26 September, 2001 by declaring it a 'terrorist organisation' and kept extending the duration of the ban from time to time. The United States also banned SIMI in the aftermath of the incident of 11 September, 2001 and declared it to be a terrorist organisation. Despite being banned in India, the underground activities of SIMI continued. The *Ansars* (those who help in propagating teachings of Islam) of SIMI created other organisations to continue with its activities. An important link of this decision was Indian Mujahideen, which can be considered to be a terrorist branch of SIMI.

On 6 December, 1992, following the demolition of the Babri mosque, the activities of SIMI received a boost and, in this link, on 27 February, 2002, Muslim extremists set fire to coach number S-6 of '*Sabarmati Express*' train in Godhra of Gujarat by dousing it in petrol. As many as 59 Hindus who were returning to Gujarat from a religious pilgrimage to Ram Janmabhumi, Ayodhya was killed. Those killed included several women and children. After this Godhra massacre, riots broke out in Gujarat in which about 1,000 people belonging to both Hindu and Muslim communities lost their lives.

Muslim fundamentalist organisations cited the 2002 riots as an excuse and vowed to 'take revenge', as part of which a conspiracy was hatched to kill senior leaders of the Bharatiya Janata party (BJP). Large number of training camps were organised in Kerala at Binanipuram (2006), Vagamon Kannur (December, 2007-January, 2008). In addition to Kerala, terrorist training camps were also organised in Hubli, Belagavi, Bengaluru, Castle Rock at Karnataka and Pavagarh in Gujarat. In these camps, people from the Popular Front of India (PFI) also participated besides those from SIMI and Indian Mujahideen. Jungle warfare, rock climbing, tracking, firing practice and

making bombs from locally-available ingredients to cause explosions were an integral part of the training. A conspiracy was hatched at the Binanipuram training camp to kill the then Chief Minister of Gujarat Narendra Modi and Home Minister Amit Shah.

The name of Indian Mujahideen started to emerge and gained prominence after these training camps. They were given terrorist training by Pakistan's ISI and terrorist organisation Lashkar-e-Tayyaba in the jungles of Muzaffarabad, the capital of Pakistan-occupied Kashmir. These people included more than about two dozen terrorists from Azamgarh in Uttar Pradesh. This Azamgarh module of Indian Mujahideen was behind the largest number of bomb explosions in India. Terrorists Riyaz Bhatkal, Iqbal Bhatkal, Yasin Bhatkal alias Mohammad Ahmad Siddhi Bappa from the coastal town of Bhatkal in North Karnataka, and Amir Raza Khan from Kolkata were instrumental in providing training in Pakistan to these terrorists. The major role in identifying Muslim youth in Uttar Pradesh, Karnataka, Maharashtra, Gujarat, Madhya Pradesh, Bihar, Jharkhand and West Bengal and including them in Indian Mujahideen, and later getting them trained in Pakistan was played out in the Bhatkal town of Karnataka and in Dubai. From Dubai they were sent to Pakistan and after their training was completed, they were sent on forged passports from Karachi to Nepal. They faced no problem in entering India from Nepal. The Indian Mujahideen was instrumental in causing about 700 deaths across India in the national capital, Delhi and in other places of religious, financial, cultural and tourist significance. Details of these incidents are given in this book.

Terrorists of Indian Mujahideen used to send e-mails to media houses prior to causing terrorist incidents. The first such e-mail was sent to media houses in Noida on 23 November, 2007 about 3-4 minutes before explosions in court buildings at Lucknow, Ayodhya and Varanasi. For the first time, the organisation also took the responsibility for causing the explosions in Delhi (29 October, 2005), Dashashwamedh Ghat, Varanasi (23 February, 2005), Mumbai local trains (11 July, 2006) and at Lumbini Park and Gokul Ghat in Hyderabad (25 August, 2007). In order to mislead the police, the e-mail mentioned that the organisation had no role in the explosions at Malegaon, in '*Samjhauta Express*' and Makka Masjid, Hyderabad.

The Indian Mujahideen also mentioned that they had no connection whatsoever with Pakistan's ISI, Lashkar-e-Tayyaba, Harkat-ul-Jihad-al-Islami (HUJI) and that it was an organisation of Muslims in India only, whereas the fact is that the organisations named herein were behind the formation of Indian Mujahideen and training them. The Indian Mujahideen mentioned that the immediate reason for causing explosions in three courts was the framing of two 'innocent' persons by Uttar Pradesh police in the terrorist incident in Dashashwamedh Ghat explosion, and the fracas with lawyers in Lucknow High Court premises where lawyers also decided not to fight their case. They claimed that this is why they had targeted three courts so that they could kill a large number of lawyers.

In the same manner, a detailed e-mail of 13 pages was sent regarding the Ahmedabad explosions (26 July, 2008) which, for the first time, also carried a logo of Indian Mujahideen. The e-mail contained *aayats* of Quran and comments in English, making hateful and insulting phrases against Hindus, Hinduism and Hindu religious deities. The text told the Hindus to adopt Islam in order to remain alive and that even their gods-goddesses and security forces would not be able to protect them. Just 20 days after the Ahmedabad explosions, another 7-page e-mail was sent which carried images of a 'boat-shaped bomb' and the cars used in the Ahmedabad blasts. This e-mail also tried to mislead the police and Indian security agencies.

A terror e-mail was sent following the Sheetala Ghat explosion (7 December, 2010) which was dated 6 December, 2010. It appears that the terrorists wanted to cause the explosion on 6 December, 2010 – the anniversary of the Babri mosque demolition, but the blast took place a day later, on 7 December, 2010. This e-mail also contained *aayats* of Quran with comments in English, and also phrases insulting Hindus and threatening them.

The Batala House police encounter took place on 19 September, 2008 in Delhi, in which M.C. Sharma, an Inspector of Delhi Police, was martyred and the North India commander of Indian Mujahideen Atif Amin (Sanjarpur, Azamgarh) and his accomplice Sajid, were killed. It was a huge setback for the Indian Mujahideen. In a show of retaliation, it caused an explosion in a car near the Jama Masjid of Delhi and also opened fire on a bus carrying foreign tourists, injuring many people. On this occasion also, the Indian Mujahideen sent a 5-page e-mail, which contained *aayats* of Quran, besides comments and threats in English. This e-mail had signature in the name of Al-Arabi in capital letters in English.

All the e-mails sent by Indian Mujahideen have been reproduced in their original form in this book and these would be eye-openers for the readers. These e-mail messages also reveal the intention of Indian Mujahideen and other terrorist organisations, which is primarily one – to convert India into an Islamic country at any cost, for which bloody *jihad* is the only way.

I have served in the police service for over 37 years and I have been in-charge of crime, law and order, STF and ATS for four-years-and-a-half. In the year 2011-12, I was the Director-General of Police in a vast State like Uttar Pradesh. I have tried to present my long experiences through this book, which is based upon terrorist incidents from the beginning of the decade in 1980. In addition to my experiences, this book is also based on interrogation reports of terrorists and authentic descriptions in police records.

Many political parties in the country have indulged in petty politics on terrorist incidents. I have also brought to the fore such facts so that the people would become aware and alert. Leftists, fundamentalists, media under the influence of certain political parties, NGOs and some writers also tried to mislead the people on terrorist incidents. Besides unravelling such efforts, this book will prove to be a useful reference for police organisations. Knowledge gained by experience is much more useful than academic knowledge. In the course of discharging my responsibilities during my long police tenure, I also became the target of some political persons and had to face many difficulties. I have learnt a lot from the ups and downs of my life's experiences. I still remember a verse recited by Obaidur Rahman Sahab, my mathematics teacher in Class 10 in the year 1970 and which I present here in honour of my *guru*:

'Rang lati hai hina, patthar par ghis jaane ke baad; Surkhuru hota hai insaan, thokrein khaane ke baad.'

(The colour of henna unveils itself after being grounded on a stone; a man becomes stronger only after suffering setbacks.)

—Brij Lal

Acknowledgements

I undertook a lot of research while writing this book. I express my gratitude to Shri Rajeev Sabbharwal, ADG, Meerut Zone, Shri Tej Bahadur Singh, Deputy SP, Shri Pradeep Kumar Srivastava, retired Joint Director (Prosecution) and my colleagues in Uttar Pradesh ATS and STF for their help in my research. I am also grateful to Dr. Narendra Kumar Amin, retired IPS officer of Gujarat, whom I could not meet in person, but who gave me correct and factual information on my questions asked over telephone.

I am also grateful to Shri Rambhai H. Mokariya, Member of Rajya Sabha from Gujarat, who not only provided me the copy of the ruling of the court on Ahmedabad serial blasts, but also provided me the Hindi translation of the main portion of the ruling written in Gujarati.

I am grateful to Vipin Kumar Shukla, Constable in Uttar Pradesh Police, for his valuable contribution to the Hindi edition of this book. He took out time after his duty hours to help me complete this book.

I am grateful to Mr. Ratan Mani Lal, a prominent journalist and former editor in *The Times of India*, *Hindustan Times* and the Bhaskar Group, for agreeing to supervise and edit the English text.

—Brij Lal

Contents

1
Usaba Committee

A few years before the terrorist organisation called Indian Mujahideen came into existence, a meeting of some fundamentalist Muslim leaders was convened in the year 2002 in Bhatkal town of North Karnataka, at which it was decided to launch a 'holy war' against India. It was decided at this meeting to constitute an Usaba Committee. '*Usaba*' is an Arabic word used for a group or a congregation that has more than 11 men, but less than 40. The newly-formed Usaba Committee had as its members the residents of Bhatkal in Karnataka:

1. Iqbal Bhatkal, son of Ismail Shah Bandari, resident of Bhatkal, Karnataka (living in Pakistan).
2. Riyaz Bhatkal, son of Ismail Shah Bandari, resident of Bhatkal, Karnataka (living in Pakistan).
3. Yasin Bhatkal, son of Zarrar Siddhi Bappa, resident of Bhatkal, Karnataka (sentenced to death for terrorist activities).
4. Zasim Saeedi, son of Iqbal Saeedi, resident of Maqdoom Colony, Bhatkal, Karnataka.
5. Salim Ishaqi, son of Hasan Ishaqi, resident of Bhatkal Madina Colony, Karnataka (living in Pakistan).
6. Sajid Salfi, son of Dr. Arif, resident of Bhatkal Madina Colony, Karnataka (living in Oman).
7. Shabbir Gandavali, resident of Bhatkal, Karnataka.
8. Sultan Armar, son of Husain Armar, resident of Bhatkal

Madina Colony, Karnataka (living in Pakistan).

9. Shafi Armar, son of Husain Armar, resident of Bhatkal Madina Colony, Karnataka (living in Pakistan).
10. Farhan Damda, son of Syed Ghafoor, resident of Bhatkal, Karnataka (living in Pakistan).
11. Ismail Gora (White Uncle), resident of Bhatkal, Karnataka.

The Usaba Committee was formed on the inspiration of Basheer Hasan to motivate Muslim youth towards fundamentalism. Basheer Hasan and Shabbir were brought to Bhatkal by Yasin Bhatkal alias Mohammad Ahmad Siddhi Bappa. The idea of launching a war against India was discussed at meetings held in the house of Iqbal Bhatkal. It was decided that Muslims must launch a *jihad* to establish Islamic rule in the entire world including India and to enforce *sharia* law. Everyone present at these meetings agreed that it was not possible to convert India into an Islamic country by democratic means and that a bloody *jihad* was the only way to establish an Islamic country (*Gajwa-e-Hind)*. Trained young men were required to launch such a war against India, for which a plan was prepared to train fighters with the assistance of Lashkar-e-Tayyaba, the terror organisation headed by Hafiz Sayeed and by Pakistan's ISI.

Mohammad Ahmad Siddhi Bappa alias Yasin Bhatkal was associated with Usaba Committee since the beginning. He went to Dubai where he stayed for about two years, till 2004. His father Zarrar Siddhi Bappa was already living in Dubai. There, Yasin Bhatkal met Tariq Anjum and Gauhar Aziz and Riyaz Bhatkal introduced Yasin Bhatkal to Amir Raza Khan of Kolkata. Incidentally, Amir Raza Khan was the brother of terrorist Asif Raza Khan. On 7 December, 2001, Asif Raza Khan was killed in a police encounter in Gujarat. Asif was connected to Pakistan's terror organisation, Jaish-e-Mohammad. He was being taken by the Gujarat police for interrogation when he complained of uneasiness and asked for water to drink. The accompanying policemen unlocked his handcuffs and gave him water. Suddenly, Asif snatched the AK-47 gun of a policeman and shot at the policemen. In return firing by the policemen, Asif was killed. He was involved in the kidnapping for ransom of Rajkot businessmen Paresh Shah and Bhaskar Parikh on 12 November, 2000. He had also kidnapped Pratim Roy Burman, the proprietor of Khadim Shoe Company, in Kolkata on 25 July, 2001. At that time, Burman was released after the payment of a ransom of Rs. 3 crore 75 lakh. This money was sent to a Dubai-based terrorist Aftab Ansari. He was closely connected to Mohammad Umar Sheikh Sayeed, the Pakistani commander of Jaish-e-Mohammad. Umar was arrested in the year 1994 with RDX explosives at Adarsh Nagar in Delhi. However, on 24 December, 1999, Umar Sheikh along with Azhar Masood was released at Kandahar in Afghanistan in lieu of the release of passengers of hijacked flight IC-814 of Indian Airlines.

In retaliation to Asif's killing, Amir Raza Khan had formed ARCF (Asif Raza Commando Force) and while living in Pakistan, he had come in close contact with Hafiz Sayeed of Lashkar-e-Tayyaba, Al-Qaeda, Pakistan's ISI, HUJI, Jaish-e-Mohammad and other terrorist organisations. Amir Raza Khan had played a major role in getting terrorists of Indian Mujahideen trained in Pakistan.

Amir Raza Khan used to go frequently to Dubai from Karachi. It was through Amir that Yasin Bhatkal had gone for training from Dubai to Karachi in December, 2005 and from there, he was sent to Lashkar-e-Tayyaba training centre at Muzaffarabad, Pakistan-occupied Kashmir, (PoK). The entire expense of this training was borne by Amir Raza Khan. In the training spread over 50 days, he was trained in dismantling and assembling weapons, operating pistols, AK-47, Indian SLR, Chinese rifles, LMG and using grenades. The explosives training was the most significant aspect in which he was trained in using locally-available ingredients. Bhatkal had acquired the expertise of using hydrogen peroxide (H_2O_2) for making bombs in Pakistan and this technique was used in executing the Sheetala Ghat explosion on 7 December, 2010 in Varanasi. In the beginning of January, 2006, Yasin Bhatkal completed his training and went to Dubai and expanded his contacts with Muslim fundamentalists in Dubai.

□

2
Karnataka Forum for Dignity (KFD)

In Dubai, Yasin Bhatkal came into contact with Abdul Rahman Berry of Karnataka, who had formed an organisation named Karnataka Forum for Dignity (KFD) to seek revenge for communal riots in Karnataka, in January 2006. This organisation was later merged into Popular Front of India (PFI). While in Dubai, Yasin also met Khalil of KFD, Abu Bhai alias Ahmad Baba, Nawaz, Razzaq, Sameer, Fakeera alias Fakir Ahmad. The objective of KFD was to ensure the presence of a group of trained personnel in the event of a riot to seek revenge against Hindus. Firing practice was provided with an airgun at Abdul Rahman Berry's house in Dubai and training to make bombs was provided with material easily available in India. Yasin Bhatkal came to India with some of his friends and set up a training centre in the farmhouse of Abdul Rahman Berry at Hakkal, Mavai Kudregaddi Koppa, district Chikmagalur. A local resident named Shakeel gave him 8 acres of land onlease. Training was organised in firing airguns and making bombs using potassium chlorate, potassium permanganate and ammonium nitrate. Burnt mobil oil and gelatin were also used in this process. Yasin fabricated a container in the shape of a wooden boat and the bomb thus made was known as the 'boat-shaped bomb' that proved to be quite effective. It is from here that Yasin became an expert in making bombs and occupied a high place in Indian Mujahideen.

□

3
SIMI (Students' Islamic Movement of India)

SIMI was constituted on 25 April, 1977 at Aligarh, Uttar Pradesh. Its founder-president was Mohammad Ahmadullah Siddiqui, a Professor in English and Journalism at Western Illinois University in the USA. This organisation of young extremist students had announced to launch a *jihad* against India. It was SIMI's objective to either forcibly convert all non-Muslims in India to Islam or turn India into Darul Islam (land of Islam) through use of violence. They believed that it was not possible to do so through democratic means. Democracy has deep roots in India and it is the world's largest democratic country. Therefore, they decided that 'violent *jihad*' was the only means to achieve this. Because of the communal riots that took place in India in 1980 and 1990, fundamentalist Muslim youth rapidly turned towards SIMI. On 6 December, 1992, the Babri mosque structure was demolished by *kar sevaks*, leading to widespread communal riots across India. Members of SIMI took part in these riots and clashed with the police and activists of Vishwa Hindu Parishad and other Hindu organisations in the nationwide violence.

This organisation had openly turned into a terrorist organisation, as a result of which the Government of India banned it several times and outrightly banned it completely on 8 February, 2006. In the aftermath of the attacks of

11 September, 2001, the USA also banned it on 26 September, 2001. However, despite the ban, the underground activities of SIMI continued unabated at a greater pace. Several incidents of bomb explosions and communal riots in the country were linked to SIMI.

The members of SIMI changed the name of the organisation in the year 2002 to Indian Mujahideen and organised terrorist incidents under this name. SIMI also used to publish and distribute provocative material throughout the country.

□

4
SIMI training camps

(Plot was hatched in Vagamon Camp to assassinate Narendra Modi)

SIMI had set up several terrorist training camps in the South Indian state of Kerala. Because of the laxity of the Kerala Government, SIMI organised several terrorist training camps in Kerala and some of them were as follows:

Binanipuram Camp

A camp was organised at Binanipuram near Aluva in Ernakulam district of Kerala, in 2006. About 40-50 members of SIMI were imparted commando training and jungle warfare tactics in this camp.

Vagamon Camp (December, 2007-January, 2008)

A camp was organised at Vagamon in Thangalpara of Idukki district of Kerala. Participants in this camp were imparted training in commando action, jungle warfare tactics, tracking, rock climbing, rappelling and herbal medicines. Provocative speeches were delivered to incite the participants to launch a war against India. About two dozen participants from Hubli, Belgaum and Bangaluru were trained by explosives expert Abdul Shubhan Qureshi to make bombs with easily-available ingredients. Ammonium nitrate is a commonly available chemical fertiliser. Camp participants were trained to make bombs by mixing some other chemicals with ammonium nitrate. Hydrogen peroxide is also easily available in the market and prototypes of liquid bombs made with this chemical were used for the first time at the Vagamon camp. Youths from Kerala were recruited in terrorist organisations before being sent for training to Lashkar-e-Tayyaba training camps in Pakistan.

It was in Vagamon camp that a conspiracy was hatched to assassinate the then Chief Minister of Gujarat Narendra Modi and the state's Home Minister Amit Shah. It was planned to cause explosions in Ahmedabad and Surat in Gujarat. **On 26 July, 2006, a car bomb explosion was caused in the civil hospital at Ahmedabad as part of this plot. Out of the total 56 victims who lost their lives in this blast, 28 were killed in the car bomb explosion at the hospital gate. The terrorists had expected the Gujarat Chief Minister and Home Minister to visit the hospital to meet the victims admitted there and thus be killed in the explosion. Fortunately, the two leaders were unharmed.**

Castle Rock Camp, Karnataka

In April, 2007, SIMI organised a terrorist training camp at Castle Rock near Hubli, in Karnataka. Hubli is an important city of Karnataka and the twin city of Hubli-Dharwad is largest in North Karnataka, in terms of size and population. During this time, there was a surge in activities of extremist Muslim organisations in North Karnataka.

Pavagarh Camp, Gujarat

A training camp was organised on an abandoned piece of land near the Khundpir (also known as Khundmir) Dargah at Pavagarh in Gujarat, in January 2008. Finishing touches were given to carry out bomb explosions in Ahmedabad and Surat and assassinate Gujarat Chief Minister Narendra Modi and Home Minister Amit Shah. Terrorists of SIMI and Indian Mujahideen were trained here to cause bomb explosions in Ahmedabad and Surat.

Kannur Camp (23 April, 2013)

On 23 April, 2013, a terrorist training camp was organised in a building of the Thanal Foundation Trust at Mayyil Narath area of Kannur district of Kerala. It was organised jointly by SIMI and Popular Front of India (PFI), In a raid by the police, country-made bombs, a human effigy and ingredients for making bombs were recovered, and 21 persons were arrested. Police investigations revealed that the camp was organised by activists of PFI and its political arm Social Democratic Party of India, and terrorists of Indian Mujahideen also participated in this camp.

□

5

Two sides of the same coin – SIMI and Indian Mujahideen (IM)

Iqbal Bhatkal, Riyaz Bhatkal, Amir Raza Khan (Kolkata) and Yasin Bhatkal had established deep connections with Pakistan's ISI and terrorist organisation Lashkar-e-Tayyaba. Pakistan was engaged in terrorist activities in India through its terror organisations – Lashkar-e-Tayyaba, Jaish-e-Mohammad, Al Burq, HUJI, Hijbul Mujahideen, etc. The involvement of Pakistan in terror incidents in India was being revealed at the international level, although Pakistan had been denying this. The incident on 11 September, 2001 (known as the 9/11 incident) in the USA shook the entire world. Onthis date, terrorists of Al-Qaeda hijacked four commercial aircraft and crashed two of them into the World Trade Centre in New York. The incident caused the deaths of about 3,000 people, including 19 terrorists. One aircraft was crashed into the western part of Pentagon, the US Department of Defence headquarters, causing extensive damage. The third aircraft was being flown towards Washington DC, but the passengers clashed with the terrorist hijackers and the aircraft crashed in the fields of Pennsylvania. The terrorists had apparently targeted the US Capitol in Washington DC or the White House, the US President's residence. The incident shook not only the US but also its allies in Europe. The US attacked Afghanistan after this incident.

Earlier, when terror incidents used to take place in India,

hardly any note was taken by the rest of the world. But after the terror incident in the US, the global community came together and decided to take stern action against terrorists. The international community knew that the links of terrorists were connected to Afghanistan as well as Pakistan. It was quite natural for Pakistan to face the heat.

There used to be involvement of Pakistani terrorists in terror incidents in India and their number increased significantly in Kashmir. On 24 December, 1999, an Indian Airlines plane IC-814 was hijacked shortly after taking off from Tribhuvan Airport at Kathmandu in Nepal. It was then taken to Kandahar in Afghanistan and the then Taliban Government in Afghanistan gave full support to the hijackers. **In order to seek the security of the aircraft and the passengers, the Indian Government was forced to release dreaded Pakistan terrorists Maulana Masood Azhar, head of the Jaish-e-Mohammad, Ahmad Zargar and Sheikh Ahmad Umar Sayeed, from captivity in Indian jails.**

The pressure of the global community increased on Pakistan. The involvement of Pakistan in terrorist incidents in India increasingly came to light. In this situation, Pakistan resorted to training Indian fundamentalist Muslims and then getting them to strike terror in India, so that Pakistan could clearly tell the global community that such incidents were being caused by Muslims of India. Although SIMI had been banned in India, but its underground activities were continuing. Pakistan directed the formation of Indian Mujahideen by bringing SIMI cadres together and it was decided to train them at the Muzaffarabad training centre of Lashkar-e-Tayyaba headed by Hafiz Sayeed.

Riyaz Bhatkal, Iqbal Bhatkal, Yasin Bhatkal of Karnataka and Amir Raza Khan of Kolkata played important roles in the establishment of Indian Mujahideen. These people were looking for a suitable individual who could bring more recruits to Indian Mujahideen from North India, besides from South India. Their search was for a young, educated and energetic man, who could strengthen the organisation. Iqbal and Riyaz Bhatkal used to visit Mumbai frequently. There is a significant presence in Mumbai of people from eastern Uttar Pradesh.

One day, the Bhatkal brothers met Mohammad Sadiq Sheikh, a programming engineer from Azamgarh, Uttar Pradesh. Sheikh lived at Cheeta Camp in Trombay, Mumbai. On meeting him, the Bhatkal brothers felt that their search had come to an end. They associated him with the Usaba Committee and sought his help in launching a war against India. It emerged in their discussions that it was not possible to launch such a war without proper training. The Bhatkal brothers gave him the responsibility of bringing around more young men from Eastern Uttar Pradesh and sending them to Pakistan for training.

Sadiq Sheikh came to Azamgarh and his first meeting was with an electrician named Arif Badr. Sadiq was on the lookout for a man who was proficient in the working of electrical appliances as well as of radio sets. Arif Badr knew both as he ran an electronic appliances shop at Sanjarpur in Azamgarh. He was also an expert in repairing mobile phones and radio sets. On Sheikh Sadiq's advice, Arif Badr shifted his shop from Sanjarpur to Sarai Meer, also in Azamgarh. Sadiq Sheikh used this man in making electronic switches to cause bomb explosions. It was found later that electronic switches made in Azamgarh were used in several bomb explosions across the country.

After consulting Riyaz and Iqbal Bhatkal, Sadiq Sheikh started recruiting young men for his campaign. In the first move, Sadiq sent Azamgarh's Arif Badr and Dr. Shahnawaz Alam to Dubai for an onward journey to Muzaffarabad in Pakistan-occupied Kashmir for their training at Lashkar-e-Tayyaba training centres. Sadiq Sheikh was instrumental in training about a dozen-and-a-half terrorists from Azamgarh and they eventually joined the Indian Mujahideen to become responsible for causing bomb explosions that led to the death of more than 700 people.

Riyaz and Iqbal Bhatkal strengthened the organisation by

bringing together people from Karnataka, Andhra Pradesh and Maharashtra. The number of members of Indian Mujahideen grew steadily and these included those from Azamgarh in U.P., Maharashtra and Karnataka who were already 'Ansars' as members of SIMI. In the fund-raising exercise for this new terrorist organisation, a lot of money was collected, including funds from those living in Gulf countries, in the name of launching *jihad* in India. Through the efforts of Bhatkal brothers and Amir Raza Khan, a lot of funds were raised from Dubai for *jihad*. Now they started thinking about raising a new terrorist organisation in place of Usaba Committee. In the beginning, they sought the help of Bangladesh-based terror organisation HUJI.

Prior to this, terrorist Asif Raza Khan living in Kolkata had been arrested and Gujarat police had taken him to Rajkot in December, 2001. Through him, an international ring of terrorists was busted. He had revealed to the police that the kidnapping of Kolkata's footwear-tycoon Partho Pratim Burman was to raise money for *jihadi* organisations, and that the mastermind of this plot was Dubai-based Aftab Ansari, who hailed from Varanasi. This organisation had kidnapped diamond merchants Bhaskar Parikh and Paresh Shah from Rajkot in Gujarat for *jihad* funding through the ransom money. The Rajkot police gained important information about the terrorist network across India after interrogating Asif Raza Khan, but he was killed on 7 December, 2002 in a police encounter while trying to escape. Asif's brother Amir Raza Khan sought revenge of his brother's killing and formed an organisation named ARCF (Asif Raza Commando Force) by seeking help from terrorist organisations in India, Pakistan and Bangladesh.

□

6
ARCF (Asif Raza Commando Force)

Asif Raza Khan was killed in an encounter while trying to escape from police custody in Rajkot, Gujarat, on 7 December, 2001. After his death, his brother Amir Raza Khan set up in December, 2001 itself, an organisation by the name of Asif Raza Commando Force or ARCF with help from HUJI, the terrorist outfit from Bangladesh. The motive behind forming this group was to seek revenge of Asif's killing. Aftab Ansari, alias Farhan Malik from Varanasi, Uttar Pradesh, was made its chief. Aftab Ansari was arrested on 23 January, 2002.

Asif Raza Khan had been arrested in Delhi in October, 2001 by Delhi police and a police team from Rajkot had brought him from Delhi to Rajkot in the case of kidnapping Bhaskar Parikh and Paresh Shah for ransom. A substantial quantity of ammunition and 14 kg of RDX explosive was recovered in November, 2001 from Patan district of Gujarat following interrogation. Along with Asif, a Pakistani national named Arshad Khan was also arrested. Asif and Aftab Ansari were also involved in the kidnapping of Varanasi's Nand Kishore Rungta for ransom. The international terror links of Asif and Aftab had come to light following their arrest. They also had links with Pakistani terrorist organisations Jaish-e-Mohammad and Lashkar-e-Tayyaba. They had also developed close contact with Pakistani terrorist Mohammad Umar Sheikh who was lodged in Delhi's Tihar Jail. Through this link, the duo had also developed deep links with Pakistani terrorist organisations and Al-Qaeda. A massive plot was hatched to generate funds for international terrorism by extracting ransom after kidnapping big Hindu businessmen at the behest of Pakistani organisations. Umar Sheikh Sayeed was set free in return of releasing the Indian Airlines flight IC-814 and its passengers. Umar had recruited Asif Raza Khan for carrying out terrorist activities in Delhi.

□

7

Attack on the American Cultural Centre

An attack was launched on the American Cultural Centre (ACC) in Kolkata at 6 in the morning of 22 January, 2002 - seven days after Asif Raza Khan's *chalisvan* (ritual on 40 days after someone's death) to seek revenge for his killing. Terrorists had used AK-47 rifles in this attack and in the resultant firing, constables Piyush Sarkar, Ujjawal Burman, Suresh Hembrem and Anil Mondal of the 5th Battalion of Kolkata Armed Police were killed. Another person belonging to a private security agency was also killed. Initially, HUJI owned responsibility for the attack, whereas Aftab Ansari had called Kolkata CID on phone to tell them that it is an act by ARCF. Four days later, Shamim and Zahid, both belonging to ARCF, were killed in an encounter with Delhi police at Hazaribagh, Jharkhand. While seriously injured, both mentioned Aftab Ansari alias Farhan Malik to be the mastermind behind this act.

Aftab lived in Dubai and was responsible for kidnapping of Partho Roy Burman from his office in Kolkata on 25 July, 2001 and had extracted a ransom of Rs. 3 crore 75 lakh. He was also responsible for kidnapping diamond merchants Bhaskar Parikh and Paresh Shah from Rajkot on 12 November, 2000. The kidnappers sought a ransom of Rs. 20 crore to raise funds for terrorist activities. Parikh was released after paying ransom of Rs. 1.50 crore, while Paresh paid crores of rupees in ransom. Aftab was known to be in contact with Sheikh Mohammad Umar Sayeed of Jaish-e-Mohammad and the two kidnapping incidents were executed at Umar's directions. A substantial part of the ransom money was sent through Umar to Al-Qaeda, the terror organisation headed by Osama Bin Laden. About US$ 1 lakh out of the ransom received in Partho Burman's kidnapping was sent by Umar to Mohammad Atta, the Egypt-based terrorist who was responsible for the 11 September, 2001 aerial attack on America's business centre Twin Towers.

Aftab Ansari fled to Pakistan after the attack on the ACC and proceeded to strengthen his links with terror organisations. The ISI facilitated the issue of a Pakistani passport number J-872142 for him in the name of Shakeel Mohammad Rana of Lahore. Aftab travelled to Dubai on this Pakistani passport and started living there. The US was hugely upset by the attack on the ACC and the then Director, FBI, Robert Mueller, rushed to Dubai and asked the administration not to allow the country to become a safe haven for terrorists. As a result of US pressure, Aftab Ansari and his accomplice Raju Sharma alias Rajendra Kumar were arrested in Dubai on 23 January, 2002, and repatriated to India on 9 February, 2002. On 28 April, 2005, a special CBI court found Aftab Ansari and six others guilty of attack on the ACC. Aftab and his accomplice Jamaluddin Nasir were sentenced to be hanged, whereas Rehan Alam, Musharraf Husain, Adil Hasan, Ashraf Alam and Shakir Akhtar were given life term. On 5 February, 2010, the Kolkata High Court upheld the death sentence to Aftab and Jamaluddin Nasir, while the imprisonment of three others was reduced to seven years.

□

8
Popular Front of India (PFI)

PFI was established on 22 November, 2006. It had come into existence after the merger of three Islamic extremist organisations – National Development Front (NDF) of Kerala, Karnataka Forum for Dignity (KFD) of Karnataka and Manitha Neethi Pasarai (MNP) of Tamil Nadu. These three organisations had come together after the demolition of the Babri structure in Ayodhya and had decided to form PFI. On the face of it, the PFI had claimed that it aimed to launch a struggle for the rights of Muslims, Dalits and backwards classes, but their main objective was the same as that of the SIMI (Students' Islamic Movement of India) – convert India from Darul Harb to Darul Islam.

The role of PFI came to light durng the communal riots in many states. This organisation made headlines on 4 July, 2010 when its workers chopped the right wrist of T.J. Joseph, a professor in Kerala, for what they believed was sacrilege as he had prepared a question paper which hurt sentiments of Islamic beliefs. This cruel act had sent shock wavess and abhorrence across India. The extent of terror caused by the incident can be understood by the fact that even the church authorities who normally are very vocal in Kerala, refrained from supporting Professor Joseph. The Newman College, Thodupuzha, run by Christian missionary bodies where Joseph was employed as a Malayalam teacher, had sacked him. His 49-year old wife Salomi had committed suicide by hanging herself in her bathroom as she was the chief witness in the attack on her husband. She was under great stress as she had been receiving grave threats to her life and feared for her family. The family had been facing serious financial crisis after Joseph had lost his job. The court of Chief Judicial Magistrate of Thodupuzha on 15 November, 2013 acquitted Joseph and found that the question paper had not been prepared with the intention of hurting religious feelings. On the one hand, Joseph had his right wrist chopped off and on the other, he faced charges of hurting Islamic religious feelings.

After this cruel act, PFI started spreading its activities across India. As SIMI had been banned in 2001, several members of SIMI started joining PFI and at that time no effective action was taken against it.

There are several cases where PFI activists indulged in extreme cruelty. In 2019, its workers mercilessly killed a Pattali Makkal Katchi (PMK) leader V. Ramalingam a few hours after a debate on religious conversion. On 5 February, 2019, Ramalingam had noticed that activists connected with PFI had started a religious conversion campaign in a neighbourhood comprising Dalits. He could not tolerate it and opposed this activity. There was a heated discussion between fundamentalist *maulvis* and Ramalingam, but matters cooled down after the intervention of some people. Ramalingam was returning home when five persons stopped his car and dragged him out. His arms were slashed with sharp weapons. He was rushed to a government hospital in Kumbhakonam where his situation turned critical. He was shifted to Thanjavur Medical College where he died. The PFI activists involved in the attack were S Nizam Ali, Sarbuddin, Rizwan, Mohammad Azharuddin and Mohammad Riaz.

In an affidavit filed by Kerala police in the High Court in 2014, mention was made of 27 cases of murder, 85 cases of attempt to murder and 106 cases of communal riots against PFI activists. The Kerala police also told the High Court that

PFI was a new version of the banned terrorist organisation SIMI. However, no strict action was taken against PFI and it continued to receive funds from Gulf States. It created a wide network all over India. The organisation responsible for cutting the wrist of Professor Joseph founded the 'Campus Front of India' with presence in many universities. It can well be imagined how this organisation would have spread the poison of fundamentalism among students. An example was seen in the form of the row over *hijab* in Karnataka.

In 2022, some girl students wearing *hijab* were not allowed entry into the class. The PFI had, under a well-thought-out strategy, sent the Muslim girls wearing *hijab* to college, disregarding the college dress code. In view of the controversy, the Karnataka government on 5 February, 2022 banned the wearing of *hijab* in colleges. The case reached the Karnataka High Court and escalated to the extent that the state government had to order closure of schools and colleges for some days. This controversy was raised in other states also. While in a conservative country like Iran, there is a popular uprising against wearing *hijab* and the government has killed hundreds of people in an attempt to quell the unrest, a controversy was raised in a secular country like India in favour of wearing *hijab*.

On 20 February, 2022 at 9 p.m., a 26-year-old Bajrang Dal worker named Harsh was attacked with knives and killed at Kamat petrol pump in Shimoga of Karnataka. Harsh had been opposing the wearing of *hijab* in schools and colleges and his murder was planned by PFI to cause widespread communal riots and create terror across Karnataka. The Karnataka government handed over the investigation to NIA. On 2 March, 2022, the Karnataka police arrested Mohammad Kashif, Syed Nadeem, Rihan Sharif, Asifullah Khan, Abdul Afnan, Nihan, Faraz Pasha, Abdul Qadar Jilan, Abdul Roshan and Zafar Sadiq, under charges of murder and Unlawful Activities (Prevention) Act, 1967. NIA submitted a 750-page chargesheet in the Special Court in Bengaluru. The NIA found in its investigation that

Harsh was murdered with a view to create an environment of hatred and terror in the society.

PFI is a part of the international conspiracy to establish a prototype of Egypt's Ikhwan-ul-Musalmeen or Muslim Brotherhood in India. The objective of this organisation was to disseminate in India the ideology of the prominent fundamentalist Maulana and founder of Jamaat-e-Islami Syed Abul Ala Maudoodi and Al Qutub, the fundamentalist leader of Muslim Brotherhood. When this fundamentalist organisation of Egypt came to power after winning an election, then its supporters unleashed such a wave of violence in Egypt that the Egyptian Army and the people had to topple the government and oust the organisation from power. PFI was working on the lines of the Muslim Brotherhood. When a case was launched in Egypt against the top leader of Muslim Brotherhood, Mohammad Morsi, for instigating violence, then PFI activists created a big ruckus outside the Egyptian Embassy in New Delhi. In its brief rule in Egypt, Muslim Brotherhood spread the venom of fundamentalism in the Egyptian society. The then Army Chief of Egypt, General Sisi, during a visit to Al-Azhar University – considered the centre of Islamic education in the world – was forced to say it was not possible that Muslims contemplated to eradicate all non-Muslims living in the world and poison the Muslim society.

Muslim Brotherhood has been banned not only by Egypt but also, by many Islamic countries, like Saudi Arabia and United Arab Emirates (UAE.) Only some countries like Turkiye and Qatar are supporting the Muslim Brotherhood. When there was an uproar in India over the statement by Nupur Sharma, then an anti-India trend was seen on the online media that started from countries like Egypt and Qatar, where Muslim Brotherhood is active. The first country to raise protest was the Government of Qatar, which is closely related to Muslim Brotherhood.

The demand to ban an anti-India organisation like PFI had been raised in the wake of the riots over the Citizens'

Amendment Act (CAA). PFI too was aware of the possibility that it would be banned and had made preparations to deal with such a situation. On 28 September, 2022, the Government of India banned the PFI and the organisations affiliated with it, for five years. But PFI had already made many dummy office-bearers so that the actual leaders could be saved from any legal action. Thus PFI had posed a tough challenge before the security agencies for an effective implementation of the ban.

On 8 September, 2022, NIA launched a crackdown in connection with the Phulwari Sharif terrorist module in Darbhanga, Araria, Chhapra, Patna and many other places in Bihar. Among the evidence material recovered from the PFI hideout in Phulwari Sharif were documents that outlined the strategy to convert India into an Islamic country by the year 2047. The Imarat-e-Sharia in Phulwari Sharif had been established on 26 June, 1921 by Maulana Abul Muhasin Muhammad Sajjad. It is a prominent centre of study of Islamic theology. PFI and many other Islamic extremist organisations had been active in Phulwari Sharif. Investigations revealed that funds were provided to PFI by Turkiye and many other Muslim countries. Illiterate, poor and unemployed Muslim youth were brainwashed and given terrorist training by PFI, which called instructors for this purpose from other states. PFI was engaged in anti-national activities before it was banned and, in the conspiracy to convert India into an Islamic country by 2047, Phulwari Sharif was a financially strong pillar. Money from abroad was sent to the bank accounts of the suspected terrorists captured from there, as well as their family members.

PFI Misguided People from the Scheduled Castes

The Citizenship (Amendment) Act, 2019 was passed by Parliament of India on 11 December, 2019. Under this Act, provision was made to give Indian citizenship to religious minorities in Pakistan, Afghanistan and Bangladesh as they were being persecuted there. Hindu, Sikh, Buddhist, Jain,

Parsi and Christian minorities who were persecuted in these countries and who reached India before 31 December, 2014, were given Indian citizenship. A section of people opposed the Act after it was passed and it was alleged that the law was against Muslims – which was completely baseless.

A protest demonstration was organised in Delhi's Shaheen Bagh against the CAA, in which Muslim women were sent to participate. This protest continued from December, 2019 to 24 March, 2020. The protestors carried copies of the Indian Constitution and photographs of Dr. B.R. Ambedkar, the force behind the Constitution. The entire protest was organised and funded by PFI and it used Ambedkar and the Indian Constitution to attract people from the Scheduled Castes. They were told that there was an attempt to change the Constitution drafted by Dr. B.R. Ambedkar. Chandra Shekhar, the founder of Bhim Army in western Uttar Pradesh, reached Daryaganj in Delhi and opposed the CAA. After being released on bail, he also reached the Jama Masjid along with his supporters and staged a protest.

Incidentally, all the people given Indian citizenship under the CAA, about 75 per cent were Dalits. Most of them were Namo Shudra and Matua from the then East Pakistan, now Bangladesh, and they had agreed to stay in Pakistan on the advice of Jogendra Nath Mandal, Pakistan's first Law and Labour Minister. Jogendra Nath Mandal was the most influential Dalit leader after Dr. B.R. Ambedkar and he decided to stay on in Pakistan despite the advice to the contrary by Dr. B.R. Ambedkar. Mohammad Ali Jinnah appointed Mandal as the first Law and Labour Minister of Pakistan. After the formation of Pakistan, there was widespread persecution of Hindus, Sikhs and other non-Muslims; there were mass killings and forcible conversions to Islam. Jogendra Nath Mandal could ensure security to Hindus and especially Dalits who had listened to him and stayed back in the newly-created Islamic country, thinking that it was their country. Mandal himself fled to India on 8 October, 1960 and sent his resignation from the government headed by Liaquat Ali Khan. Mandal led rest of his life in obscurity and died in Kolkata on 5 October, 1968.

Despite there being a majority of Dalits among those given Indian citizenship under CAA, many Dalit leaders fell into the PFI trap and joined the protests against CAA. These Dalit leaders were not aware of the life and history of Jogendra Nath Mandal and did not know that there were 75 per cent Dalits among those made Indian citizens. Left-oriented historians eliminated from history the facts about Jogendra Nath Mandal and the persecution of Dalits by Muslims in Pakistan.

Citizenship had been given to those who were persecuted on religious issues because of which they were forced to quit their country and escape to India. At the time of Partition of India, the population of Hindus and Sikhs in West Pakistan (now Pakistan) was 24 per cent, which has now dwindled to 1.5 per cent. Similarly in East Pakistan (now Bangladesh), the Hindu population has come down from 28 per cent to 8 per cent.

Organisations Merged with PFI

Three Islamic extremist organisations merged into PFI. Their description is as follows:

1. Manitha Neethi Pasarai (MNP) : Manitha Neethi Pasarai was set up as a Muslim extremist organisation in Tamil Nadu. Its founder was a prominent Muslim journalist M. Ghulam Mohammad. On the face of it, this organisation claims to work on issues related to minorities, Dalits and backward communities in Tamil Nadu. It was a registered society under the Tamil Nadu Societies Act with registration number 51 of 2001. It published a Tamil magazine, titled *Vidiyal Velli* which carried Islamic teachings and had 23,000 associates. It was the largest Muslim magazine in Tamil Nadu. The ideology of MNP was the same as that of SIMI. After the Government of India banned SIMI in 2006, MNP became a part of PFI.

2. National Development Front (NDF) : The organisation created a large base in the Malabar area of Kerala after getting inspired by pan-Islamic campaigns in India in the wake of the demolition of the Babri structure in 1992. NDF had mainly Muslim youths as members and Kerala police found during investigations that NDF was a new version of ISIS. In order to win the confidence of Muslims, NDF actively encouraged the claim that it represented their rights. It had 19 members in the Supreme Council and included Professor P. Koya, who had been one of the founder-members of SIMI. In 1997, NDF organised a national conference on human rights. After consensus, a new organisation was formed, named CHRO. People associated with CHRO worked with Human Rights Watch International (HRWI). It is well-known that HRWI is an anti-Indian organisation and is routinely engaged in maligning India.

In the years 2004, 2005 and 2006, NDF organised 'Be an Islamic Warrior' rallies on the occasion of India's Independence Day on 15 August every year, and it became a routine activity. In 2007, it organised an 'Empower India' conference in collaboration with PFI. In 2022, NDF also provided food and water to those engaged in protests over the *hijab* issue. In 2002, members of NDF were found to be engaged in the Marad massacre in Kerala and it was referred to as a terrorist organisation.

Marad is located near the sea-beach in the Kozhikode district of Kerala. In 2002, the issue of drawing water from a public tap turned into a communal issue between Hindus and Muslims, in which many people were killed. NDF played a key role in this incident and its members were actively involved in killing of Hindus and arson in their houses. A Judicial Inquiry Commission was formed under the chairmanship of Justice Thomas P. Joseph to investigate the Marad communal riots. The police told the Commission that the funding of NDF was done by Pakistani ISI and many other Islamic countries. NDF also received millions of rupees from abroad for its training programmes. Assistant Police Commissioner (Special Branch) A.B. George of Ernakulam told the Marad Inquiry Commission that NDF had been sending people to Pakistan for years, to undergo terrorist training. NDF merged with PFI in 2006.

3. Karnataka Forum for Dignity (KFD) : It was an Islamic extremist organisation in the state of Karnataka and was established in 2006. It was active in Karnataka's coastal city of Mangalore, Udupi, South Kannada, Kodagu (Coorg) of Karnataka and Kasargode of Kerala. As a public face, this organisation claimed to be a platform for equality and justice to minorities, Dalits and backwards. Its area of influence was coastal Karnataka, especially Udupi and South Kannada. Its membership drives attracted attention from colleges, institutions and social groups. With active association of K.L. Ashok, Prasanna and some other so-called progressive thinkers and writers, this organisation tried to make inroads into Dalit and backward communities, but it was basically an extremist Islamic organisation.

KFD had been established mainly to seek revenge for the January, 2006 communal riots in Karnataka. Its objective was that in case of riots, Muslims should have a trained group of their own which could confront and fight the Hindus. KFD activists were trained in the house of Abdul Rahman Beri in Dubai and were given firing practice by airguns. Training was also given in making bombs with ingredients available easily in India. KFD was related to SIMI and after SIMI was banned on 22 November, 2006, it merged with PFI.

Khilafat Movement and Kerala

More than 30 countries were part of World War I. There were two sides – the Allies comprising more than 17 countries, such as Britain, Russia, France, Japan, Italy, Serbia, USA, etc. On the other side were the Central Powers comprising Germany, Austria, Hungary, Bulgaria and the Ottoman Empire. The Central Powers lost the war, the Ottoman Empire disintegrated and Turkey was separated after the Khalifa was deposed.

Muslims all over the world and even in India considered the Sultan of Turkey as their spiritual leader (*khalifa*). The aftermath of WW-1 was considered as an insult of the Khalifa and Muslims all over the world harboured a grudge against Britain and its allies.

In India, a movement was launched between 1919 and 1924 to reinstate the position of Khalifa of Turkey and it was named the 'Khilafat Movement'. To launch this campaign, a Khilafat Committee was set up in Mumbai in March, 1919. The brothers Mohammad Ali and Shaukat Ali besides many other Muslim leaders talked with Mahatma Gandhi in this regard to make it a public movement. Mahatma Gandhi also felt there was a need to launch a widespread campaign against the British in India. He felt that it was necessary to take Hindus and Muslims together for a widespread movement.

During 1919-1922, two public movements were launched in India against British rule – the Khilafat movement and the Non-Co-operation Movement. The Congress and the Muslim League organised many joint political protests during this period. Through the Non-Cooperation Movement, the cruel and repressive face of the British rule related to Rowlatt Act, 1919, martial law in Punjab and the Jallianwala Bagh massacre came to light.

The Khilafat movement against the British was also launched in Kerala. The meetings organised in support of Khilafat in Malabar were responsible for stoking communal feelings among the Moplah Muslims. Most of the landowners (*zamindars*) in Malabar were Namboodiri Brahmins and Nairs, whereas the farmers were Moplah Muslims. Provoked by the aggressive speeches of Muslim clerics and the prevailing anti-British sentiments, the Moplah Muslims launched a violent agitation. They attacked not only the British but also the landowners and Hindus. The day of 20 August, 1920 is remembered as a black day in the history of Kerala. The Moplah uprising in Malabar started on this day and the anti-British agitation soon acquired a communal colour. During the violence, the Moplah Muslims in Malabar killed thousands of Hindus, raped Hindu women and thousands of Hindus were forced to convert and become Muslims. More than 10,000 Hindus were killed in communal massacres. About 300 temples were destroyed and damaged. Property worth millions of rupees was looted and houses and shops belonging to Hindus were set on fire. During the Khilafat movement, Arya Samaj leader Swami Shraddhanand went to Kerala and re-converted the forcibly converted Muslims into Hinduism. This ultimately proved to be the reason behind his murder. On 23 December, 1926, a man named Abdul Rashid seeking to meet Swami Shraddhanand for some work, went to his *ashram* and killed him. It was later revealed that Abdul Rashid was against the Swami's '*shuddhikaran*' programme.

The religious fanaticism that grew in Kerala in the wake of the Khilafat movement also added to religious fundamentalism among Muslims in Kerala. All the Islamic extremist organisations formed in recent times have their roots in Kerala.

Kerala: The Hub of Fundamentalism

The state of Kerala has been a major centre of spices export since the era before Christ and it is also known as the 'garden of spices'. The spices of Kerala attracted traders from ancient Arabia, Babylonia and Egypt in 2nd and 3rd centuries B.C. Trade ties had been established between India and the Arab countries much before the time of Prophet Mohammad. People from Arabic countries had settled on the western coast of India much before the advent of Jewish and Christian settlers. The king of Calicut used to encourage these settlers. It is said that Cheraman Perumal of the Cher dynasty went to Mecca from here and adopted Islam. He is said to be the first converted Muslim. He then invited Muslim clerics and missionaries to Kerala. A Muslim faithful from Arabia named Malik bin Denar came to Kerala to propagate Islam and in the year 629, got the first mosque constructed in Kodungalur and it was made in the life-time of Prophet Mohammad. Later, mosques sprang up in Quilon, Kasargode, Shrikantapuram, Dharmapattanam, and Chaliam. The number of Muslims in Kerala kept on rising because of the large presence of traders from Arabic countries. In the 15th, 16th and 17th centuries, Muslims in Kerala became prosperous and their numbers also increased at a rapid pace. The Muslims of Kerala are also known as Mappilahs and all of them speak Malayali language. They follow a mix of Arabic and Malayali culture. Islam is the second largest faith in Kerala after Hinduism. In the decade of the 1950s, the oil boom in Saudi Arabia and Gulf countries also caused a spurt in prosperity in Kerala. People here already had a close association with the Gulf countries and on the basis of these connections, a large number of people went to the Gulf States for employment and proved instrumental in bringing about prosperity in their families. Especially in northern part of Kerala, at least one member from every household went to work in the Gulf. And when they returned, they brought the riches and also a rich dose of culture and fundamentalism from there.

Most of the Muslims in Kerala belong to the Sunni sect. From the point of view of jurisprudence, Islam is divided into four schools of thoughts, known as Hanfi, Maliki, Salafi and Hanbali. These names are based on the names of their founders – Abu Hanifa Al-Numan, Malik Ibn Anas, Muhammad Ibn Idris Al-Shafi and Ahmad Ibn Hanbal. Most of the fundamentalist Muslims in the Gulf countries follow the Hanbali stream which has the highest dose of Islamic fundamentalism. Among Kerala Muslims also the influence of the Hanbali ideology is the strongest. It can be said that the Islamic thought that came to India via the sea route had the highest component of religious fundamentalism. It is also notable that among the Muslims from India who went to join the ISIS, the largest number was from Kerala.

□

9
Kidnapping for terror funding

Kidnap of Partho Pratim Roy Burman

Huge funds were needed to run terrorist organisations and the perpetrators decided to extract ransom running into crores of rupees after kidnapping wealthy Hindu businessmen. A beginning was made by kidnapping Partho Pratim Roy Burman, a wealthy footwear tycoon, who was chairman and managing director of Khadim Shoes. On 25 July, 2001, he was kidnapped from his office at C.N. Road, Tiljala, Kolkata. A ransom of Rs. 3 crores 75 lakh was extracted through *hawala* in Hyderabad. Partho was kept in captivity near Purulia, 24 Parganas and was released on 2 August, 2001 after ransom was paid. The mastermind of this incident was Aftab Ansari alias Farhan Malik, and the main kidnapper was Asif Raza Khan alias Rajan. Asif was arrested in Delhi on 29 October, 2001. He had told the police that his 'commander' Aftab Ansari had sent US$ 1 lakh out of the ransom money to Pakistani terrorist Umar Sheikh Sayeed (he was among those terrorists released from Indian jails in return for the release of hijacked plane IC-814.) Umar had then sent US$ 1 lakh to the Egyptian-origin terrorist Mohammad Atta in US. This Mohammad Al-Amir Awad-el Sayed Atta had hijacked the American Airlines plane and had himself piloted the plane on 11 September, 2001 to crash into the north tower of World Trade Centre.

Besides Asif Raza Khan, another person involved in the kidnapping of Partho Burman was Jalaluddin Mulla alias

Amanullah Mondal alias Babu Bhai, a resident of Bangladesh. He was a HUJI terrorist and was arrested in Lucknow in June, 2007. In this kidnapping case, 13 persons including Aftab Ansari had been sentenced to life imprisonment on 25 May, 2009 by the court of Additional District Judge of Kolkata, Biswaroop Bandopadhyaya.

Kidnapping of Diamond Merchants Bhaskar Parikh and Paresh Shah

Another kidnapping by Aftab Ansari to raise money for terror funding was that of two diamond merchants from Rajkot, Gujarat – Bhaskar Parikh and Paresh Shah, on 12 November, 2001. It was planned by Asif Raza Khan and Aftab Ansari and was backed by Pakistani terrorist organisation Lashkar-e-Tayyaba, headed by Hafiz Sayeed. Earlier, ISI used to give Rs. 25 crores every year to Indian Mujahideen through Riyaz and Iqbal Bhatkal for carrying out terrorist activities in India. But later, the funding amount was reduced and they were told to raise money through their own efforts. The scheme to extort ransom after kidnapping wealthy Hindu businessmen was prepared on the advice of Hafiz Sayeed of Lashkar-e-Tayyaba.

In the diamond merchants' kidnapping, the chief conspirator was Pakistani terrorist Mohammad Umar Sheikh Sayeed. A ransom of Rs. 20 crores were demanded from the two businessmen. Paresh Shah was released through the efforts of Gujarat police but Bhaskar Parikh was brought by a lawyer named Shailendra Jat in his car to Delhi, and he arranged to send Rs. 1.5 crore of ransom money to Aftab Ansari in Dubai through *hawala*, while retaining a substantial amount for himself. Aftab Ansari acquired arms and ammunition from this ransom money. At the time of this kidnapping, Aftab Ansari was running his gang in Dubai and was in close contact with Pakistani *jihadi* organisations. A part of this ransom money was sent to Pakistani terrorist Umar Sheikh Sayeed, who further sent it to Al-Qaeda.

Kidnapping of Nand Kishore Rungta

Nand Kishore Rungta, also known as Nandu Babu, was a big businessman of coal and had his office at Bhelupur, Jahawar Nagar in Varanasi. Rungta was also the treasurer of International Vishwa Hindu Parishad. On 22 January, 1997, he was kidnapped by Ataur Rahman 'Babu', a resident of Mahrupur Mohammadabad in Ghazipur. He was a close aide of mafia don Mukhtar Ansari and the chief shooter of Mukhtar's gang. Babu was also related to Mukhtar Ansari, being the cousin of the latter's father in-law. Ataur Rahman, posed as a businessman and a coal dealer from Hazaribagh, went to Rungta on the pretext of a business deal. After a brief discussion, he called Rungta outside on the pretext of showing some papers and of having tea with him. He mixed some drug in the tea, making Rungta unconscious. Babu then called up Rungta's family members and told them about the kidnapping, seeking a ransom of Rs. 3 crores. After extorting the ransom money, Rungta was killed and his body was thrown in Jhusi on the bank of River Ganga at Allahabad (now Prayagraj). Ataur Rahman fled to Nepal with the ransom money. Mukhtar Ansari called Ataur Rahman from Nepal in December, 2005 for killing the Bharatiya Janata Party leader Krishnanand Rai. Ataur Rahman's accomplice Shahabuddin alias Shahabu of Ghazipur fled to Ghazipur and Ataur Rahman himself spent his time in Pakistan and Bangladesh. It was rumoured that a part of the ransom money received after Rungta's kidnapping was sent to terrorists based in Pakistan. Aftab Ansari and Asif Raza Khan had developed contact with Pakistani Umar Sheikh Sayeed lodged in Tihar Jail of Delhi and Umar Sheikh was also involved in the killing of American journalist Daniel Pearl in Pakistan.

□

10
Attacks on Ram Janmabhumi, Ayodhya, CRPF Group Centre, Rampur and the Indian Parliament

1. Terror Attack on Ram Janmabhumi: Five Terrorists of Jaish-e-Mohammad Killed

Jaish-e-Mohammad, a terrorist organisation, sent terrorists to launch an attack on Ram Janmbhumi in Ayodhya. On 5 July, 2005, five terrorists armed with AK-47 rifles and grenades made in Pakistan, attacked the makeshift temple constructed after the demolition of the erstwhile Babri mosque structure. All the five terrorists were killed in the encounter with personnel of Uttar Pradesh police and the CRPF. These terrorists had entered India from Karachi via Nepal. Posing as pilgrims, they had travelled in a Tata Sumo vehicle to Ayodhya from Akbarpur, near Kichhauchha Sharif. In Faizabad, they left this vehicle and rented another vehicle, a jeep, which was driven by driver Rehan Alam. They reached near the Ram Janmabhumi, pushed the driver out and crashed the vehicle into the road barrier. At 9.05 a.m., they threw M-67 grenades and broke the security ring, killing a guide, Ramesh Pandey. Firing indiscriminately, the five terrorists entered the Sita Rasoi, where they were stopped by personnel of the CRPF and U.P. police. In the resultant encounter, all the terrorists were killed. Among the items recovered later from their possession were one rocket propelled grenade launcher

RPG-7, five AK-56 rifles, five M-1911 pistols, several M-67 grenades and a lot of *jihadi* literature.

2. Attack on CRPF Group Centre, Rampur

At around 1 a.m. on the intervening night of 31 December, 2007/1 January, 2008, terrorists armed with AK-47 rifles and grenades attacked the CRPF Group Centre in Rampur. This night of the New Year eve 2008 was very cold and the guards and other CRPF Jawans were warming up their hands around a small bonfire. In the attack by Lashkar-e-Tayyaba terrorists, seven CRPF jawans were killed. Those arrested after the encounter were Shabauddin, India commander of Lashkar-e-Tayyaba, a resident of Madhubani in Bihar, two Pakistani terrorists Imran Shahzad and Mohammad Farukh, Mohammad Sharif alias Sohail Ansari from Rampur, Jang Bahadur Khan from Moradabad and Fahim Ansari from Goregaon, Mumbai. A case against all of them was registered at Rampur *kotwali* on charges of waging war against India, killing of CRPF personnel, Arms Act and use of forged passports.

3. Shabauddin, India Commander of Lashkar-e-Tayyaba

Shabauddin was a resident of Madhubani in Bihar and had studied at Aligarh Muslim University. In Aligarh, he came in contact with *jihadi* elements, quit his studies and joined the path of *jihad*. From Aligarh, he was sent to Kashmir and then onwards to Pakistan. He was trained in the Muzaffarabad training centre run by the Lashkar-e-Tayyaba terrorist Hafiz Sayeed. The 20- or 22-year-old Shabauddin was trained in the 21-day *daura-e-aam* (initial training) and also in using AK-47 rifles, pistols, light machine gun and grenades.

I had myself interrogated him. It was ascertained from him that Hafiz Sayeed was impressed by Shabauddin's enthusiasm and sent him to the three-month long *daura-e-khaas* (special training). He was made to rise very early in the morning and after the *fazr namaz*, a *maulvi* used to come and tell him that Muslims were being ill-treated and tortured in India. Some videos with fake visuals were also shown to them that aimed at making terrorists out of them. They were told that they had to fight a war against *kafirs* (non-Muslims) and establish the rule of Islam (Dar-ul-Islam) in India. They were told that one day there will be only one faith and that would be Islam, and *jihad* was aimed to achieve this goal. In *Daura-e-Khaas*, officers of Pakistan Army and the ISI also came to train the participants. They were trained in electronic surveillance, chatting through e-mail, besides making and exploding bombs, using ingredients available locally. After completing his training, Shabauddin stayed for some days at the Lashkar headquarters in Muzaffarabad. Thereafter, a fake Pakistani passport was arranged for him and he was sent from Karachi to Dhaka. From Dhaka, he crossed the Bangladesh-India border, came to Tripura and reached his native place Madhubani in Bihar. His family members were under the impression that after completing his studies in Aligarh Muslim University he would uphold the family name, but they did not know that this son had transformed into a ferocious terrorist of Lashkar-e-Tayyaba. The Lashkar headquarters then ordered him to move to Kathmandu. Sometime later, his fake identification papers with a Hindu name were prepared and he was admitted to a school in Bangalore (now Bengaluru) on this fake Hindu name. He made arrangements to stay in a private, rented room. Then he was called to Kashmir and given two AK-47 rifles, 400 cartridges and six Chinese grenades. He kept all these articles in a students' bag and came by train to Bangalore. A few days later, a Pakistani terrorist, namely Hamza came to Bangalore by crossing the Bangladesh border.

They were instructed by Hafiz Sayeed to attack and destroy the Indian Space Research Organisation (ISRO) in Bangalore. Shabauddin and Hamza went on a recce to the site but could not do so in view of the tight security. Then in the last week of December, 2005, a convention of Indian Science

Congress was being held at the Indian Institute of Science (IISC) in Bangalore. On 28 December, 2005, the two terrorists entered the IISC premises in a white Ambassador car at 7.20 p.m., when all delegates were coming out of the J.N. Tata Auditorium at the end of the conference and were going to the dinner venue. Suddenly, the terrorists in Army uniforms with black face masks opened indiscriminate firing with AK-56 rifles. Professor Munish Chandra Puri, a mathematics professor from IIT, Delhi, was riddled with bullets. Three other scientists and a laboratory assistant were wounded. Among the injured was a pregnant woman scientist. It was learnt that besides Shabauddin and Hamza, some other Lashkar-e-Tayyaba terrorists were also involved in this incident.

Shabauddin and Hamza then fled from Bangalore. While Shabauddin reached his home in Madhubani, Hamza went to Bangladesh and then to Karachi. After living in Madhubani for a few days, Shabauddin reached Kathmandu. He revealed in his interrogation that the India commander of Lashkar earlier used to be a Pakistani and conducted the outfit's activities in India while living in Kathmandu. But after the IISC attack, Hafiz Sayeed was highly pleased with him and made him – not a Pakistani – the India commander. He used to be in touch with thc Lashkar headquarters through a Thuraya satellite phone. He was also given the task of attacking an Army convoy between Bareilly and Lucknow but could not do so because of tight security.

4. The plan to attack the Rampur CRPF Group Centre

As per the plan, Mohammad Sharif alias Sohail Ansari, a resident of Rampur, was chosen for the attack. After completing his studies in a *madarsa* in Rampur, he had gone to Saudi Arabia in 1990. He was a driver and earned good money there. He revealed in his interrogation that in Saudi Arabia, he met a *maulvi* in 2004 who inducted him in *jihad*. After taking leave on the pretext of going to India, he went to Karachi and joined the Lashkar-e-Tayyaba terrorist training camp at Muzaffarabad. After the training, he along with some Pakistanis was sent to Kashmir, from where he made his way to Rampur. He was told that he would receive Rs. 6 lakhs through a *hawala* channel to buy a pre-used truck and ply it from Kashmir. He received the money in Bareilly, bought a truck as instructed and started plying it from Kashmir to Moradabad and Bareilly. While in Kashmir, he was given two AK-47 rifles, about 500 cartridges and eight Chinese grenades. He hid these items in his truck which was laden with cardboard and brought them to Rampur. He came with these items to Patti Pratapgarh and hid them in a pit in the house of a friend, Mohammad Kausar. Initially Kausar was reluctant to help but Mohammad Sharif convinced him by saying that it was all in the name and cause of faith.

Mohammad Sharif was married to the only daughter of his in-laws, who belonged to Azamgarh. His wife's uncle was a *maulvi* in Rampur and used to teach Quran in a *madarsa*. The uncle's sons went to Saudi Arabia to earn their livelihood. The uncle arranged Mohammad's Sharif's marriage. Sharif and his wife were the sole owners of all the property of the in-laws' family. The *maulvi's* son knew that Sharif had become a terrorist. He thought that if Sharif was caught, then he could get control of all the property. He sent an anonymous letter to the SSP, Azamgarh. Somehow no one paid any attention to this important letter and a constable from the police station went to Sharif's house to inquire of his whereabouts. Sharif was at home but his wife misled the policeman by saying that he was not there.

But an alerted Sharif then left Azamgarh and reached Shabauddin, the India commander, in Kathmandu. Accompanied by him and Jang Bahadur alias Baba Khan, Shabauddin went to Bangladesh and talked to the Lashkar commander there. They were told that in western U.P., a large number of Hindus could be killed during the Kawar Yatra in the month of *Savan*. Among the means to achieve this was poisoning the food or drinking water meant for the pilgrims, or cutting the tower of the overhead high tension (HT) wires during the Kawar Yatra in such a manner that the tower fell on the pilgrims, killing several of them by electric shock as well as the fall. They were trained for this in Bangladesh.

On a request from Shabauddin, Hafiz Sayed again sent Rs. 6 lakhs through *hawala* to Mohammad Sharif, and he was helped in setting up a small shop at Birgunj in Nepal. Having found a means to earn his livelihood, he called his wife to Birgunj.

5. Pakistani *Fidayeen*

Hafiz Sayeed also sent two *fidayeen* (suicide attackers) from Karachi to Kathmandu. They were Imran Shahzad, resident of Bhimber *tehsil* in Pakistan-occupied Kashmir and Mohammad Farukh, from Gujranwala in Pakistan's Punjab. Both had been trained by Lashkar-e-Tayyaba and had volunteered to lay down their lives as *fidayeen*. Hafiz Sayeed had sent Rs. 4 lakh each to their family members. These two had played the main role in the attack on CRPF Group Centre in Rampur.

6. Recce of the CRPF Group Centre

Shabauddin accompanied both the *fidayeen* from Kathmandu to Gorakhpur in India via the Sonauli-Maharajganj border. Then he moved to Mohammad Sharif in Rampur and conducted a recce of the CRPF Group Centre. They had planned to enter through the main gate while firing indiscriminately and killing several CRPF Jawans. After the recce, the team returned to Kathmandu and Sharif was told to bring the arms and ammunition from Patti Pratapgarh to Rampur. Sharif went to Mohammad Kausar's house and very carefully brought out the stuff. Sharif was pleased to see that the AK-47 rifles and ammunition, smeared with grease and then wrapped in plastic, were in good shape and not spoiled while buried in the pit. He brought these to Rampur and hid them in a garage in a relative's house.

7. IB tipped off

The Intelligence Bureau (IB) had been tipped off about the attack. They had informed the CRPF and the DGP, U.P., as well as myself about the possibility of such an attack. The intelligence report said that the attack was most likely during the recruitment at the CRPF Group Centre. I informed the Group Centre in Rampur as well as the SP, Rampur. I ordered the closure of a public thoroughfare through the Group Centre despite the objections of residents of nearby areas. My decision was to ensure that the attackers did not enter the Centre through this passage.

8. The Attack

There was heightened alertness at the CRPF Group Centre and security was beefed up. But there was some laxity as soon as the recruitment was over. The terrorists had planned the attack on the night of 30 December. A railway line passes close to the Centre and as per the terrorists' plan, the two Pakistani *fidayeen* Imran Shahzad and Mohammad Farukh were to meet below a railway underpass at 11 in the night. Mohammad Sharif and Baba Khan had told them that if they could not meet because of any reason, then they would meet at the same spot the next day, which was 31 December, 2007. Sharif could not bring out the arms and ammunition from Mohammad Kausar's garage on 30 December because of some repair work going on there, so the meeting could not take place.

Sharif told me during the interrogation that on the night of 31 December, he met Baba Khan and Shabauddin at the railway underpass. He had brought along roasted chicken, lamb brain curry and *parathas* made in *desi ghee* for the *fidayeen*, as he wanted them to have a feast on the last night of their lives. Both *fidayeen* also knew that it was the last meal of their lives and that they could be killed in the attack. But they were happy that after being killed, they would go straight to heaven where they would be welcomed by 72 *hoors* (beautiful young women). During the training at Hafiz Sayeed's training centre, the *maulvi* had told them that as soon as they died, they would become 28–30-year-old men, regardless of their actual age, and remain so till eternity. Then they would be able to lead a life of luxury with the young women as much as they wanted.

Mohammad Sharif, Shabauddin and Baba Khan along with the two *fidayeen* reached close to the gate of the CRPF Group Centre around midnight. The trio hugged the two *fidayeen* and bade them goodbye, saying, "Remember us in your wishes, *khuda hafiz*." They instructed that the attack should take place after an hour so that the three of them could get away as far as possible from the spot.

It was a very cold night. The heavily-armed Imran Shahzad and Mohammad Farukh wrapped themselves in blankets and reached the gate of the Centre. The CRPF officers had gone back to their residences after the New Year party, and the *fidayeen* noticed that the CRPF guard was away from the gate, warming himself along with some colleagues. As Fate would have it, a rickshaw-puller too had joined them at the bonfire. The two *fidayeen* tip-toed to the gate and opened fire at the rate of 600 bullets per minute from their AK-47 rifles. The Jawans warming themselves at the bonfire were riddled with bullets and died before they could understand what had happened. The two attackers entered the Centre and killed a few more Jawans. In all, seven CRPF personnel and a rickshaw-puller were killed in the attack. The two terrorists fled from the scene, dumped their AK-47 rifles in a pond on the way and caught a train to reach Moradabad in the night itself. They then went to Gorakhpur and, then along with Shabauddin, the two Pakistani *fidayeen* went to Nepal via the Sonauli Maharajganj border.

At that time, I was the Additional Director-General of Police (ADG), Law and Order, as well in charge of the newly formed ATS and STF. Our team worked very hard and arrested the two Pakistani *fidayeen*, the India commander Shabauddin, Mohammad Sharif Ansari, Baba Khan and Mohammad Kausar. Fahim Ansari, a resident of Goregaoan in Mumbai was also arrested and from his possession, handmade maps of the places attacked on 26 November, 2008 were also recovered. A huge cache of arms and ammunition was also recovered from these terrorists.

9. The Mumbai attacks could have been averted

Fahim Ansari had hand-drawn detailed maps showing roads from Haji Ali to Mantralaya, Mumbai CST (previously VT) Station, Taj Mahal and Trident hotels. He revealed during interrogation that Hafiz Sayeed had entrusted him with this task after the training in Pakistan. He was to hand over this map at the Pakistani Embassy in Kathmandu, from where it would have reached Hafiz Sayeed. To complete this task, he had been shown these places on Google Search during his training at Karachi. Being a resident of Goregaon in Mumbai, he himself was familiar with all these places. Fahim Ansari used to work in Saudi Arabia and had taken to terrorism after being convinced by a *maulvi*. He was sent to Iran by sea route and thereafter to Pakistan, by road. He received training at the Lashkar training centre. He used to stay in hotels in Mumbai for many months and had also obtained forged certificates and driving licence made in the name of Sahil Pavaskar. He had received training at a computer centre in Mumbai.

After arresting Fahim Ansari, our team took him to Mumbai and visited those places where he used to stay under the name of Sahil Pavaskar. The Mumbai police were apprised of the maps prepared by him and the fake documents, but the Mumbai police did not even lodge a report against him. On 26 November, 2008, the 10 Lashkar-e-Tayyaba *fidayeen* attacked these places in South Mumbai that had been depicted in the maps drawn by Fahim Ansari. In the attack on this day, 175 people including nine Pakistani *fidayeen* were killed and more than 300 injured. Among those killed were IG (ATS) Hemant Karkare, Additional Commissioner Ashok Kamte, Inspector Vijay Salaskar, Inspector Shashank Shinde and Assistant Sub-Inspector Tukaram Omble. In the battle with terrorists, Major

Sandeep Unnikrishnan of NSG and NSG Commando Havaldar Gajendra Singh Bisht also lost their lives.

Three railway employees were killed at the Chhatrapati Shivaji Maharaj Terminus railway station (formerly Bombay VT).

After the 26/11 incident, the Mumbai police took Shabauddin and Fahim Ansari to Mumbai and submitted a charge-sheet against them as well as the lone surviving *fidayeen* Mohammad Ajmal Aamir Kasab for the conspiracy behind Mumbai attacks. But Shabauddin and Fahim Ansari were acquitted by court because of insufficient evidence.

If the Mumbai police had taken seriously the facts presented by the Uttar Pradesh police and initiated timely action, then the 26 November, 2008 on Mumbai could have been averted.

10. Charge-sheet against terrorists in CRPF Camp attack case and the unsuccessful attempt by Akhilesh Government to withdraw It

The charge-sheet against all the terrorists was prepared after a thorough investigation and sent to the court. The hearing in the case had started in the Rampur Court but in March, 2012, Akhilesh Yadav became the Chief Minister of Uttar Pradesh. He initiated the withdrawal of 14 cases related to terrorist actions and it included the case pertaining to the terror attack on CRPF Group Centre in Rampur. The Allahabad High Court stayed the withdrawal of cases. The case was heard by the court of ADJ, Rampur.

On 9 December, 2019, the court of Sanjay Kumar Singh, ADJ, Rampur, sentenced Shabauddin, Pakistani *fidayeen* Imran Shahzad, Mohammad Farukh and Mohammad Sharif alias Sohail Ansari of Rampur to death by hanging. Jang Bahadur Khan was jailed for life and Fahim Ansari was sentenced to 10 years' rigorous imprisonment. Mohammad Kausar was acquitted for lack of evidence. All these terrorists were trained at the Lashkar-e-Tayyaba headquarters run by Hafiz Sayeed.

The plot to carry out terrorist activities in India by ISI and Lashkar-e-Tayyaba was unravelled during interrogation of the arrested terrorists. They had revealed that it was the Lashkar chief Hafiz Sayeed who had planned the attacks at different places in India.

11. Attack on Indian Parliament

On 13 December, 2001, five Pakistani terrorists of Jaish-e-Mohammad armed with AK-47 rifles and explosive belts entered Parliament House in Delhi in an Ambassador car, which displayed a forged vehicle entry pass issued by the Home Ministry. The winter session of Parliament was in progress. Present inside the building were several ministers, including Home Minister L.K. Advani, Minister of State for Defence Harin Pathak and many MPs. The terrorists crashed their car into the official car of Vice President Krishna Kant and that was parked near the gate number 12. The Vice President was inside the building. The terrorists started firing as soon as they entered the premises, in which nine persons were killed, including Jawans of Parliament Security, Delhi police and Kamlesh Kumari of CRPF. Those killed were Jagdish Prasad Yadav, Matbar Singh Negi of Rajya Sabha Secretariat Security, Kamlesh Kumari, Sepoy Nanak Chand and Rampal of CRPF, Delhi Police ASI Om Prakash, Bijendra Singh, Head Constable Ghanshyam and Gardener Deshraj of Rajya Sabha support staff. The security forces shot down the five terrorists.

The Government of India took this attack on Parliament very seriously and the Indian Defence Forces rushed towards the Pakistan border. War was almost imminent but it was somehow averted with the intervention of the international community.

Pakistan had always maintained that it had no role in these terrorist incidents. The Government of India drew the attention of the international community towards the terrorist acts committed by Pakistani terrorists in India and it led to considerable embarrassment for

Pakistan. This was the reason that it was put in the 'Grey List' of terrorist funding. To save itself from further embarrassment, Pakistan initiated the setting up of Indian Mujahideen in India with help from Lashkar-e-Tayyaba and HUJI, and also facilitated its training and funding in Pakistan. The objective of Pakistan was to ensure that the terror acts were committed by Indian terrorists so that Pakistan could claim that Muslims in India were behind this.

□

11
The Batala House encounter

Prior to the Batala House encounter, a series of bomb explosions were launched in Delhi on 13 September, 2008 in which 30 persons were killed and 90 were injured. These explosions were carried out at five different places in Delhi. The first blast was conducted in Ghaffar Market at Karol Bagh area. It is a prominent market place for electronic goods and is quite crowded in the evenings. Targeting this crowd, the terrorists triggered a bomb blast at 6.07 p.m., leading to many casualties. This was followed by two explosions in Connaught Place and two more in M Block Market of Greater Kailash. Two bomb blasts were conducted near Prince Paan Corner and Levi store. Four other blasts that could not materialise were planned at India Gate, Regal Cinema and on Parliament Street. These explosions within 50 minutes shook entire Delhi.

These blasts were planned by Riyaz Bhatkal and Atif Amin. Riyaz Bhatkal had instructed Yasin Bhatkal alias Mohammad Ahmad Siddhi Bappa to prepare 10 IED units and hand them over to Atif Amin. Mohammad Saif and Khalid from the Azamgarh module of Indian Mujahideen had gone to Udduki in Karnataka by the '*Mangala Express*' train on 26 August, 2008. They obtained the IEDs from Yasin Bhatkal, returned to Delhi on 30 August, 2008 and handed over the explosives to Atif Amin. Hakim Ahmad of Azamgarh had carried small steel balls that were used for making the IEDs.

The serial blasts caused serious concern in the Government of India. The then Home Minister Shivraj Patil called a meeting of IB Director P.C. Haldar, Delhi Police Commissioner Y.S. Dadwal and other senior officers of Delhi police and apprised them of the concern of the Prime Minister Manmohan Singh. It was mentioned in the meeting that the incident had sent a wrong message to the world and if the perpetrators were not apprehended quickly, then India would be known as an insecure country. It was a cause of serious concern for Shivraj Patil since such incidents had been happening with alarming regularity. Just 50 days prior to this, Ahmedabad was rocked by serial blasts on 26 July, 2008, killing 56 persons and injuring more than 200. More alarming was the fact that terrorists aimed at killing the Gujarat Chief Minister Narendra Modi and Home Minister Amit Shah. On the same day, blasts of a greater intensity were planned in Surat but these could not take place because of a circuit failure in the device. About four months earlier, serial blasts had rocked Rajasthan capital, Jaipur, on 13 May, 2008, killing 63 persons and injuring more than 200. Before this, on 11 July, 2006, serial blasts had taken place in the local trains in Mumbai – the capital of Patil's home state of Maharashtra – in which 209 persons were killed. The Ghatkopar blasts in Mumbai (28 July, 2003), Gateway of India and Jhaveri Bazar blasts (25 August, 2003) had killed 58 persons. In Hyderabad, the capital of then Andhra Pradesh (now Telangana), serial blasts had taken place at Gokul Chaat House and Lumbini Park on 25 August, 2007, killing 42 people. Explosions had taken place in court buildings in the capital of Uttar Pradesh Lucknow as well as in Ayodhya and Varanasi, in which 15 persons had died. The national capital Delhi and other major cities including state capitals were at the target of terrorists. In Delhi itself, serial blasts had taken place in Delhi on 29 October, 2005, taking a toll of 62 lives and injuring 210 others.

All these incidents had tarnished the image of India in rest of the world. It was harming India's tourism industry and the country's economy. Many countries were advising their citizens not to travel to India.

The Delhi Police Commissioner Y.S. Dadwal convened a meeting of all the senior officials of the force and instructed them to arrest the terrorists as soon as possible. This responsibility was given to the Special Cell of Delhi Police that had been following the terrorists' activities. Many terrorists involved in Ahmedabad blasts had been arrested and many of them had links with SIMI. The car used as a bomb in Ahmedabad blasts had been stolen from Mumbai and brought to Ahmedabad. The car theft was planned by Afzal Usmani, a resident of Shivaji Nagar, Govandi, in Mumbai and originally a resident of Mau in U.P. The Mumbai police had arrested and jailed him for car theft on 25 August, 2008. Afzal Usmani had a mobile number from Uttar Pradesh and it had been kept on surveillance. A number from Delhi was also linked to it and this too was put on surveillance. The Delhi police had come to know that the conversation on this number was not related to terrorist activities, but it was used very frequently to order food from some restaurants. This number was on suspect list and surveillance showed its location in Jamia Nagar in New Delhi.

From this number, the Delhi police got the location of a house where terrorists could be hiding, although the police did not have any confirmed information about them. Inspector Mohan Chand Sharma of Delhi police led a team to Batala House in the morning of 19 September, 2008 and knocked at the door. The door was opened after a while and someone peeped out. The police team barged into the room and the inmates did not know that these were men from the Delhi Police Special Cell. There was commotion inside and the terrorists opened fire. In the firing that ensued, Atif Amin of Sanjarpur, Azamgarh and the North India commander of Indian Mujahideen, along with an accomplice Mohammad Sajid were killed. Atif Amin was involved in the serial blasts in Delhi on 13 September, 2008. Mohammad Saif managed to escape and at the advice of some acquaintance of his, he reached the office of the Indian news television channel Aaj Tak, and blurted out the entire story including his involvement in the incident. This was broadcast live by the TV channel. Saif realised that he could be killed in a police encounter and the TV appearance could save his life. **Mohammad Saif revealed for the first time that his terrorist organisation was named Indian Mujahideen and that it was involved in most of the bomb explosions in the country.**

Inspector M.C. Sharma was killed in the firing by the terrorists in the Batala House incident and several policemen were injured. Many terrorists belonging to the IM were arrested after this encounter even though Ariz Junaid from Azamgarh and Shahzad Pappu had managed to escape along with Mohammad Saif. Inspector Sharma, who had earned six police medals for bravery, was honoured posthumously in 2009 with the Ashok Chakra for his commendable action.

After Mohammad Saif's arrest, the U.P. ATS launched a crackdown on Indian Mujahideen terrorists. All the terrorists involved in the Batala House encounter belonged to Azamgarh. The U.P. ATS arrested Hakim alias Bagga, an IM terrorist and resident of Azamgarh, from Lucknow's Integral University in January. 2009. Hakim had brought to Atif Amin the steel balls used in the IEDs that caused the Delhi serial blasts on 13 September. 2008. Salman alias Chhotu was arrested from Badhni in Siddharth Nagar on the India-Nepal border on 5 March. 2010. He was sentenced to death by a Jaipur Court on 20 December. 2019 for his involvement in the serial blasts in Jaipur. Also sentenced to death along with him were IM terrorist Mohammad Saif, Mohammad Sarvar and Saifur Rahman.

Shahzad alias Pappu was arrested by U.P. ATS on 1 February, 2010 from Azamgarh and he was handed over to Delhi police. He was sentenced to life imprisonment by the Court of Additional District Judge of Delhi, Rajendra Kumar Shastri on 25 July, 2013. Azamgarh resident Ariz Junaid escaped to Nepal after the Batala House encounter and got a passport made for himself in the name of Mohammad Salim. He lived in Palapa, Kapilvastu, Gorakha till the year 2014. Riyaz Bhatkal called him to Saudi Arabia and he went there to work for three years. During this time, he had regular meetings with Riyaz Bhatkal, Iqbal Bhatkal, Amir Raza Khan and others from SIMI. Riyaz Bhatkal gave Shahzad some money and sent him back to Nepal. Shahzad kept coming to India frequently from Nepal and continued his efforts to strengthen Indian Mujahideen. But he was arrested by the Delhi police on 14 February, 2018 from Banbasa, Uttarakhand. Ariz Junaid was sentenced to death by a Delhi Court on 15 March, 2021 for his role in Batala House encounter.

Saifur Rahman was arrested on 12 April, 2009 from Jabalpur by a team of U.P. ATS and Madhya Pradesh ATS. He was travelling on a train from U.P. to M.P. and personnel of the U.P. ATS were keeping a watch on him. Some over-enthusiastic official conveyed this information to the government and then orders came that Saifur Rahman should be arrested in M.P. and the M.P. police should also be involved in the arrest. U.P. ATS was engaged in demolishing the Azamgarh module of IM but the then Chief Minister Mayawati was concerned that this might anger her Muslim vote-bank. Her advisors were telling her that members of the Muslim community were angry with her Bahujan Samaj Party and this might upset her chances in the 2012 Assembly election.

At that time, veteran Congress leader Digvijay Singh was visiting the houses of the terrorists from Azamgarh and claiming that the Batala House encounter was fake. Maulana Aamir Rashadi had constituted the Ulema Council for helping the terrorists. Azamgarh has been a stronghold of Samajwadi Party and the party supremo Mulayam Singh Yadav, as well as his son Akhilesh Yadav, were Members of Parliament from there. The Samajwadi Party too was standing in support of the terrorists and their supporters. Shadab Ahmad alias Mister, father of IM terrorists Shahnawaz Alam Khan and Mohammad

Saif, had campaigned for the Samajwadi Party in the Assembly elections of 2012, 2017 and 2022, as well as the Lok Sabha elections of 2014 and 2019. He was also the vice president of the Ulema Council. A description of politics by different political parties on the issue of terrorist activities has been given in a separate chapter in this book.

□

12
The aftermath of Batala House encounter

Following the investigations by the intelligence and police agencies, a search was launched for terrorist members of Indian Mujahideen in South India also. On 19 September, 2008, as soon as Yasin Bhatkal alias Mohammad Ahmad Siddhi Bappa saw the news on TV about the Batala House encounter, he along with South India commander Riyaz Bhatkal and Kayamuddin Kapadia and Akbar Ali, set off for Hyderabad by bus via Shimoga and Hubli in Karnataka. He then went to Pune and asked his associates to arrange for a rented accommodation for Kayamuddin and Akbar. Then Yasin, Riyaz and Iqbal Bhatkal came to Delhi and started living in a flat in Shaheen Bagh belonging to an old associate Tariq Anjum alias Dablu, son of Badruzzaman, a resident of Nalanda, Bihar. Tariq had been involved in SIMI activities since 1998 and in 2000, he had got admitted to the Anjuman Engineering College in Bhatkal, Karnataka, to study BE, Civil Engineering. It was then that he came into contact with Riyaz Bhatkal, Iqbal Bhatkal, Yasin Bhatkal, Maulana Shreesh, Afiq and Sultan – all residents of Bhatkal. By the end of 2003, there was a discussion at the residence of Iqbal Bhatkal to set up an organisation. At that time, 11 persons including Riyaz, Iqbal, Yasin, Maulana Shreesh, Afiq, Sultan and White Uncle had come together to form a core committee, named Usaba. Yasin and Tariq Anjum maintained contact even when they were in Dubai. Tariq had returned from Dubai to Okhla in Delhi, in 2007 and in February, 2008, he had met Yasin Bhatkal in Gurgaon and Delhi.

After the Batala House encounter on 19 September, 2009, Yasin Bhatkal had left Koppa Farm in Karnataka and arrived at Shaheen Bagh in Delhi to meet Tariq Anjum, and he was accompanied by Riyaz Bhatkal, Iqbal Bhatkal and Mohsin Chaudhary, who had adopted pseudonyms of Shahid, Habib and Ashfaq, respectively during their stay in Delhi.

□

13
The arrest of Shahzad alias Pappu

Shahzad was arrested by a team of U.P. ATS in a dramatic manner from his village Khalispur in Azamgarh. The plan for this arrest was made by me and the DIG, ATS, Rajiv Sabbarwal, (IPS, 1993), after which Shahzad was arrested on 1 February, 2010 from Azamgarh. Shahzad was on the ATS radar and was under surveillance for a long time. I sent a team of ATS to Azamgarh led by Deputy SP, Ravindra Kumar Singh assisted by Inspector, Tej Bahadur Singh. The team also had 20 sharp and aggressive Jawans and they were instructed not to share the information of this operation with Azamgarh police. Although the then SSP of Azamgarh, Ramit Sharma, was a good officer, but in view of the sensitive nature of the operation, even he was not taken into confidence about this operation. It was found in surveillance that the staunch followers of Shahzad were regularly changing his location in Azamgarh. Khalispur is a Muslim-dominated village and it was not possible for the ATS team to stay for long and keep an eye on him. I and Rajiv Sabbarwal then decided on a different strategy. A handpump of India Mark-II was bought from the market and the local people were told that the government had sent a team to install a handpump for water supply in minority areas. The members of the ATS team, along with the Gram Pradhan and some others, were conducting fake ground testing with fake machines. In Lucknow, the in-charge of the surveillance team, Inspector Ashok Banerjee, was sitting in the ATS office and constantly sharing the information about Pappu's location with the ATS field team.

I consulted Rajiv Sabbarwal as to what could be the fall-out of Shahzad's arrest. We suspected that after his arrest, his followers would try to mislead the villagers and try to free him from police custody, and this is what happened. We suspected that the supporters would block not only the exit from the village but also the roads leading out of Azamgarh, and try to create a law-and-order situation with communal overtones, leading to a possible communal flare-up. To avert this, we did a quick recce and chose a way which passed through places not having Muslim inhabitants. The passage from Azamgarh to Mau, Varanasi and Jaunpur has a predominant population of Muslims, therefore, we chose the road from Azamgarh to Jiyanpur, Dohrighat and Gorakhpur. I and Rajiv Sabbarwal were constantly in touch with the field team, which was conducting fake ground-testing experiments on locations sent by Inspector Ashok Banerjee and the villagers were not suspicious at all. On 1 February, at around 11 a.m., the team got the location of Shahzad in the house of his uncle (*mausa*). They immediately entered the house and caught him and started off on the Gorakhpur route. The fundamentalist elements of the community immediately informed other supporters on mobile phone calls and blocked the roads leading out of Mau, Varanasi, Jaunpur and other places. They also placed burning tyres at many places so as to stop the ATS vehicles from driving on. Rumours were spread that some miscreants had kidnapped Shahzad Pappu. In fact, they had blocked all roads leading out of Azamgarh even before complaining to the Azamgarh police. They had also come to know that the so-called water handpump installing team was actually the ATS team. They knew very well that Pappu was a terrorist with a reward of Rs. 5 lakh on his head, as announced by the Delhi police. The supporters also spread a rumour that Shahzad could be killed in an encounter. Even after knowing that a police team had arrested Shahzad, they continued spreading the rumour of it being a case of kidnapping by miscreants.

Efforts were rapidly being made to cause a law-and-order problem. I then informed SSP, Azamgarh, Ramit Sharma, about the operation and asked him to deploy the Force to control the crowd. He announced before the crowd that Shahzad had been arrested by an ATS team but the extremist Muslims gathered there disbelieved him and continued spreading rumours.

To control the situation, I called a briefing of the electronic media at 1.30 p.m. at the Chief Minister's office in Annexe Building in Lucknow, and told them that the U.P. ATS had arrested Shahzad Pappu and that he was involved in the Batala House encounter and carried a reward of Rs. 5 lakh on his head as announced by the Delhi police. As soon as this news was telecast on TV, the situation started getting under control. I then informed the Delhi police about Shahzad's arrest. A team from their Special Cell rushed to Lucknow, produced Shahzad in court and took him off to Delhi.

Shahzad Pappu was a literate young man and wanted to become a commercial pilot. He had been taking money from his father on the pretext of getting pilot training but actually never joined any commercial pilot training course. His father had been dreaming of the son becoming a pilot and making lots of money, adding to his stature in the community. But Pappu was caught in the net of Indian Mujahideen's North India commander Atif Amin and turned into a *jihadi*. Remarkably, no one in Atif Amin's team had ever studied in a *madarsa*, but all had studied in good schools and even pursued higher studies, such as MBA, computer science, media and engineering at institutions in Delhi. Whenever these recruits told Atif Amin that their careers will be ruined if they were caught engaged in terror activities, then Amin would reply that the police would look for *madarsa* students wearing *kurta* and *pyjama* and would never suspect such boys in modern dresses, such as jeans and T-shirts.

Shahzad had turned into a full-fledged *jihadi* and had come from Azamgarh to Delhi on 1 September, 2008. He had told his father that he was going to Delhi to get his passport made for Australia, then he would get a visa from the Australian High Commission and proceed for Australia to work as a commercial pilot there. His father was overjoyed and gave him the money he wanted. After coming to Delhi, Shahzad played a key role in serial blasts on 13 September, 2008 in Karol Bagh, Greater Kailash, India Gate and picnic spot that led to the killing of 26 people and injured 133. He had managed to escape during the Batala House encounter on 19 September, 2008 and narrowly escaped being hit in police firing. The Delhi police submitted a chargesheet against Shahzad and three others on 28 April, 2010 in a court. The Additional Sessions Judge-2, South-east Delhi, Rajendra Kumar Shastri, found Shahzad Pappu guilty and on 25 July, 2013 and sentenced him to life imprisonment.

□

14
The Darbhanga module of Indian Mujahideen

In Delhi, Gauhar Aziz met Yasin Bhatkal. One of Gauhar's relatives, Fasih Mohmmad, was a resident of Badh Samela in Darbhanga in Bihar, and he had studied in Bhatkal. It was here that Yasin Bhatkal met Kateel Siddiqui through Gauhar Aziz and he was inducted into IM. It was with the help of these terrorists that Yasin then set up a new unit of IM in Darbhanga. Riyaz Bhatkal, Iqbal Bhatkal and Mohsin Chaudhary also came from Delhi and lived in Darbhanga. After some time, the three of them went to Jaynagar on Bihar-Nepal border and proceeded to Nepal. The ISI of Pakistan got its agents to make Nepalese passports for all of them and they went off to Dubai. By September, 2009, one by one, they reached Pakistan. After Azamgarh, Darbhanga became a prominent centre of IM terrorists and was known as the 'Darbhanga Module'.

Yasin Bhatkal wanted to constitute a new team of IM members in India. He contacted Riyaz Bhatkal and Iqbal Bhatkal, then living in Pakistan and asked them to arrange for explosives. Bhatkal already was in close touch with the terrorist organisation HUJI of Bangladesh and there was no problem in arranging explosives. Yaseen Bhatkal and Kateel Gauhar Siddiqui went to Kolkata and obtained the explosives through the HUJI operatives. At that time, the Kolkata police had also launched a crackdown and they caught Yasin Bhatkal while he was going in a taxi, but they found nothing suspicious on him. Yasin Bhatkal had hidden his mobile phones in the taxi itself and he told his identity to the Kolkata police as Ashraf, resident of Badh Samela of Bihar. The police asked him if he was carrying fake notes. This made Yasin realise that the police did not actually know his real identity and he accepted the exchange of fake notes. After some initial questioning lasting six or seven days, the Kolkata police could not find out anything about Yasin Bhatkal and he was charged for a non-serious offence under Section 381 IPC. Yaseen was lodged in the Presidency Jail in Kolkata and was released on bail from there on a personal bond of merely Rs. 30. He then came to Delhi with Kateel Gauhar Siddiqui and stayed in a rented house. He set up an illegal arms factory there and remained in constant touch with Iqbal Bhatkal, Riyaz Bhatkal and Amir Raza Khan in Pakistan planned and executed several terrorist incidents all over India.

□

15
Death of terrorist Khalid Mujahid by heatstroke

Terrorist Khalid Mujahid, involved in the court explosions, had died from heatstroke in Barabanki district hospital after returning from an Ayodhya Court. On this date, he had been taken on a police Braj van from Lucknow Jail to Ayodhya court for an appearance at 10 a.m. While returning from Ayodhya, he suddenly fell ill near Ram Sanehi Ghat in Barabanki District around 4.40 p.m. The policemen on escort duty immediately rushed him to the Barabanki District hospital where doctors declared Khalid to be dead at 5.25 p.m. When Khalid's family members reached the hospital, preparations for conducting a post-mortem examination were being made. In the meantime, his uncle Zaheer Alam Falahi and others from the Ulema Council alleged that Khalid was murdered and started demanding that an FIR be registered against the police. They said they would agree on a post-mortem examination only after an FIR was lodged. On a verbal submission by Khalid's uncle Zaheer Alam Falahi, son of Abdul Razzak, resident of Madiyahu in Jaunpur, a case was registered in the *kotwali*, Barabanki at 3.30 a.m. on 19 May, 2013, as crime number 295/13, under Section 302/120B IPC, in which the following police officials were named:

1. Brij Lal, the then Additional Director-General of Police, Uttar Pradesh

2. Chiranjeev Nath Sinha, Deputy SP
3. Manoj Kumar Jha, Additional Superintendent of Police
4. Vikram Singh, the then Director-General of Police, U.P.
5. S. Anand, Additional Superintendent of Police

In addition, some officials of the IB were also named, totalling 42 persons.

Zaheer Alam Falahi had alleged that the R.D. Nimesh Commission had found Khalid Mujahid to be not guilty and the case against him had been withdrawn by the U.P. Government, but it had been stayed by a Barabanki Court. If Khalid Mujahid was acquitted by court, then it would have caused a problem for many police officials and that is why all of them had conspired and planned his murder.

Two days after his death, the then Chief Minister of U.P., Akhilesh Yadav on 20 May, 2013 handed over the inquiry into his death to the CBI. However, the CBI declined to conduct the inquiry and listed many reasons for this, including the fact that the inquiry committee constituted to inquire into Khalid's death did not find any evidence of murder. The U.P. Government had constituted this committee headed by a senior IPS officer Javed Akhtar to look into Khalid's death and the committee had found it to be a natural death.

After the CBI's refusal, Khalid Mujahid's relatives and the president of Rihai Manch Mohammad Shoeb, a lawyer, filed a petition in the Lucknow Bench of the High Court, seeking investigation by CB-CID. Justice Ajay Lamba and Justice V.K. Srivastava of the High Court passed an order on 2 November, 2015 that the investigation be handed over to Uttar Pradesh Crime Branch-CID. At the same time, it stayed action on the final police report submitted in Barabanki Court. Then the CB-CID continued investigation into this case and it faced pressure to fabricate evidence against the named police officials. An officer of IG rank of the CID himself tried planting evidence against the other police officials but could not succeed. In March, 2017, there was a change of government in Uttar Pradesh and Yogi Adityanath became the Chief Minister of the state. In July, 2017, the final report was submitted in the case and this episode came to an end.

Rihai Manch

A lawyer from Lucknow, named Mohammad Shoeb, had formed this organisation named Rihai Manch and it staged an agitation in front of the Vidhan Bhawan in Lucknow to demand arrest of all police officials named in the case filed in Barabanki *kotwali*. Shoeb was the advocate in Nimesh Commission as well as in the case of terrorist Khalid Mujahid and Tariq Kasmi, related to the Lucknow and Ayodhya Court explosions. The agitation continued for several months in which besides Shoeb, Rihai Manch General Secretary Rajiv Yadav, Magsaysay Award-winner Sandeep Pandey, former IG

S.R. Darapuri (IPS, 1972) also participated. The Samajwadi Party government wanted to jail all police officials named in the case with an eye on the Muslim vote-bank.

□

16
Emergence of Ulema Council

The Indian Mujahideen, Azmgarh module was exposed after the Batala House encounter and several arrests were made. In order to protect the terrorists, Maulana Amir Rashadi constituted the Ulema Council. This Maulana's son had earlier been arrested by the ATS, Gujarat. In the aftermath of Batala House encounter, the Ulema Council booked two trains to take thousands of people to Delhi for holding protest demonstrations. Such demonstrations were held in Lucknow as well and it was demanded that a judicial inquiry be conducted into the encounter.

The Ulema Council also formed a political party and in the year 2009, Dr. Javed Akhtar, father of the terrorist Asadullah alias Haddi, contested the election from Azamgarh on the Ulema Council ticket, but he lost. Later in the Assembly elections, Maulana Rashadi put up more than a dozen candidates on the Ulema Council ticket from U.P. and Bihar, but all of them lost. Dr. Javed Akhtar was a well-known orthopaedic surgeon of Azamgarh and his son turned a *jihadi* after he went to Delhi and was involved in several terrorist incidents across the country. He was arrested in 2013 from near the Bihar-Nepal border, along with Yasin Bhatkal alias Siddhi Bappa, and he was given the death penalty in the German Bakery blasts case.

The Ulema Council is no longer as active an organisation as it was during the arrests of terrorists of the Azamgarh module in 2008. Courts sentenced a large number of terrorists after they were caught. In the Ahmedabad blasts case, five terrorists from Azamgarh – Mufti Abu Bashar Sheikh of Binapar, Sarai Mir, Saifur Rahman, Mohammad Arif Naseem Ahmad Mirza of Sanjarpur, Sarai Mir, Mohamad Shadab Ahmad of Sanjarpur, Zeeshan Ahmad Sheikh of house number 311, Mohalla Baz Bahadur, Azamgarh – were sentenced to be hanged till death. Asadullah Haddi and Ariz Junaid have been sentenced to death in the German Bakery blasts case and Batala House encounter case, respectively. Shahzad Pappu has been jailed for life in the Batala House encounter case. Atif Amin and Mohammad Sajid of Sanjarpur have been killed in the police encounter at Batala House. The Ulema Council, though weakened, kept showing its presence from time to time by supporting these terrorists.

On 7 March, 2017, an ISIS terrorist identified as Saifullah from Kanpur was killed by the U.P. ATS in an encounter in Lucknow, and at that time the U.P. Assembly elections were going on. Just a day before the polling ended, the police got to know about the presence of terrorists in a house in a sensitive locality, in west Lucknow. As soon as the police surrounded the house, the terrorists opened fire. In the encounter that lasted for many hours, terrorist Saifullah kept firing at the police despite being told by the police to surrender and lay down his arms. After he was shot dead by the police, a huge cache of arms, ammunition and ISIS flags and literature were recovered. Saifullah's father Sartaj had refused to even take the body or conduct the last rites of his son's body, saying that the deceased was a traitor.

On 10 March, 2017, Maulana Amir Rashadi of Ulema Council reached Saifullah's house in Kanpur and alleged that the encounter was fake. He also tried to arouse the Muslim community but Saifullah's father did not even listen to him. A case was then registered in Chakeri police station in Kanpur against Maulana Amir Rashadi for trying to incite religious unrest by delivering provocative speeches. Maulana Rashadi had tried to revise the importance of Ulema Council but he failed in his efforts.

□

17
The Nimesh Commission Report

On 31 August, 2012, Justice R.D. Nimesh had submitted his recommendations to the state government and these were presented in the U.P. Vidhan Sabha on 16 September, 2013. These are some of the recommendations:

"The facts regarding the arrest of Tariq Kasmi, son of Riyaz Ahmad, resident of village Sammopur, police station Rani Ki Sarai, District Azamgarh, and Khalid Mujahid, son of Jamir Mujahid, resident of 37, Mahatwana Mohalla, police station Madiyahu, District Jaunpur, on 22 December, 2007 under crime number 1891/2007 in police station *kotwali*, District Barabanki, appear questionable." The above case is under consideration in District Court, Barabanki; therefore, at this level, no liability can be fixed against anyone with regard to this case.

The Commission gives the following suggestions in connection with such cases:

1. In a terrorism incident, a gazetted officer of a department other than police should be the witness of recovery.
2. Video recording should be made of the interrogation of the so-called accused.
3. The investigation should be done by a gazetted officer of any other branch of the police.
4. Special courts should be constituted for disposal of such cases.

5. There should be no compulsion of fixing a quota of case disposal for the presiding officers of such courts.
6. Skilled and efficient advocates/prosecution officers should represent the state government from the prosecution side.
7. A separate prosecution cell should be constituted for such cases to facilitate early disposal of cases.
8. A system should be laid down to dispose such cases quickly and within a maximum of two years, and a time limit should be fixed for action at every level. A review should be done if cases are not disposed in time and action should be taken against the person responsible for the same.
9. There should be provision for giving adequate compensation to the aggrieved party.
10. There should be provision for giving reward to officials and employees for good work.
11. There should be provision for punishment after fixing responsibility for implicating innocent persons.
12. Full security should be provided to officials, employees and presiding officers of courts connected to such cases."

Thus, Justice R.D. Nimesh had prepared the background for exonerating the terrorists Khalid Mujahid and Hakim Tariq Kasmi and a foundation had also been created for implicating me, the then DGP Vikram Singh, Additional Superintendent of Police Manoj Kumar Jha, S. Anand, Deputy Superintendent of Police R.K. Srivastava and others. When the case is pending in court after investigation, then how can the Commission say that the arrest of the two terrorists in Barabanki and their involvement in the incident is questionable? During the hearing by the Commission, we had provided undeniable evidence to establish that Tariq Kasmi and Khalid Mujahid were terrorists, but Justice Nimesh did not include these in his report.

Undeniable Evidence

Mohammad Amin Wani alias Khalid alias Zia alias Naeem, son of Mohammad Sabir Wani, resident of Bankoot, police station Banihal, District Doda, was the chief of the Harkat-ul Jihad al-Islami (HUJI) in Jammu & Kashmir. The Delhi police arrested him on 21 December, 2006 and recovered Rs. 4 lakh 50 thousand from his possession. He was interrogated by the Delhi police and Central Intelligence organisations. An amount of Rs. 5 lakhs had been sent via *hawala* channel from Pakistan by Taukir, the head of terrorist organisation HUJI, to Azamgarh. Hakim Tariq Kasmi had made this money available to this terrorist in Delhi after deducting his cut of Rs. 50,000. This fact had been established in the interrogation of Tariq after his arrest in the court blasts case. In a report prepared by Delhi police at that time, Amin Wani had been quoted as saying that he had met Khalid Mujahid and his accomplice 16-year-old Rakib (from Assam) in a *madarsa* in Amroha. Both had been sent to Kashmir for terrorist training in 2003-2004, where Rakib was killed and Khalid fled for his life, and came to his house at Madiyahu in Jaunpur. Wani went to jail, but after getting released on bail, he came to Jaunpur and met Khalid Mujahid. Khalid had organised his meeting with Hakim Tariq Kasmi of Azamgarh.

After this meeting, Hakim Tariq Kasmi had handed over the money from *hawala* to Mohammad Amin Wani in Delhi and Wani was arrested the same day, but Tariq managed to escape. Khalid Mujahid wanted to set up a terrorist base in Jaunpur. Mohammad Amir Wani had organised a conversation on Khalid's mobile phone with Pakistan-based Taukir on the latter's mobile number 0092-3005154737 on 29 November, 2006. Khalid had declined to accept the *hawala* money but instead suggested the name of Hakim Tariq Kasmi. Khalid had told Wani in his house that he could arrange the supply of fake Indian currency notes and he had also provided a sample of five-hundred-rupee fake notes. Khalid had also suggested getting involved in heroin and morphine supply business to earn lots of money that could be used in *jihadi* activities. He wanted to use the money thus earned to purchse AK-47 and other weapons. He also wanted to assassinate a gangster of Azamgarh and an MP with criminal records. This MP had taken a large sum of money from Khalid Mujahid for running the business of fake Indian currency notes and had refused to return it. Khalid had told him that he could easily procure AK-47 guns from the ULFA, a terror organisation of Assam. He had developed good contacts with terrorists in Assam through Rakib.

A terrorist Bashir Ahmad alias Hejaji, son of Habibullah Mir, resident of Kuchhal Chatru, District Kishtwar in Kashmir, had been killed in a police encounter and from his possession a Nokia 1110 mobile phone bearing mobile number 9906753203 had been recovered. Bashir Ahmad alias Hejaji was a dreaded terrorist and was formerly the head of HUJI in Kashmir. This organisation had been formed in Bangladesh and it was active in India and Pakistan also, besides in Bangladesh. It had been banned by the Bangladesh Government in 2005. Its operational commander was Iliyas Kashmiri and he had been killed in an US drone attack in southern Waziristan on 4 June, 2011. After his death, the local Taliban commander Shah Sahib was made his successor. This organisation was involved in the Varanasi bomb blasts and Delhi High Court blast in 2006, Delhi bomb blast in 2011, killing of a police officer in Hyderabad and other terrorist activities. Details obtained from the SIM card in Hejaji's phone provided direct links between him and Tariq Kasmi and Khalid Mujahid. Tariq Kasmi had, from his mobile number 9450047342, talked to Hejaji on 27 May, 2007 at 9.47 a.m. and 9.56 a.m. Khalid Mujahid had three mobile numbers – 9889569370, 9451253363 and 9889810588 – and had talked to Hejaji on the latter's mobile number (9906753203). He had talked to Hejaji on 8 June. 2007, 12 November, 2007, 13 November, 2007 (thrice), 2 December, 2007 and 19 December, 2007. Khalid and Tariq had also been in regular touch.

□

18

Undeniable evidence of Khalid Mujahid and Tariq Kasmi having links with HUJI

A graphic description of the call details related to mobile numbers of Khalid Mujahid, Tariq Kasmi and HUJI Kashmir leader Hejaji establishes the links between them. Also, the terrorists' links had been provided as evidence to Justice Nimesh but the latter did not include these in his report, apparently because he wanted to please the then Samajwadi Party government and be in its good books. He got rewarded for this also. The Samajwadi Party government expected the judge to do this as per its appeasement policy and the judge obliged. As a reward, he was made the Chairman of the Tappal Commission constituted to look into the violent stir by farmers of Aligarh in August, 2010.

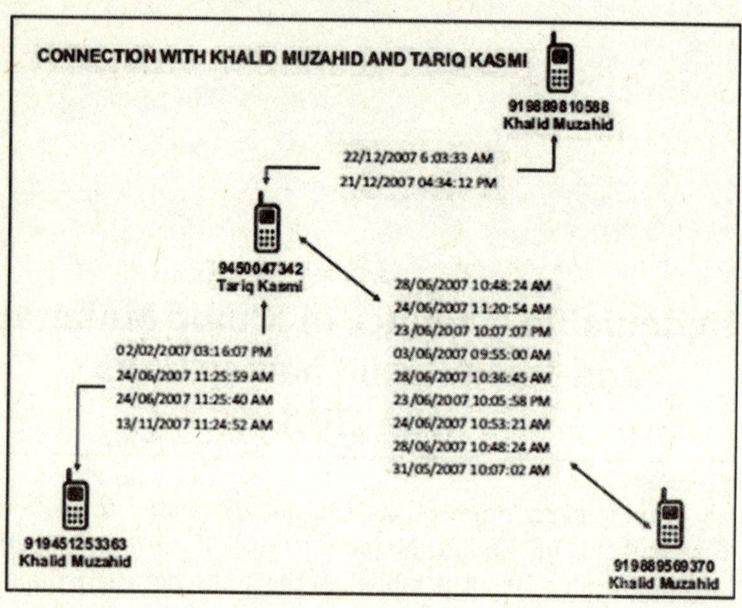
CONNECTION WITH KHALID MUZAHID AND TARIQ KASMI
919889810588
Khalid Muzahid
22/12/2007 6:03:33 AM
21/12/2007 04:34:12 PM
9450047342
Tariq Kasmi
28/06/2007 10:48:24 AM
24/06/2007 11:20:54 AM
23/06/2007 10:07:07 PM
03/06/2007 09:55:00 AM
28/06/2007 10:36:45 AM
23/06/2007 10:05:58 PM
24/06/2007 10:53:21 AM
28/06/2007 10:48:24 AM
31/05/2007 10:07:02 AM
02/02/2007 03:16:07 PM
24/06/2007 11:25:59 AM
24/06/2007 11:25:40 AM
13/11/2007 11:24:52 AM
919451253363
Khalid Muzahid
919889569370
Khalid Muzahid

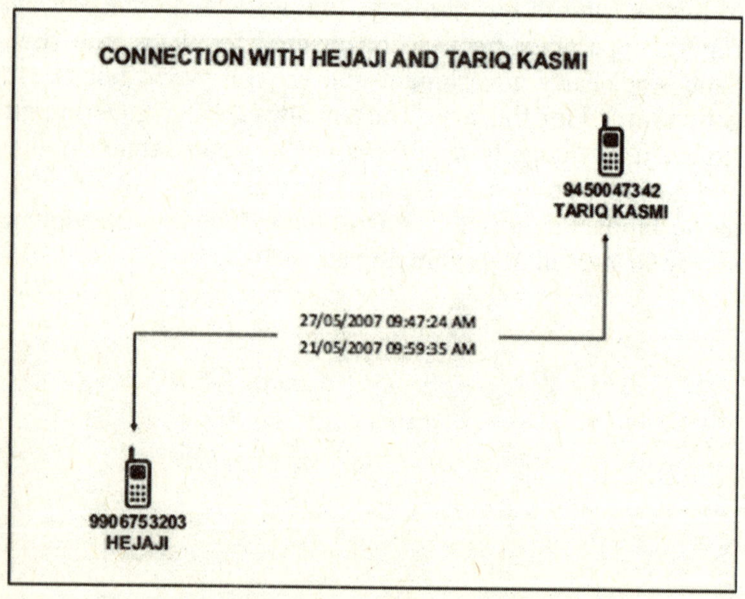
CONNECTION WITH HEJAJI AND TARIQ KASMI
9450047342
TARIQ KASMI
27/05/2007 09:47:24 AM
21/05/2007 09:59:35 AM
9906753203
HEJAJI

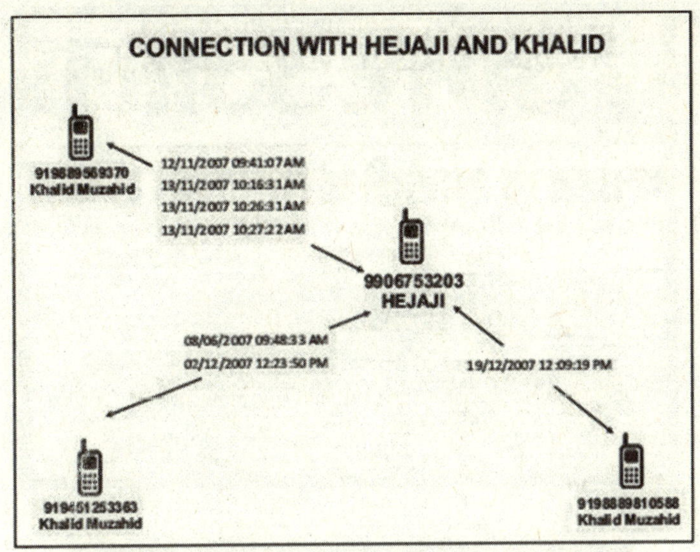

प्रतिष्ठित अखबार "अमर उजाला" ने तारिक कासमी और खालिद मुजाहिद के हूजी आतंकवादी संगठन से रिश्ते के सम्बन्ध में 28 मई 2013 को समाचार प्रकाशित किया था।

अमर उजाला

तारिक और खालिद के थे हूजी से रिश्ते

आईबी का दावा- दोनों चार साल पहले से थे आतंकियों के संपर्क में

SUNDAY

अमर उजाला

ब्लास्ट के आरोपी की हिरासत में मौत

पेशी के बाद फैजाबाद से लौटते वक्त बिगड़ी तबीयत, गृह सचिव ने शुरू की जांच, न्यायिक जांच भी होगी

सुबह से बिगड़ने लगी थी तबीयत

खालिद की मौत की सीबीआई जांच होगी

राज्य सरकार ने केंद्रीय गृह मंत्रालय को भेजी सिफारिश

लखनऊ, बाराबंकी और फैजाबाद जेल के अफसरों से मांगी रिपोर्ट

19
Ruling of the Barabanki Court

The Akhilesh Yadav government in Uttar Pradesh had on 18 April, 2013 ordered the withdrawal of the chargesheet filed in the case registered in the Barabanki *kotwali* against terrorists Hakim Tariq Kasmi and Mufti Khalid Mujahid. These two terrorists had been arrested by U.P. STF on 22 December, 2007 from near the Barabanki railway station in connection with the bomb explosions in Lucknow and Faizabad (now Ayodhya) courts. Besides *jihadi* literature, 1.25 kg RDX and three detonators were recovered from their possession. A case was registered against these two terrorists in Barabanki *kotwali* in crime number 1891/2007, under Sections 121/121A/124A/332 IPC and Section 4/5 of Explosive Substances Act. After investigation, the chargesheet against the two terrorists were submitted for perusal of the court.

The Barabanki Sessions Court did not allow the withdrawal of the chargesheet as proposed by the U.P. Government and the trial was initiated. The ADGC (Criminal), Barabanki was persuaded to proffer a weak prosecution in this case. The then Chief Minister was upset with the ADGC because the chargesheet in the case of these terrorists could not be withdrawn in the Barabanki Sessions Court despite the order from the state government, apparently because of weak representation. The ADGC bore the brunt of the government's ire as he was dismissed. The case was then taken forward by Pradeep Kumar Srivastava, the JD (Prosecution) of U.P. ATS and he too was persuaded by the DG (Prosecution) to offer weak arguments, so that the terrorists were not prosecuted. The then DGP and Principal Secretary (Home) were repeatedly calling the officials to put pressure on them that the chargesheet against the terrorists had to be withdrawn, come what may, and that this task had to be completed within a fixed time limit.

The Samajwadi Party had announced as part of the pre-election manifesto in the 2012 Assembly election that after forming the government, the cases against jailed innocent Muslims would be withdrawn. A Samajwadi Party government was formed in the State in March, 2012 and there was a lot of confrontation in the Yadav family on the issue of who will become the Chief Minister. Mulayam Singh Yadav's younger brother, Shivpal Singh Yadav, strongly put forward his claim for the post, but eventually Mulayam Singh Yadav succeeded in making his 38-year-old son Akhilesh Yadav the next Chief Minister of the state. Among the main faces of the Muslim community in the Samajwadi Party government were leaders like Azam Khan, Ahmad Hasan, Shahid Manzoor, Iqbal Masood, Yasser Shah (all Cabinet Ministers), Anis Ahmad Khan, Akbar Husain (Ministers of State, independent charge), Mahboob Ali and Shahzil Islam Ansari (Ministers of State). However, the main face of the community was Azam Khan. He did not give any importance to Akhilesh Yadav and did not even attend Cabinet meetings if he was upset with him. He was at the forefront in putting pressure about withdrawing cases against, the terrorist's specailly terrorist involved in CRPF Rampur attack case.

On 31 December, 2007/1 January, 2008, the CRPF Group Centre in Rampur was attacked by Lashkar-e-Tayyaba terrorists in which seven CRPF personnel were killed. On an initiative led by me, India commander of Lashkar Sabauddin (Madhubani, Bihar), Sharif alias Sohail Ansari (Rampur), Mohammad Farukh and Imran Shahzad (Pakistani *fidayeen*), Jang Bahadur Khan alias Baba (Moradabad) and Fahim

Ansari (Goregaon, Mumbai), were arrested. A huge cache of ammunition and AK-47 rifles were recovered from their possession. Azam Khan was most interested in the withdrawal of chargesheet in this case, since he belonged to Rampur and he had promised before the elections that he would ensure that the case was withdrawn. Azam Khan used to claim at various meetings with officials that the case was fake and innocent Muslims were implicated in it. According to him, there was a celebration of New Year at the CRPF Personnel Group Centre, Rampur and the drunk CRPF personnel had fought amongst themselves, leading to firing in which seven persons had been killed. This story had been conveyed among all fundamentalist Muslims in the entire state.

Muslim ministers in the government and fundamentalist Muslims in the state were putting pressure on the Chief Minister Akhilesh Yadav as well as on the then president of Samajwadi Party, Mulayam Singh Yadav, to implement the promises made in the manifesto. Mulayam Singh Yadav himself wanted the cases against the terrorists to be withdrawn as soon as possible since Muslims constituted the core vote-bank of his party and he did not want it to shift away. He often used to say in election rallies that he had ordered firing on *kar sevaks* on 30 October and 2 November, 1990 in which about a dozen Ram *bhakts* at Ayodhya were killed at Ayodhya In an election rally in Moradabad, on 10 April, 2014, he had said that it was wrong to punish men in cases of rape as young men often make mistakes. According to him, it was misuse of the law. He even went on to say that in case any friendship between boys and girls went sour, the girls slapped rape charge on the boys to seek revenge and the poor innocent boys were punished.

He had given the statement to please the Muslim vote-bank in the aftermath of the punishment awarded by a court to Mohammad Kasim Hafiz, Sheikh alias Kasim Bangali, Siraj Rahman Khan, Mohammad Salim Ansari, Mohammad Ashfaq Sheikh and two minors for the rape of a photo-journalist in Shakti Mills, Mumbai on 22 August, 2013. The Mumbai Sessions

Court had, on 20 March, 2014, found five adults and two minors guilty of gang rape. The sentence was announced on 4 April, 2014 in which three accused were sentenced to death and two were given life imprisonment. The minor accused were sentenced on 15 July, 2015 to three years' imprisonment each and they were lodged in the Nashik Probation Home. However, the Mumbai High Court later, on 25 November, 2021, changed the death sentence of the three accused to life imprisonment (to be jailed till death). Apparently, Mulayam Singh Yadav saw his Muslim vote-bank in the accused since all of them were Muslims.

Earlier in 1993, when Mulayam Singh Yadav had become the Chief Minister for the second time, he had ordered withdrawal of the chargesheet in cases of the attack on PAC picket in Meerut on 26 January, 1993, terrorist attack on Nauchandi PAC Camp on 13 July, 1992 and the blowing up by RDX of U.P. Roadways bus number U.P.07-4326 going from Delhi to Saharanpur on 23 July, 1993. In these cases, chargesheets were filed against Mohammad Ayub, Yunus, Mohammad Yaqub, sons of Haji Munshi resident of 335, Islamabad, Abdul Malik of 269, Kidwai Nagar, Amir Hamza of 164 Kidwai Nagar, Dr. M. Irfan of 164 Kidwai Nagar, Salim alias Salim Patla of 197 Islamabad and Salim Mota of 48 South Islamabad, all from Meerut. In addition to various sections of IPC, there were also charged under Explosives Act and Terrorists and Disruptive Activities Prevention Act (TADA). However, because of court's intervention, Mulayam Singh Yadav could not withdraw the cases in these three terrorist incidents and the court sentenced the terrorists to life imprisonment.

Taking forward the policy of Muslim appeasement of his father, Akhilesh Yadav too wanted to put me and the then DGP, Vikram Singh besides 42 other police officials in jail in the fake case of the death (actually by heatstroke) of terrorist Khalid Mujahid. It was aimed to send out a message of Muslim appeasement, on the strength of which the Samajwadi Party could get Muslim votes en masse in the 2014 Lok Sabha elections. All of us had to engage private lawyers to defend ourselves. If the terrorists were acquitted from Barabanki Court, then the Akhilesh government would have got a reason for prosecuting the police officials in this fake case.

The report of the R.D. Nimesh Commission was presented in the U.P. Vidhan Sabha on 16 September, 2013. As per the Samajwadi Party's vote-bank politics, it was planned to punish all the police officials. The Additional Sessions Court of Barabanki did not agree to the recommendation of the state government to withdraw the chargesheet in this case. A case was heard in the Court of Special Sessions Judge S.P. Arvind against Tariq Kasmi. The Special Judge of Barabanki Court awarded life imprisonment to Tariq Kasmi on 24 April, 2015 for possession of RDX and detonators. He was also sentenced to jail for life in cases of blasts in Golghar, Gorakhpur and blasts in Courts in Lucknow and Ayodhya.

□

20

Activities of Indian Mujahideen in the aftermath of Batala House encounter

The activities of IM were uncovered after the Batala House encounter. Among its founders, Iqbal Bhatkal, Riaz Bhatkal, Mohsin Chaudhary and Amir Raza Khan (brother of the deceased Asif Raza Khan) of Kolkata, fled to Nepal from Bihar. The ISI got their Nepalese passports made in Nepal and sent them to Pakistan via Dubai. The two Bhatkal brothers and Amir Raza Khan developed strong contacts in Pakistan with the Pakistani intelligence agency ISI and Pakistani terrorist organisations Jaish-e-Mohammad and Lashkar-e-Tayyaba. From there, they continued to plan and execute terrorist incidents in India. Dr. Shahnawaz Khan of Azamgarh, Mohammad Sajid alias Bada Sajid, Khalid, Abu Rashid, Asadullah Haddi and Salman Chhotu also fled to Nepal and were transported to Pakistan with help from ISI.

The activities of IM were weakened because of the arrests but the IM terrorists sitting in Pakistan were active. Their Pakistani handlers kept prodding them to conduct terrorist actions in India. It is to be remembered that IM was formed by the ISI with help from Lashkar-e-Tayyaba and HUJI. ISI wanted to ensure that in terror acts in India, the involvement of Pakistani organisations, such as LeT, JeM, HUJI and Hijbul Mujahideen, was not established.

Many IM terrorists were caught after the Batala House encounter and their activities were exposed. In the first terror mail sent by IM after the court blasts in U.P. on 23 November,

2007, it was clearly mentioned that they were not related to the neighbouring country's ISI, LeT and HUJI, and that it was purely an organisation of Indian Muslims.

In the interrogation after the arrest of IM terrorists Mufti Abu Bashr, Shahzad Ahmad alias Pappu, Salman alias Chhotu, Mohammad Saif, Mohammad Sadiq Sheikh, Asadullah Haddi etc, the network of Pakistani terrorist organisations came to light. Pakistan's ISI had trained the IM terrorists in the training camps of LeT at Muzafarabad in PoK. The terrorists were sent from India to Dubai and then to Pakistan. After training, they were given fake Pakistani passports and sent to Karachi, then to Kathmandu and then back to India. They were trained in operating AK-47, grenades and pistols, and also in making bombs with locally available ingredients. Amir Raza Khan and Iqbal Bhatkal planned terrorist incidents in India in co-ordination with Pakistan-based terrorist organisations and the ISI. Riaz Bhatkal supplied explosives from Karnataka and the explosive material used in the blasts in courts in U.P., as well blasts in Sankat Mochan, Dashashwamedh Ghat, Shitla Ghat, '*Shramjivi Express*' train, Golghar, Gorakhpur, Jaipur, Ahmedabad, Gokul Chat centre, Lumbini Park and blasts in Delhi was supplied mainly from Bhatkal in Karnataka. Bhatkal, a coastal town in North Karnataka, is inhabited mostly by Muslims. The outline of setting up *jihadi* organisations prior to IM, such as Usaba Committee, Karnataka Forum for Dignity and Asif Raza Commando Force was formed in Bhatkal. Terrorists of SIMI had constituted IM through Pakistani agencies in which funding, training, directions, supplies of explosives, etc. was mainly done by Iqbal Bhatkal, Riaz Bhatkal, Yasin Bhatkal alias Mohammad Ahmad Siddhi Bappa in association with Amir Raza Khan of Kolkata.

After the crackdown, many IM operatives fled to Pakistan but the organisation wanted to establish that it may have become weak but was not finished. Incidents like blasts in Shitla Ghat, Delhi's Jama Masjid, firing on bus carrying foreigners, blasts in Bodh Gaya, Pune, Patna, German Bakery, Jhaveri Bazar and Opera House were conducted to reinforce its presence.

□

21
The Azamgarh module of Indian Mujahideen

Immediately after the Batala House encounter, Mohammad Saif alias Carry On alias Rahul Sharma, a resident of Sanjarpur in Azamgarh was caught, leading to further exposure of incidents carried out by IM. Ample information about IM activities was also gathered after the arrest of Mohammad Shahzad from Azamgarh by U.P. STF. It is Mohammad Sadiq Sheikh alias Imran, son of Israr Ahmad, a resident of Cheeta Camp, Trombay, Mumbai, who was mainly responsible for brainwashing young men from Uttar Pradesh into joining terrorist activities. Originally a resident of Azamgarh, he worked as a computer engineer in Mumbai. He got associated with SIMI in 1996 and came into contact with Riaz Bhatkal in Cheeta Camp itself. One of his relatives, Mujahid Salim, created his E-mail ID, and saying that someone important would contact him soon, advised him to check his mail regularly. Three months later, in the year 2001, he met Zaheer in Madina Hotel in Cheeta Camp. Zaheer called him to visit Kolkata, where he came to know that Zaheer was actually the dreaded terrorist Asif Raza Khan. The latter was eventually killed in an encounter with Gujarat police in December, 2001.

It was Asif Raza Khan who had organised a meeting of Sadiq Sheikh with Azhar in Tipu Sultan Masjid at Dharamtalla in Kolkata in July, 2001. It was later learnt that Azhar was actually Aftab Ansari of Varanasi. Aftab had sent Sadiq Sheikh to Pakistan for training through the Bangladeshi terror organisation HUJI. Asif's brother Amir Raza Khan lived at Karachi in Pakistan and used to visit Dubai quite frequently. Sadiq Sheikh had met Azam Cheema of Lashkar-e-Tayyaba in Pakistan, and Sadiq had also completed the primary and advance terrorist training programmes known as *daura-e-Aam* (20 days) and *daura-e-khaas* (30 days), respectively. The advance training was organised by Azam Cheema in a desert which focused on organising bomb explosions and operating grenades. After completing the training, Sadiq Sheikh came from Karachi to Kathmandu and then to India. He then motivated youths from Azamgarh to join IM and sent them to Pakistan for training. Sadiq Sheikh often went to Dubai from Mumbai. Amir Raza Khan had set up an electronics shop for him in Dubai in association with Mohammad Yahya. After living in Dubai for about eight months, he came to Azamgarh at the end of 2002 and set up a group comprising Arif Badr, Dr. Shahnawaz Alam, Rashid, Akmal, Dr. Majid, Atif Amin, Sarfuddin and others. This group was later known as the 'Azamgarh Module' of IM which was responsible for executing several bomb blasts in the country, leading to more than 700 deaths.

Over two dozen operatives of this Azamgarh Module had got trained from LeT in Pakistan. Among them, Atif Amin ended up to bc the most aggressive and got associated directly with the founders of IM, namely Iqbal Bhatkal, Riaz Bhatkal and Amir Raza Khan, eventually becoming the North India commander of IM. Those associated with him in playing a leading role in terrorist incidents in India were 1. Sadiq Sheikh, 2. Asadullah Haddi, 3. Dr. Shahnawaz Alam, 4. Arif Badr, 5. Mohammad Shadab Ahmad, 6. Ariz alias Junaid, 7. Bada Sajid, 8. Abu Rashid, 9. Mohammad Saif, 10. Khalid, 11. Chhota Sajid, 12. Shakeel, 13. Zeeshan Ahmad Sheikh, 14. Shahzad alias Pappu, 15. Mohammad Salman alias Chhotu, 16. Mufti Abu Bashar Sheikh, 17. Saifur Rahman, 18. Shadab Doosra, 19. Mohammad Sarvar Azmi, 20. Shaqib, 21. Sarfuddin, 22. Mohammad Arif Naseem and 23. Zia.

These incidents executed by this Azamgarh Module of IM included Golghar Gorakhpur blasts, Court blasts in Lucknow, Ayodhya, Varanasi, Dashshwamedh Ghat blast, Sankat Mochan blast, Sheetla Ghat blast (all in Varanasi), '*Shramjivi Express*' blast in Jaunpur, Mumbai local train blast, Delhi blasts in Sarojini Nagar, Paharganj serial blasts, Ghaffar Market, Connaught Place, Greater Kailash, Regal Cinema, Jama Masjid, serial blasts in Jaipur, Ahmedabad serial blasts and blast attempt in Surat. Explosives were provided to them by Riaz and Iqbal Bhatkal, and these were carried to Mumbai and then sent to Azamgarh for preparing IEDs there. The switch for triggering the blast was made by Arif Badr who ran an electronics shop in Sarai Mir in Azamgarh. The plans to cause explosions were often made at meetings held by Atif Amin. Dr. Shahnawaz Alam, Asadullah Haddi, Saifur Rahman, Mohammad Saif and Ariz Junaid at Arif Badr's shop. The IEDs were initially prepared by Arif Badr but later, Atif Amin and Dr. Shahnawaz Khan had also acquired the expertise to make these. A boat-shaped bomb was designed by Yasin Bhatkal which was used to cause explosions in Ahmedabad, Gokul Chat Centre and Lumbini Garden in Hyderabad and one incident in Delhi.

Of these terrorists, Mohammad Atif Amin, commander of the Azamgarh Module and Chhota Sajid were killed in the police encounter in Batala House in Delhi on 19 September, 2008, in which Delhi Police Inspector M.C. Sharma was also killed. Mufti Abu Bashar Sheikh of village Binapar, Saifur Rahman and Mohammad Arif Naseem of village Sanjarpur and Zeeshan Ahmad Sheikh – all residents of Azamgarh – were sentenced to death on 18 February, 2022 by court for Ahmedabad blasts.

Mohammad Salman alias Chhotu, Mohammad Sarvar Azmi, Saifur Rahman and Mohammad Saif, all residents of Azamgarh, were sentenced to death on 20 December, 2019 for Jaipur blasts.

Asadullah Haddi, along with Yasin Bhatkal, Tehsin Akhtar and Ejaj Sheikh were sentenced to death by NIA court on

13 December, 2016 for the German Bakery blast in Pune. Ariz Junaid was sentenced to death by a Delhi court on 15 March, 2021 for Batala House police encounter and in the same case, Shahzad alias Pappu was sentenced on 30 July, 2013 to life imprisonment. Notably, all of them belonged to Azamgarh.

Zia-ur-Rahman Teli of Parikshitgarh, Meerut, Mohammad Shakeel Lohar of Aurangabad, Bulandshahar and Mohammad Tanvir of Najibabad, Bijnore, were sentenced to death on 18 February, 2022, for the Ahmedabad blasts.

Dr. Shahnawaz Khan and Bada Sajid fled to Pakistan via Nepal and later joined the Al Qaeda. It is learnt that both were killed in Syria.

□

22

Terrorist incidents caused by the Azamgarh module

1. Dashashwamedh Ghat blast – seven killed, nine injured (23 February, 2005)

The terrorists trained in Pakistan were put to work to cause explosions in India. Sadiq Sheikh contacted Amir Raza Khan and conveyed to him that he had the trained boys ready but lacked the explosives. Amir Raza Khan contacted Riaz Bhatkal who directed him to Babu Bhai in Varanasi. Babu Bhai is learnt to have provided him 20 kg of a black coloured explosive substance, a dozen detonators and three timers.

Sadiq Sheikh came with this material to Arif Badr's shop in Sarai Mir. The plot to cause the first blast in Dashashwamedh Ghat in Varanasi was hatched in Arif's shop. Arif made the switches and put them in aluminium boxes to prepare two bombs. Atif Amin and Dr. Shahnawaz Khan and their accomplice placed these IED bombs in Dashashwamedh Ghat and caused the explosions, in which seven persons were killed and nine were injured. However, Atif Amin was not happy with the outcome as he had anticipated the death of dozens of persons.

2. '*Sharamjivi Express*' Train Blast – 13 killed, over 50 injured (28 July, 2005)

The plot to cause explosions on '*Shramjivi Express*' train was hatched by Atif Amin, Mohammad Sadiq Sheikh and

Dr. Shahnawaz after the incident at Dashashwamedh Ghat. Atif Amin was now in direct touch with Amir Raza Khan, thus having grown in stature. A suitcase bomb was made with the explosives left over from that given by Babu Bhai. Sadiq Sheikh and Atif Amin conducted a recce in Varanasi and took a room on rent near the Varanasi Cantonment railway station. On the day of the incident, both went to the station and placed the suitcase bomb in a toilet of a coach. As the '*Shramjivi Express*' halted on the station, they came out. The train left for Delhi on right time and the bomb exploded at 5.15 p.m. as the train approached Jaunpur. Thirteen persons lost their lives and more than 50 were injured in the incident.

3. New Delhi bomb blasts – 62 killed, 210 injured (29 October, 2005)

Atif Amin came to Delhi after the '*Shramjivi Express*' blast and lived in a rented room at Jasola. He kept visiting Azamgarh and, with Mohammad Sadiq Sheikh, planned a bigger incident in Delhi. He felt that such an incident in Delhi would have an all-India impact. Atif then called over Sadiq Sheikh from Azamgarh and, along with the trio of Shakeel, Shaqib and Mohammad Shadab, made the preparations. Atif Amin had arranged the explosives. Arif Badr and Atif bought two pressure cookers and one tiffin box, and later Arif Badr prepared bombs out of these utensils in Atif Amin's house.

Atif was looking for a time when the explosion could cause the highest casualties. He waited for the festival of Diwali, since Saroijini Nagar, Govindpuri and Paharganj markets were places where a large number of people gathered for festive shopping. The markets became crowded as Dhanteras approached. On 29 October, 2005, bombs were placed by Atif Amin in Paharganj, by Mohammad Shadab in Sarojini Nagar, while Shakeel and Shaqib placed them in Govindpuri. The explosions were caused between 5.38 p.m. and 6.05 p.m., leading to deaths of 62 people and injuring 210.

4. Sankat Mochan blasts–28 killed, 101 injured (7 July, 2006)

After the Delhi blasts, Atif Amin and his associates came back to Azamgarh as he had run out of explosives. He spoke to Amir Raza Khan who promised to send more explosives after consulting Riaz Bhatkal. Amir also gave him Riaz Bhatkal's mobile number. Later, Riaz provided 6 kg of explosives to Abu Rashid in Mumbai. Abu Rashid also belonged to Sanjarpur in Azamgarh. This explosion looked like a silver-coloured powder. Rashid gave this explosive to Dr. Shahnawaz Khan in Mumbai, who came to Azamgarh and handed over this material to Atif Amin. A meeting of the conspirators was held in Arif Badr's shop in Sarai Mir. Atif Amin wanted to target religious places in Varanasi, besides the railway stations. Atif and Sarvar went to Varanasi and rented a room in front of Saba Hospital. Later, Sarwar, Asadullah Haddi, Arif Badr and Ariz Junaid also came there. Atif decided to cause a blast in the Sankat Mochan temple on Tuesday as on this day a large number of devotees assamble there. At that time, examinations of CBSE/ISC were also being held and several students came to the temple to seek blessings of Lord Hanuman, adding to the already large number of devotees. The terrorists decided to cause the explosion at the time of the evening *arti* in the temple, when the number of devotees would be at its peak and the gathering of people large at the railway station also. Two cooker bombs were made by Arif Badr. One of them was placed by Atif Amin and Ariz Junaid in Sankat Mochan temple, while Sarwar placed it at the Cantonment railway station. The first explosion took place at Sankat Mochan at 6.20 p.m. when the *arti* was in progress. Immediately thereafter, the other explosion took place at the Varanasi Cantonment railway station, when the Delhi-bound '*Shiv Ganga Express*' was stationed there. The explosions led to the death of 28 persons while 101 were injured.

5. Mumbai Local Train Serial blasts - 209 killed, 714 injured (11 July, 2006)

The terrorists ran out of explosives after the Varanasi blasts. Then a plot to cause blasts in the local trains in Mumbai, the financial capital of India, was hatched in Azamgarh by Sadiq Sheikh and Atif Amin. They also decided to target the first-class coach in which mostly Gujaratis travel, as they wanted to avenge the 2002 riots in Gujarat. Atif and Sadiq conveyed this plot to Amir Raza Khan in Pakistan. Amir told Riaz Bhatkal to arrange explosives. Atif and Sadiq came to Delhi and directed Dr. Shahnawaz Khan and Abu Rashid to reach Mumbai and take a flat on rent to put their plan into action. Sadiq Sheikh reached Mumbai in June 2006 and ten days later, Abu Rashid and Dr. Shahnawaz followed suit. They started living in a rented flat in Sewri locality. Abu Rashid worked in a shop named GKB Opticals in Andheri West and lived with his uncle in Sewri.

Towards the end of June, 2006, Atif Amin also came from Delhi to Mumbai to give final shape to the Mumbai local train blasts and started living in a rented flat in Sewri. He then asked Amir Raza Khan to deliver the explosives. Atif contacted Riaz Bhatkal on a number provided by Amir. Riaz said he would provide explosives in Mangalore, Karnataka. Atif then went to Mangalore and obtained about 35-36 kg of explosive material from Riaz Bhatkal. It was a light cream-coloured material packed in a bag on which 'Amin Explosive Bomb' was written. The group decided to make seven cooker bombs this time. Mohammad Sadiq Sheikh had obtained the timers from Arif Badr and brought them to Mumbai. The seven cooker bombs were made in the Sewri flat and a timer was set to cause the explosion after four-and-a-half-hours. They had done a recce of the local trains based on the timetable. Mohammad Sadiq Sheikh, Atif Amin, Abu Rashid, Sajjad and Dr. Shahnawaz decided to plant the bombs. Atif Amin and Dr. Shahnawaz carried two bombs each in a bag and the rest three took one each. The blasts were timed between 6.24 p.m.

and 6.35 p.m. and exploded accordingly. The blasts caused the death of 209 persons which included 22 foreigners and injured 714 others. The IM commander Amir Raza Khan, Riaz Bhatkal and Atif Amin were highly pleased at these explosions. Sadiq and Atif Amin went to Azamgarh on 13 September, 2006, Dr. Shahnawaz Khan went to Lucknow and Abu Rashid and Sajjad stayed in Mumbai to work as usual.

6. Golghar, Gorakhpur Blasts – 4 injured (22 May, 2007)

Atif Amin and Mohammad Saif reached Arif Badr's house in Sarai Mir in 2007 and handed him 12 kg of cream-coloured explosive material and four detonators. They asked them to make three bombs in milk cans. Arif Badr did likewise and set a timer of 1.30 p.m. In the third week of May, 2007, Atif Amin, Mohammad Saif, Mohammad Shadab, Mohammad Salman alias Chhotu and two others gathered in Sarai Mir and went by bus to Gorakhpur. They conducted a recce of some places and returned the same day. On the second day, that is 22 May, 2007, Atif Amin, Sadiq Sheikh came to Arif Badr's house in Sarai Mir and took away the three bombs to Gorakhpur. Atif, Shadab, Salman, Saif and Hakim Tariq Kasmi bought three cycles from a shop in Gorakhpur. These were parked in Baldev Plaza, Golghar and Bal Vihar. One IED was placed on each cycle. The terrorists had used bicycles in the anticipation that a blast from some height would lead to more casualties. However, no one was killed in these explosions but four persons were injured. Atif and his associates were highly disappointed as they expected more than a dozen fatalities. The chargesheet of this terror incident was ordered to be withdrawn by the then Chief Minister Akhilesh Yadav on 5 March, 2013 but it could not be done because of the court's intervention. After the case was heard in the court, Hakim Tariq Kasmi was sentenced to life imprisonment on 21 December, 2020.

7. Lumbini Park, Gokul Chat Centre, Hyderabad Blasts – 42 killed, 54 injured (25 August, 2007)

In July, 2007, Riaz Bhatkal directed Aniq to go to Hyderabad and take up a flat on rent. Aniq did as he was told and rented a flat, 25 days before the actual blasts. He then called Riaz Bhatkal, who sent Akbar from Pune to Hyderabad. The plot was hatched by Riaz Bhatkal who provided gelatine to Yasin Bhatkal to make three bombs. Yasin was directed to make deadly bombs that could cause high fatalities. Riaz gave him boat-shaped wooden frames, made out of 3 inches wide and 11 inches long wooden boards. It was Yasin who had designed boat-shaped IEDs made out of wooden planks bought from Shimoga in Karnataka. It was decided to pre-test the bombs, but instead, they were actually put to deadly use in Lumbini Park and Gokul Chat Centre in Hyderabad. Riaz had himself planted the bomb at Gokul Chat Centre, Aniq had planted them at Lumbini Park and Akbar had placed them in Dilsukh Nagar. The explosions took place on 25 August, 2007 between 7.45 p.m. and 9.00 p.m., but only two bombs exploded – the Dilsukh Nagar device failed to explode. There were 42 casualties and 54 were injured. Riaz then met Yasin Bhatkal and both were pleased at the high toll with just two blasts. The boat-shaped bombs were made to cause blasts in Ahmedabad and Surat, and they were tested successfully in Hyderabad.

8. U.P. Courts blasts – 15 killed, 40 injured (23 November, 2007)

A terror accused Waliullah was scheduled to appear in Lucknow High Court in November, 2007. He was a *maulvi* in a mosque at Phulpur in Prayagraj (then Allahabad). He had been arrested on 7 March, 2006 in connection with the blasts in Sankat Mochan temple in Varanasi and was lodged in Dasna Jail at Ghaziabad. He had been brought from jail to the Court of Justice Suresh Chandra Chaurasia and Justice Imtiaz Murtaza in Lucknow Bench of the Allahabad High Court, and was being taken back to Ghaziabad when some lawyers accosted him and assaulted him.

Riaz Bhatkal told Yasin Bhatkal that lawyers in Lucknow had assaulted a *mujahid* and it had to be avenged. Riaz promised all help to the Azamgarh group including explosives. He revealed that the Azamgarh group of IM was behind Mumbai local train blasts and the explosives were arranged by him in July, 2006. Mohammad Sadiq Sheikh then talked to Riaz Bhatkal and sought material to cause blasts in the Courts of Uttar Pradesh. Mohammad Saif told Arif Badr in Sarai Mir that Sadiq Sheikh had instructed from Mumbai that bombs should be prepared for causing blasts at some places. Arif prepared six timers. Atif and Mohammad Saif then provided 18 kg of explosives (2 kg black coloured, 10 kg white and 6 kg grey) sent by Riaz Bhatkal in Mumbai to Arif Badr. They had also brought with them 6 kg of steel ball bearings, six detonators, six medium-sized tin boxes, 12 medical plaster tape spools and three bags. Arif Badr was instructed to make the bombs before 16 November, 2007 but he could not do so. The six bombs were prepared a week later. They comprised tin boxes filled with 3 kg of explosives in each. The timer was sent between 1.05 p.m. and 1.40 p.m. and they were provided to be placed on 23 November, 2007. Atif Amin made three groups for further action:

Varanasi: Mohammad Saif, Chhota Sajid, Shadab Ahmad

Faizabad: Shadab alias Malik, Saifur Rahman, Hakim Tariq Kasmi

Lucknow: Atif Amin, Ariz Junaid and one other person as per plan, explosions were caused in Courts in these three places. The bombs were placed in cycles. Two bombs exploded in Varanasi, but one bomb each exploded in Faizabad and Lucknow. Some people were injured in Lucknow, four were killed and a dozen injured in Faizabad, whereas the toll in Varanasi was the highest at 11 dead and more than three dozen injured.

At that time, I was posted as ADG (Law and Order) and

was also in charge of STF. After the incidents, I and the then DGP Vikram Singh went to the blast site in Lucknow Court and then flew to Faizabad and Varanasi to examine the blast sites. The then Chief Minister Mayawati also visited the explosion sites. We had a meeting with the Chief Minister in the Varanasi Airport lounge and it was decided to constitute a separate organisation named Anti-Terrorist Squad (ATS) to prevent terrorist incidents and related action.

Formation of ATS in Uttar Pradesh

Three days after the Court blasts in U.P. on 23 November, 2007, the U.P. ATS was formed on 26 November, 2007. I was made its first ADG In-charge and Rajiv Krishna (IPS, 1991) was made the first IG, ATS. Prior to the formation of ATS, the U.P. STF used to take action against terrorist organisations.

□

23

Indian Mujahideen sends E-mail to take responsibility for blasts

A few minutes before the Lucknow court blasts, an E-mail was sent to a media house in Noida. In this mail, written in English, it was mentioned that within a few minutes, bomb blasts are going to take place in some cities in U.P., and these were caused by Indian Mujahideen. In this same E-mail, the Indian Mujahideen took responsibility for the Delhi blasts (29 October, 2005), Varanasi blasts (7 March, 2006), Mumbai local train blasts (11 July, 2006), Lumbini Park and Gokul Chat Centre, Hyderabad blasts (25 August, 2005).

Later investigations showed that the following seven bomb blasts, prior to the U.P. courts blasts, had also been caused by Indian Mujahideen:

1. Dashashwamedh Ghat blast (23 February, 2005), 7 killed, 9 injured
2. Shramjivi Express blast (28 July, 2005), 13 killed, 50 injured
3. New Delhi blasts (29 October, 2005), 62 killed, 210 injured
4. Sankat Mochan blast (7 March, 2006), 28 killed, 101 injured
5. Mumbai local train blast (11 July, 2006), 209 killed, 714 injured
6. Golghar Gorakhpur blasts (23 May, 2007), 4 injured

7. Lumbini Park and Gokul Chat Centre, Hyderabad blasts (25 August, 2007), 25 killed, 54 injured

Hakim Tariq Kasmi has been given life imprisonment for the Faizabad Court blast and the Golghar Gorakhpur blasts. The case of his arrest was proposed to be withdrawn by the Akhilesh Yadav government of the Samajwadi Party on 18 April, 2013, but it could not be done because of a court order and the case went to trial, leading to jail for Tariq Kasmi. His accomplice, terrorist named Mufti Khalid Mujahid had died from heatstroke while being transported from Ayodhya Court to Lucknow. Both these terrorists were related to HUJI and they were involved along with IM in the court blasts. While being interrogated after their arrest at that time, they had admitted to their involvement but did not reveal the names of IM terrorists. In its E-mail, IM had clearly mentioned that it was not related to HUJI, Lashkar-e-Tayyaba or ISI. As per the instructions of their Pakistani handlers, Tariq Kasmi and Mufti Khalid Mujahid had not revealed their association with the IM.

The E-mail sent by Indian Mujahideen:

BISMILLAH-AR-RAHMANIR-RAHEEM

ALLAH SAYS IN QURAN: *"AYE IMAN WALON IN KUFFAR SE LADO JO TUMHARE AAS PASS HAIN, AUR INKO TUMHARE ANDAR SAKHTI DIKHNI CHAHIYE"* [SURAH TAUBAH: VER 122]

INDIAN MUJAHIDIN

OUR BIG SUCCESSFUL ATTACKS IN INDIA

- DELHI 29/10
- VARANASI MARCH
- 7/11 MUMBAI LOCAL TRAIN BLAST.
- HYDERABAD GOKUL CHAT & PARK.
- BLAST NOT EXECUTED BY US NOR BY ANY MUSLIM
- MALEGAON
- SAMJHAUTA EXP.
- MECCA MASJID, HYDERABAD

As the bomb blast which is going to take place in two cities of U.P. within few minutes, Insha Allah has been planned and going to be executed by our Mujahindin brothers. Before I start telling the cause behind this sacred activity [Al-JIHAD], I would like to give introduction about our organisation & our Mujahidin. We are not any foreign Mujahidin, nor even we have any attachment with neighbouring countries agency like ISI, LET, HUJI, etc. We know only that much as much media has knowledge about them. We are purely Indian.

CAUSES BEHIND *JIHAD* (HOLY WAR) IN INDIA

When our Muslim brothers were fleeing from India to Pakistan at the time of Partition, **ABDUL KALAM AZAD** asked them not to go & promised them on behalf of Congress Party **(GANDHI, NEHRU & PATEL)** that all of you can stay here and they **(GANDHI, NEHRU & PATEL)** had promised to give us full rights and a brutally killed for rehabitilitation*exact contents of Indian Mujahiddin E-mail.* Everybody knows what had happened to that promise and how our brothers and children and our sisters were raped. I am not going to take you back I would like to take your attention towards 1992 massacre, the year when I realised the fact regarding their promises.

THE WOUNDS GIVEN BY THE IDOL WORSHIPPERS TO THE INDIAN MUSLIMS; They demolished our BABRI MASJID and killed our brothers, children and raped our sisters, especially in **MAHARASHTRA** this all happened with the support of party which was ruling at that time both in Centre and in **MAHARASHTRA.** Indian police which always play key role in such massacre has provided arms and full protection to the son of bitches like **SHIV SENA, RSS, VHP,** etc. This injustice does not stop here; the police officers who were pointed out by the **SHRI KRISHNA COMMISSION** for their negative role in 1992 massacre were given promotions and felicitated by the Indian government for their graveyard sin. Those who killed (revenge) only 257 people are awarded with capital and life imprisonment punishment Such type of partiality shows that if you want to be successful person in India, then you should be idol worshipper and kill Muslims.

Violence against Muslims in India is not new; nearly everyday some violence take place in India. BUT the most recent massacre which shaken not only India but the whole world was **GUJARAT RIOT (2002),** which forced us to take strong stand against this injustice and all other wounds given by the idol worshippers of India. Real picture of **GUJARAT RIOT (POST GODHRA CARNAGE)** has been already displayed by TEHELKA.COM. Such injustice reveals the pathetic condition of Muslims in India that idol worshippers can kill our brothers, sisters, children and outrage dignity of our sisters at any place and at any time and we can't resist them,

AL-HUM-DU-LILLAH now we are prepared enough to retaliate. This is not the war between two communities, but this is war for civilisation. We want to empower the society from injustice, corruption, etc. which is prevailing in the society now a days. Only Islam has the power to establish a civilised society and this could be only possible in Islamic rule, which could be achieved by only one path **JIHAD-FEE-SABILILLAH.**

THINGS TO COME AND WHY: Now the Islamic raids which is going to take place against lawyer within few minutes INSHA-ALLAH is because police nabbed two innocent groups and frame them in fake charges (TERRORIST). Lawyer of these places beaten those innocent group members and refused to take their cases and dindn't allow others to take their case.

Now our next target will be INSHA-ALLAH Indian police.

SEEN THE PATIENCE NOW FEEL THE AGGRESSION

ALLAH-O-AKBAR

□

24
The truth behind Indian Mujahideen

The court explosions were triggered by IED bombs placed on bicycles parked in court premises, leading to the death of 15 persons including lawyers. The explosions were caused by timers and cycles were used so that the height could cause greater damage and higher death toll. The Indian Mujahideen also claimed that they were in no way connected to Pakistan's ISI, Lashkar-e-Tayyaba or HUJI, and that it was a *jihadi* organisation of Indian Muslims. They claimed they had adopted the path of violence in retaliation to the demolition of the Babri mosque structure and the riots in Gujarat in 2002. At that time, it was believed that the blasts were caused by Pakistani terrorist organisations and the responsibility for the same was taken by the organisation named Indian Mujahideen just to mislead India's police and intelligence agencies.

I was the ADG, Special DG (Law and Order) and Crime, as well as in-charge of U.P. STF and ATS for four-and-a-half years from 2007 to 2011. I had directed the investigation into terrorist incidents in U.P. under my observation. I also kept in regular touch with police forces of Maharashtra, Gujarat, Delhi and Madhya Pradesh. It was found during the investigation that it was at the behest of Pakistan, that IM had written in the E-mail that it was not related to ISI, LeT or HUJI, and that they were Indian Mujahideen. However, the involvement of Pakistan was regularly being unearthed in terrorist incidents across India and Pakistan was earning a bad name. It was as a face-saving gesture that ISI and LeT had come together to set up IM, which constituted mostly of former Ansars of SIMI. This organisation was in the initial years given Rs. 25 crore per year by the ISI. Amir Raza Khan (Kolkata), Iqbal Bhatkal and Riaz Bhatkal (Karnataka) lived in Pakistan and in co-ordination with ISI and LeT, organised training in arms operation and bomb making for IM recruits at LeT training centre in Muzaffarabad. The IM was behind several other blast incidents after the court blasts such as in Jaipur, Ahmedabad and German Bakery, etc. and it had claimed responsibility for them as well. IM had sought assistance from HUJI for Dashashwamedh Ghat and '*Shramjivi Express*' blasts. Many recruits of IM had been provided training in Bangladesh with the help of HUJI in which the North India commander of IM, Atif Amin (later killed in the Batala House encounter), was also involved. The explosions caused in India by IM had led to the killing of about 700 persons and thousands were injured. It is now known that actually IM was the Indian incarnation of Pakistan's LeT that had been formed jointly by the Pakistani ISI and LeT's chief Hafiz Sayeed. Iqbal Bhatkal, Riaz Bhatkal and Amir Raza Khan planned the blasts sitting in Pakistan and IM executed them. This trio also played a crucial role in training of IM terrorists.

□

25
Terrorist incidents in Mumbai

Several terrorist incidents had taken place in Mumbai prior to the incidents connected to IM. However, no organisation had been named or found involved in these incidents.

1. Mumbai Ghatkopar blast (28 July, 2003), 4 killed, 32 injured

A bomb was planted under the seat of a city bus in Ghatkopar area on 28 July, 2003. It exploded at 9.15 p.m., leading to the death of four persons and injured 32. The Mumbai Police had arrested Syed Hanif Anis, his wife Fahmida Syed and Ashrat Ansari in this connection. This was the first incident in which a husband-wife couple was involved. It was later learnt that the couple was highly disappointed at the death of only four persons as they had planned to kill all passengers in the bus.

2. Gateway of India – Jhaveri Bazar blasts (25 August, 2003), 54 killed, 300 injured

Disappointed at the low toll in Ghatkopar blast, Syed Hanif Anis and his wife Fahmida Syed planned a bigger explosion and they involved Ashrat Ansari this time too. They caused blasts near Gateway of India and in Jhaveri market near Mumba Devi temple on 25 August, 2003, in which 54 persons were killed and 300 injured. The first bomb exploded at Gateway of India, a popular tourist spot and the second exploded near Mumba

Devi temple in Jhaveri Bazar jewellery market.

A day before the blasts, a taxi-driver named Shiv Narain Pandey was hired for Rs. 1000 by a family of four to go from Shoppers Stop in Andheri to South Mumbai. The group of four went to Gateway of India and returned to Andheri via Jhaveri Bazar. It was a Sunday and there was a big crowd at Gateway of India. Actually, it was a dry run of the terrorists and Pandey was unaware of this.

On 25 August, 2003 also, three persons travelled in his taxi to Gateway of India. After the passengers got off at 1 p.m., Shiv Narain Pandey got down to have his lunch. A few minutes later, there was an explosion in the boot of his taxi (number MH02-R 2007), damaging many vehicles parked nearby. Shiv Narain Pandey escaped unhurt. But the blast hit a group of 27 persons from Dharwad family who were getting photographed before proceeding towards Kumbh Mela in Nashik, and eight of them lay dead as the darkness caused by the explosion cleared.

A few minutes before this explosion, an explosion took place in a car parked on Dhanji Street near Mumba Devi temple in Jhaveri Bazar jewellery market. The two explosions led to the death of 54 persons within 15 minutes and 300 were injured. Highly explosive RDX was used in these blasts and the CNG cylinders fitted in the taxis proved to be lethal. The Mumbai police arrested Ashrat Ansari, Syed Hanif Anis and his wife Fahmida Syed. The culprits claimed they had caused the explosions to avenge the 2002 Gujarat riots. Investigations also revealed that all these terrorists were linked to LeT in Pakistan and they were unhappy with the low toll in Ghatkopar bus blast, apparently because of low-capacity explosive material used in it. They had used high-grade RDX to ensure that the blast was more deadly.

Cases for murder, Prevention of Terrorism Act (POTA) and other offences were lodged against them and investigation was launched. Special Judge (POTA) M.R. Puranik on 4 August, 2009 found Ashrat Ansari (32), Syed Hanif Anis (46) and his wife Fahmida (43) guilty of the murder of 54 persons and injuring 300 others. Special Public Prosecutor Ujjawal Nikam had represented the prosecution and the three terrorists were sentenced to death on 6 August, 2009.

In addition to these two major explosions, five other minor blasts also took place in Mumbai after the 2002 Gujarat riots, in which low-grade explosive material was used.

□

26

Jaipur blasts – 80 killed, 216 injured

Riaz Bhatkal and his brother Iqbal called Yasin Bhatkal to Pune and he was lodged in a rented flat belonging to Dr. Anwar Bagwa of Pune. He was not allowed to meet anyone. Later, Aniq, Sayeed and Mohsin Chaudhry of IM, Pune group, came to meet Riaz Bhatkal, who was at that time preparing to cause blasts in Ahmedabad and Surat, for which he required 100 boat-shaped bombs. The work was underway when Yasin got an urgent call from Riaz that he immediately needed 10 boat-shaped bombs.

Yasin reached Udupi, carrying the 10 items with him. There in a hotel, he met Atif Amin of Sanjarpur, Azamgarh. Yasin handed over the ten IEDs to Atif as directed by Riaz. These bombs were used to cause severe blasts in Jaipur on 13 May, 2008. In the nine explosions caused within 15 minutes, 80 people were killed and 216 were injured. The explosives were planted on bicycles and the entire operation was conducted by the Azamgarh module of IM, led by Atif Amin.

To prepare for this incident, Mohammad Saif and Bada Sajid had come to Delhi and stayed at Atif's house. While Saif went to Azamgarh to appear in his MA examination, Bada Sajid stayed back. On 8 May, 2008, Chhota Sajid, Salman Ahmad Chhotu and Saif went to Atif's house but Atif was not there. Two days later, Atif and Ariz Junaid came to Delhi with the IEDs. On 11 May, 2008, Atif Amin, Bada Sajid, Chhota Sajid, Ariz Junaid, Shadab alias Malik, Khalid, Saifur Rahman and Salman Ahmad Chhoru travelled from Delhi by bus and reached Jaipur at 3 p.m. After their recce in the city, they came to Delhi the same night. On 12 May, 2008, Atif gave Rs. 300 to each of them to buy bicycles. On 13 May, 2008, all of them reached Jaipur by bus and bought 10 bicycles. The IEDs were planted on these bicycles and they were parked at fixed places by 4 p.m. All explosions took place at 6.30 p.m., while all terrorists returned to Delhi by Jaipur-Delhi '*Shatabdi Express*'. They came to know about the blasts by 7 p.m.

Jaipur was chosen by them as the city attracts a large number of foreign tourists. The terrorists expected that the blasts would deter foreign tourists, adversely affecting the tourism industry in India. Yasin Bhatkal came to know after the blasts that the 10 IEDs he had given to Atif in Udupi had been used in the Jaipur blasts.

On 30 December, 2019, the court sentenced Mohammad Saif, Sarwar alias Mohammad Sarwar Azmi, Saifur Rahman and Salman alias Chhotu to death for the Jaipur blasts.

□

27
Recce in Agra and Prayagraj for serial blasts

1. Recce in Agra for Serial Blasts

Agra is a major tourist attraction in North India. Tourists from all over the world visit Agra to see the Taj Mahal, Agra Fort, Itmad-ud-Daulah's tomb, Akbar's grave, Sikandara and Fatehpur Sikri.

Itmad-ud-Daulah's tomb was constructed by Jehangir's wife Noorjahan in memory of her father between 1622 and 1628, much before the Taj Mahal was constructed. It is also known as the Chhota Taj Mahal. The Taj Mahal was constructed by Mughal ruler Shahjahan in the memory of his queen Mumtaz Mahal between 1632 and 1653. Built with white marble, it is India's most well-known tourist attraction and a must-see for all foreign tourists coming to India. The Agra Fort was built between 1565 and 1573 by Mughal ruler Akbar and had been the residence of Mughal rulers up to 1638, when the Mughals shifted their capital from Agra to Delhi, where the Red Fort became the new residence of the Mughals.

Fatehpur Sikri fort was also built by Akbar who lived here from 1571 to 1585, but, because of shortage of water, shifted to Agra Fort built on the banks of the Yamuna River. The *dargah* of Sheikh Salim Chishti is located within Fatehpur Sikri and it is said that with his blessings, Salim Jehangir was born to Akbar's queen Jodhabai. Akbar's grave is located at Sikandara on Agra-Mathura Road. It was built by his son

Jehangir between years 1605 and 1613 on a plot of land measuring 119 acres.

Prior to the blasts in Jaipur, Agra was on the target of IM terrorists. It was expected by them that blasts in Agra will have the most serious impact on tourism in India. Riaz and Iqbal Bhatkal had entrusted the task of conducting recce in Agra to Abu Bashar and his team from Azamgarh. In March, 2008, they had conducted a recce in busy Agra localities of Raja Ki Mandi, Subhash Bazar, Heeng Ki Mandi, Rawatpara, etc. As part of the dry run, he was parking a bicycle in Raja Ki Mandi when the local traders scolded him and made him go away. This fact came to light during the interrogation of Abu Bashar after his arrest on 16 August, 2008. Abu Bashar had realised that it was not possible to park a cycle laden with bombs in busy streets of Agra.

2. Recce of Kumbh Mela, Prayagraj

Abu Bashar of Azamgarh had tried to do a recce of Kumbh Mela at Prayagraj in March, 2007. As he was trying to enter the Mela area, he noticed that even a government vehicle with blue beacon lights was being stopped and checked by policemen who had hand-held metal detectors to check all visitors going into the area. Bashar got scared and gave up the idea of doing a recce there. If the IM terrorists had succeeded in causing explosions in the Kumbh Mela area, then thousands of lives could have been lost. It also would have had grave international repercussions since it is the world's largest fair.

□

28
Terrorist incidents in Delhi, Bangalore and Guwahati in 2008

1. Delhi blasts – 30 killed, 90 injured (13 September, 2008)

Yasin Bhatkal had been instructed by Riaz Bhatkal to prepare 10 IEDs to be given to Atif Amin. Mohammad Saif and Khalid had on 26 August, 2008 reached Udupi in Karnataka by '*Mangala Express*' train and obtained the 10 IEDs meant for Atif. They reached Delhi on 30 August, 2008 with the explosives. At that time, Atif Amin was living in a flat in Jamia Nagar and there, Atif and Bada Sajid equipped the IEDs with timers. Hakim Ahmad had brought small steel balls from Lucknow and these were used in the IEDs.

The blasts in Delhi took place on 13 September, 2008 in which 30 persons were killed and 90 were injured. The first blast took place at 6.07 p.m. in Ghaffar Market where 20 persons were injured. Then at 8.34 p.m., two blasts took place in Connaught Place and two in Gopal Das Bhawan. An explosion also took place in Central Park, Connaught Place where the bombs were placed in a dustbin. Two more bombs exploded at Prince Pan Corner in Greater Kailash and near the Levis Store. The four bombs planted at India Gate, Regal Cinema, Connaught Place and Parliament Street failed to explode.

2. Bangalore blast – 1 killed, 6 injured (25 July, 2008)

The terrorists were planning to cause bomb explosions

in Ahmedabad and Surat on 26 July, 2008, but a day earlier, on 25 July, serial bomb explosions took place in Bangalore. The first explosion took place at Madiwala Bus Depot at 1.20 p.m., the second on Mysore Road at 1.25 p.m., third at Adugodi at 1.40 p.m., fourth at Koramangala at 2.10 p.m., fifth at Vitthal Malya Road at 2.25 p.m., sixth at Longford Town at 2.35 p.m. and seventh at Richmond Town at 2.40 p.m. These blasts were executed by the Kerala module of IM and caused the death of one person, besides injuring six others.

3. Guwahati blasts – 77 killed (31 October, 2008)

Guwahati was rocked by serial blasts on Friday, 31 October, 2008 and killed 77 people. The responsibility for these blasts was taken by ISF-Indian Mujahideen. This incident was also considered related to the IM because similar serial blasts had taken place the same year in Jaipur, Ahmedabad, Bangalore and Delhi.

□

29
Ahmedabad blast – 56 killed, over 200 injured (26 July, 2008); Surat blast (26 July, 2008) – unsuccessful

Riaz Bhatkal had been planning for long to conduct explosions in Ahmedabad and Surat. He had asked Sadiq Sheikh to arrange timers and he had obtained 40 electronic switches prepared by Arif Badr. Riaz entrusted the responsibility of causing blasts in Ahmedabad and Surat to Atif Amin, the commander of IM's Azamgarh module, in view of the successful blasts at Jaipur.

In Ahmedabad, Rizwan alias Kayamuddin Kapadia made arrangements for the stay of all terrorists in a house. It was in this house that Yasin Bhatkal met Atif Amin, Bada Sajid, Chhota Sajid and Saif. Riaz asked Yasin to prepare 30 boat-shaped IEDs. Riaz then sent Yasin to Bharuch where the latter met Aniq, Fazalur Rahman alias Salauddin, who had taken a bungalow on rent near the highway and where two new cars were parked. There Yasin came to know that the IEDs prepared by him had reached Bharuch from Ahmedabad. Yasin then came to Surat where Akbar Chaudhary had taken a house on rent in the name of Yaqub. Akbar alias Saeed alias Yaqub lived there with his associates. Yasin went to Bharuch to take the IEDs and a day later, Naushad and Asif too reached there along with the timers. They began planting the IEDs on the night of 25 July, 2008 itself and on 26 July, 2008, 30 IEDs were planted.

Most of the IEDs were planted by Yasin and a few were planted by Talha alias Tanvir of Surat. After planting the bombs, Yasin went from Surat to Mumbai and then took a bus to Pune.

In all, 24 explosions rocked Ahmedabad between 6.45 p.m. and 7.55 p.m. on 26 July, 2008. Three IEDs failed to explode.

The explosions were triggered in boat-shaped IEDs. The injured were being taken to the emergency wing of Civil Hospital in Ahmedabad and about two hours after the blasts in Ahmedabad city, a car bomb exploded at the gate of the Civil Hospital, killing 28 people. In all, the Ahmedabad blasts killed 56 people and more than 200 were injured.

The cars used in the Ahmedabad blasts were stolen from Navi Mumbai by a notorious car thief named Afzal Usmani. Afzal, son of Mutalib of Firozpur village in Madhuban, district Mau in Uttar Pradesh, lived in room number L-1, plot number 43, Shivaji Nagar, Govandi. Riaz and Iqbal Bhatkal wanted to cause widespread explosions in Ahmedabad and Surat by planting explosives in cars and bicycles in order to cause high fatalities. Afzal Usmani had stolen Wagon-R and Maruti-800 cars from Mumbai and their original registered number plates had been changed many times up to Ahmedabad and Surat in order to avoid detection. These stolen cars were parked on different days and times at Kalupur railway station, Makrand Desai Pay & Park, Relief Road railway parking and different places in Surat. In all, four stolen cars with changed number plates had been made available in Ahmedabad and Surat to associates of Riaz Bhatkal. The latter had told Afzal Usmani in January, 2008 itself to arrange 10 stolen cars for the operation. Usmani had put his jail buddies Irfan and his cousin Amin alias Raja on this job. On 4 July, 2008, Irfan and Amin had stolen two Wagon-R cars (one black and the other silver coloured) from Navi Mumbai and handed them over to Tanvir Pathan Raju at Surat railway station. On the way, they had put forged Gujarat registration number plates on these cars and had stopped in Hotel Krishna in Valsad. Tanvir Pathan had given Rs. 50,000 to Afzal Usmani for both cars and had made them talk to Riaz Bhatkal on his mobile phone.

The stolen cars were used for causing explosions in Ahmedabad Civil Hospital and LG Hospital. When Afzal Usmani was coming to Ahmedabad with the stolen cars, then he had been told not to use any mobile phone. As Afzal was about to reach Ahmedabad, it had become dark and all PCOs had closed. He was then forced to use his mobile phone – having a SIM card of Uttar Pradesh – for ensuring delivery of the cars. The Gujarat police had, after the Ahmedabad blasts, analysed the 'mobile tower dump' on the Ahmedabad-Mumbai Road and found a suspicious number of U.P. Afzal Usmani's wife was at that time, living in U.P., and who was already on the radar of UP ATS. Some important leads were obtained in the surveillance of her mobile phone by the U.P. ATS. In the meantime, Mumbai police had arrested and jailed Afzal Usmani on car theft charges on 25 August, 2008. He had admitted to stealing cars and delivering them in Ahmedabad and Surat. **If the Mumbai police had shared the information of Afzal Usmani's arrest with Gujarat ATS and Central agencies, then the Ahmedabad blasts could have been averted. It was revealed in sorting the call details of Afzal Usmani's mobile phone that he had provided all the cars used in the Ahmedabad and Surat blasts.**

In Pune, Yasin Bhatkal was waiting for the news regarding the Surat blasts, but no explosions took place there. The timing for blasts in Surat was the same as in Ahmedabad, but no explosion was caused in Surat because of a malfunction in the electronic circuit. Riaz and Atif Amin were highly disappointed at the failure in Surat because if it had been successful, then the toll would have been much higher than in Ahmedabad, since the bombs were planted at 29 places in Surat.

□

30

Narendra Modi and Amit Shah were targeted in Ahmedabad blasts

The then Chief Minister of Gujarat Narendra Modi and Home Minister Amit Shah were on the target of Riaz Bhatkal and Iqbal Bhatkal. They knew that the Chief Minister and Home Minister would visit the Civil Hospital to meet the injured and therefore a big explosion was planned at that time to assassinate the duo.

The Court of Special Nominated Judge Ambalal R. Patel on 18 February, 2022 announced the verdict in the Ahmedabad blasts case. Justice Patel wrote in his ruling that those injured in the explosions would have been taken to the LG Hospital and Civil Hospital, where a huge crowd would have gathered. At the emergency gates of both hospitals, stolen Maruti cars laden with explosives and gas cylinders had been parked on the morning of 26 July, 2008. Explosions were triggered at the emergency gates of both the hospitals, leading to a big loss of life and property.

The assassination of Chief Minister Narendra Modi and Home Minister Amit Shah was planned at the Civil Hospital. A social worker named Pradeep Parmar and his friends were engaged in taking care of the injured and he too was injured in the explosion. Fortunately, Modi and Shah did not reach the hospital at that time and the plot to kill them was foiled.

□

31
E-mail sent by Indian Mujahideen in Ahmedabad blast

The IM had sent two E-mails in the Ahmedabad blast. Here is the first E-mail:

INDIAN MUJAHIDEEN

In The Name Of Allah, The Most Beneficent, The Most Merciful.

Praise be to Allah, we seek His Help and ask for His Pardon. We believe in Him and on Him we put our trust. We take refuge in Allah from our wrongs and bad deeds. Whomever Allah has Guided will not be misled, and whomever He Misled, will never be guided. I bear witness that there is no God but Allah, no associate with Him and I bear witness that Muhammad is His Servant and Messenger.

And all Praises and Glory be to Allah Alone, the Sustainer of the Heavens and the Earth, Who revealed in His Qur'an:

إِنْ تَسْتَفْتِحُوا فَقَدْ جَاءَكُمُ الْفَتْحُ وَإِنْ تَنْتَهُوا فَهُوَ خَيْرٌ لَكُمْ وَإِنْ تَعُودُوا نَعُدْ وَلَنْ تُغْنِيَ عَنْكُمْ فِئَتُكُمْ شَيْئًا وَلَوْ كَثُرَتْ وَأَنَّ اللَّهَ مَعَ الْمُؤْمِنِينَ

(O Kaafirs!) If you demand a judgment, the judgment has then indeed come to you; and if you desist, it will be better for you; and if you turn back (to fight), We (too) shall return back, and your forces shall avail you nothing, though they may be many, and (know) that Allah is with the believers. (Qur'an 8:19)

All Praises and Glory be to Allah Alone, The One, The Supreme, Who revealed in His Book:

إِنَّا بُرَآءُ مِنْكُمْ وَمِمَّا تَعْبُدُونَ مِنْ دُونِ اللَّهِ كَفَرْنَا بِكُمْ وَبَدَا بَيْنَنَا وَبَيْنَكُمُ الْعَدَاوَةُ وَالْبَغْضَاءُ أَبَدًا حَتَّىٰ تُؤْمِنُوا بِاللَّهِ وَحْدَهُ

(O Disbelievers!) We are guiltless of you and of whatever you worship besides Allah: we have rejected you, and there has arisen between us and you, enmity and hatred for ever, - unless you believe in Allah and Him alone. (Qur'an 60:4)

And Peace and Prayers be upon His Servant and His Messenger Muhammad (peace be upon him), who said:

I am commanded to fight the people unless they admit that there is none to be worshipped except Allah, and that Muhammad (peace be upon him) is the Messenger of Allah and establish prayers, and pay the zakah, so if they do this then they have saved their blood and wealth from me, except the rights of Islam and their accountability is towards Allah".

[Hadith narrated by Bukhari and Muslim].

Here we are back - the Mujahideen of India - the terrorists on the disbelievers - the radicals of Islam - after our triumphant and successful assault at Jaipur, once again calling you all, who disbelieve in Allah and His Messenger Muhammad (peace be upon him) to accept Islam and bear witness that there is none to be worshipped except Allah, and that Muhammad (peace be upon him) is the Messenger of Allah. Accept Islam and save yourselves.

O Hindus! O disbelieving faithless Indians! Haven't you still realized that the falsehood of your 33 crore dirty mud idols and the blasphemy of your deaf, dumb, mute and naked idols of ram, krishna and hanuman are not at all going to save your necks, Insha-Allah, from being slaughtered by our hands? Nor is your fictitious faith in monkeys, pigs and nude statues going to save you from the Wrath of Allah and His Humiliating Punishment. Know that it is only the true confession of the Oneness of Allah Alone, with no associates, that can save your blood from being spilled on the streets of your own cities.

We call you, O Hindus, O enemies of Allah, to take an honest stance with yourselves lest another attack of Ibn-e-Qasim sends shivers down your spines, lest another Ghauri shakes your

foundations, and lest another Ghaznawi massacres you, proving your blood to be the cheapest of all mankind! Have you forgotten your history full of subjugation, humiliation, and insult? Or do you want us to repeat it again? Take heed before it is too late!

Yes! We - the terrorists of India – THE INDIAN MUJAHIDEEN, - the militia of Islam whose each and every Mujahid belongs to this very soil of India - have returned, to execute the compulsion of Allah:

قَاتِلُوهُمْ يُعَذِّبْهُمُ اللَّهُ بِأَيْدِيكُمْ وَيُخْزِهِمْ وَيَنصُرْكُمْ عَلَيْهِمْ وَيَشْفِ صُدُورَ قَوْمٍ مُّؤْمِنِينَ

"Fight them (the disbelievers), Allah will punish them by your hands and bring them to disgrace, and give you victory over them and He will heal the hearts of those who believe." (Qur'an 9:14).

Here we begin the answer to your tyranny and oppression, raising the illustrious banner of Jihad against the Hindus and all those who fight and resist us, and here we begin our revenge with the Help and Permission of Allah, - A terrifying revenge of our blood, our lives, and our honor that will Insha-Allah terminate your survival on this land.

Remember, O you Gujarati Hindus! O you filthy, shameless and foul creatures! O you Gujarati Hindus, most immoral and the most gutless cowards! Remember whom you have fought against! You have fought against the inheritors of a Messenger of Allah, of a Prophet of Allah whose terror was cast on the enemy from a distance of a month's journey.

You have fought against the warriors who love death more than you love life, who fight for a cause that makes them enter a never-ending Paradise, who fight for an absolute purpose - the purpose of making Islam superior over all religions.

So wait! .... Await now..........! Wait only for five minutes from now! .... Wait for the Mujahideen and Fidayeen of Islam and stop them if you can - who will make you feel the terror of Jihad. Feel the havoc cast into your hearts by Allah, the Almighty, face His Dreadful Punishment, and suffer the results of fighting the Muslims and the Mujahideen. Await the anguish, agony, sorrow and pain. Await, only for 5 minutes, to feel the fear of death.

All Praise and Glory be to Allah, Who Alone Helps His slaves, Who Alone Fulfils His Promise, and Who Alone Defeats the enemy.

O leader of disbelieving cowards and eunuchs, Narendra Modi! O you base-born of illegitimate birth! O you spineless coward! You boast of the pride of Gujarat and pride of Gujaratis. You brag of your filthy faith and conviction in Hindutva. You are the one who claims to be committed and devoted to Gujarat. You sick politician who used Hinduism to complete your evil desires. Look! We are back with the Will of Allah, striking in your own land. With the Will of Allah, assaulting and ruining your own cities, raiding and ravaging your own territory! Show us where has all your Gujarati asmita (pride) gone? Look, you have incurred Allah's Wrath, You have provoked the Mujahideen to massacre you and your five and a half crore multitude of pathetic infidels who tortured us in the post-Godhra riots asking "where is your Allah"? Here He Is, The Most Supreme, The Most Sublime, with His Punishment to chastise you by our hands. We swear by Allah in Whose Hands are our lives, we will make you, O Modi, an example and a lesson, that the enemies of Islam should learn from. This is our beginning! Our commencement! Our Opening Launch! To burn you alive in your own Hell - your own Gujarat.

O You sick criminals of the Hindu Parishad! You nasty dogs of the RSS! Yes! We know you, we identify you by your ugly faces! We will not be satisfied until we make each and every criminal pay for every drop of blood you spilled and for each and every cry of the oppressed women and children. Our swords are ready to cut off your veins and to push you into the Hell Fire. This is our assurance to you, a promise to you, a pledge to you, which Allah Alone, The Most Exalted with His Will shall fulfill.

This is our Qisaas - our revenge, and in it lies our life.

In the light of the injustice and wrongs on the Muslims of Gujarat, we advance our Jihad and call all our brethren under it to unite and answer these irresolute kafireen of India. We call you, O Muslims of Gujarat, to elevate yourselves from the fear of these wretched hindus, to unify all your courage and bravery that you have in your hearts. Come! Move forward and grasp the hold of the Qur'an and the Sunnah of His Messenger (peace be upon him). Get stimulated and reinforce all your strength to revive the same valor and daring as that of the Sahaabah (companions) of the Messenger of Allah (peace be upon him) had. Show these weak-willed hindu cowards the onslaught of Khalid bin Waleed, the determination of Ali bin Abi Talib, the bravery of Saad bin Abi Waqqas, the heroism of Abu Bakr and Umar, and the guts of Talhah and Zubair. Let these spineless Hindus know that you inherit fearless courage of Salahuddin Ayyubi, Tariq bin Ziyad and Muhammad bin Qasim.

O Muslims of Gujarat! Inspire yourselves from the Qur'anic chapters of 'Anfal' and 'Taubah' and from the events of 'Badr' and 'Uhud'. I ask you: Do you still hesitate to fight these hindus? Just think how much you and we have suffered during and after the riots. Think of the fraud perpetrated on us in the name of the Nanavati Commission. Remember the blasphemy of the Government in the name of judiciary and the fast-track courts. O my brethren! I ask you and make you witness over yourself. I ask you what good these bastard police and military have ever done for us? They all are one, and they unite for only one purpose - the annihilation of Muslims.

The terms Democracy, secularism, equality, integrity, peace, freedom, voting, elections are yet another fraud with us. Have you forgotten what the Messenger of Allah (peace be upon him) said: "The believer is not stung twice by the same hole". I ask you, who has healed your wounds so far? Congress, or BJP? Do you still want the media and agencies like "Tehelka" to expose your torture and make money in return of your burnt dead bodies and present all this in front of the judiciary so that they can watch this 'drama' of your killing and laugh at you, seeing you cry and beg for justice. By Allah! This is much more humiliating for us than being killed by their hands.

O Muslim youth of Gujarat! O you force of Islam! Stand up and rise! Fulfill your duty towards Allah:

يَا أَيُّهَا الَّذِينَ آمَنُوا قَاتِلُوا الَّذِينَ يَلُونَكُمْ مِنَ الْكُفَّارِ وَلْيَجِدُوا فِيكُمْ
غِلْظَةً وَاعْلَمُوا أَنَّ اللَّهَ مَعَ الْمُتَّقِينَ

O you who believe! Fight those disbelievers who are near you and let them find harshness in you and know that Allah is with those who keep their duty unto Him. (Qur'an 9: 123)

انْفِرُوا خِفَافًا وَثِقَالًا وَجَاهِدُوا بِأَمْوَالِكُمْ وَأَنْفُسِكُمْ فِي سَبِيلِ اللَّهِ ذَلِكُمْ
خَيْرٌ لَكُمْ إِنْ كُنْتُمْ تَعْلَمُونَ

Go forth light armed or heavy armed and fight with your wealth and your lives in the way of Allah, that is better for you if you but knew.[(Qu'ran 9: 41).

Come, O Muslim Youth! Make your preparations with whatever you have. Join our ranks and help us – the ranks of Indian Mujahideen to strengthen the Jihad against the Hindus. Get ready with all the weapons you have. Plan and organize your moves. Select your targets. Target these evil politicians and leaders of BJP, RSS, VHP and Bajrang Dal, who provoke the masses against you. Target and kill the wicked police force who were watching the "fun" of your bloodshed and who handed you to the rioting sinful culprits. Target their hired informers and spies even if they are the disloyal and betraying munafiqeen (hypocrites) of our Ummah. O Muslims of Gujarat! If a petty population of Rajasthani Gujjars can use force for fulfilling their needs, then are we even more subjugated than these backwards?

With these triumphant attacks, we send our message to all those faithless infidels and their hypocrite allies from amongst the so called Muslims like Arshad Madni & Mehmood Madni who have bartered their faith in return of just one seat in the Parliament and we hereby declare an ultimatum to all the state governments of India, especially to those of Rajasthan, Uttar Pradesh, Madhya Pradesh, Andhra Pradesh, Karnataka and Maharashtra to stop harassing the Muslims and keep a check on their killing, expulsion, and encounters. We warn you of your foolish plots that you plan against us, thinking that you can curb our missions and foil our targets. Here are our demands that you must fulfill if you hope for your well being.

a) You agitated our sentiments and disturbed us by arresting, imprisoning, and torturing our brothers in the name of SIMI and the other outfits in Indore, Ujjain, Mumbai, and in other cities of Karnataka. We hereby notify you, especially the ATS and the STF and the governments of Madhya Pradesh and Andhra Pradesh, to release them all, lest you become our next targets and victims of our next attack. Don't consider us heedless about the crimes you have committed in recent Indore riots and all this will be, Insha-Allah brought to account very soon.

b) We warn the Andhra Pradesh government, specifically the Hyderabad Police, to release the imprisoned Muslim youth immediately, and to be wise with yourselves. We are watching you, and our ground-work to gun you down has already begun. Insha-Allah, we will be rid of you very soon.

c) To the Maharashtra government and the rascals like Vilasrao Deshmukh and R.R. Patil, we announce the deadline to take heed before it is too late. Don't think we are unaware of the SRPF attacks on our Masjids and our homes, the insult of our Qur'an and your enmity with the Muslims in Digras and the nearby areas in Yavatmal and of the burning alive of three Muslims in Jalna with the backing of police. Yes! It is all being recorded and you will face the ill consequences thereof. And also the troubles faced by the Madrasa students and Muslim women in Mumbai Western Railways. We wonder at your memory. Have you forgotten the evening of 7/11/2006 so quickly and so easily?

You try to fool us in the name of fast-track courts made for '93 riot cases, through which you wish to free the actual Hindu culprits like Madhukar Sarpotdar who was caught red-handed with illegal firearms while the innocent Muslims arrested in the bomb blast case are being tried in the courts for years and years. Is this the hellish justice you speak of? I urge all the Muslims of Maharashtra to denounce those Muslim MLA's who prove themselves to be the loyal dogs of Congress and NCP. Beware! O you criminals! you are already on our hit-list and our cross-hair now! We also alert Mukesh Ambani to think twice before usurping and building a citadel on a land in Mumbai that belongs to the Waqf Board, lest it turns into horrifying memories for you which you will never ever forget.

d) The news of the lawyers of the Bar Council in UP denying to fight the cases of our Muslim brethren has already reached us. Remember, you are provoking us to repeat the same blasts in civil courts that blew up your bodies into pieces.
e) Lastly, we intimidate and threaten the Media and the News channels, especially the TIMES OF INDIA and the TIMES NOW to be extra cautious in their propaganda

war against the Muslims. Your biased and impartial approach to the news and the noise and the politics you make of 'Islamic Terrorism' indicates your hostility, hatred and fear that you grudge against Muslims and your loyal allegiance to the cunning ones who call themselves the "Intelligence Bureau". You become dumb when it comes to the oppression and torture of the Muslims, faced in riots, firing, encounters, police custodies, remand homes and civil courts and your propaganda turns violent to project the 'brutality' of 'Islamic terrorists' and their 'ruthlessness' and their 'merciless mentality' and so on. We warn you to end this hypocrisy or get ready for a bloody slaughter.

The Indian Mujahideen hereby claim the sole responsibility of the Gujarat serial blasts, planned and executed by Indians only and it is our request to Lashkar-e-Toiba and other organizations, for the sake of Allah, not to claim the responsibility for these attacks.

This message is a declaration of hostility towards all those who fight Allah, His Messenger, and His Religion. While hoping for the Help and Victory from Allah we declare that such and more severe attacks shall continue irrespective of what the blamers blame us for.

سَيُهْزَمُ الْجَمْعُ وَيُوَلُّونَ الدُّبُرَ

The hosts (of the kafireen) will all be routed and will turn and flee. [Qur'an 54: 45].

We ask Allah to forgive us and Have Mercy on us and Aid us to conquer the unbelievers and Guide us to raise His Word and degrade His enemies with His Will Alone.

And peace be upon His Messenger, and all those who follow the Guidance.

AL-ARBI.

The second E-mail sent by IM in the Ahmedabad blast is:

INDIAN MUJAHIDEEN

In the Name of Allah, The Most Beneficent, The Most Merciful.

Praise and Glory be to Allah, Who helped His slaves, fulfilled His Promise and Who Alone defeated the enemies. And Peace and Blessings of Allah be upon His Messenger Muhammad (peace be upon him) and on all those who believe and honor him.

And all Praise and Glory be to Allah Alone, the Sustainer of the Heavens and the Earth, Who revealed in His Qur'an:

قُلِ ادْعُوا شُرَكَاءَكُمْ ثُمَّ كِيدُوْنِ فَلاَ تُنْظِرُوْنِ

إِنَّ وَلِيِّيَ اللهُ الَّذِيْ نَزَّلَ الْكِتَابَ وَهُوَ يَتَوَلَّى الصَّالِحِيْنَ

Say (O Muhammad to the Kafireen): "Call upon your (so called) partners (of Allah) and then plot (your worst) against me, and give me no respite! For my Protector is Allah, Who revealed the Book, and He will choose and befriend the righteous". (Qur'an 7:95-96)

Here again, the INDIAN MUJAHIDEEN addresses the escaped multitude of faithless disbelievers, praising our Lord for humiliating you by our hands at Ahmedabad and Surat and calming our hearts by chastising your bodies with a disgraceful punishment. We declare that with the Will of Allah our attacks on you will be severely intensified from now on and with our extremely lethal strikes, which are to follow successively, we shall make you weep and repent for the evil hatred and grudge against Islam and Muslims. We openly intimidate you of our new attacks about to hit you very soon and shatter all the fabricated lies that you have forged about "busting the terror module behind the Ahmedabad bomb blasts".

O you cowardly bastards of ATS Gujarat, ATS Mumbai, ACB, Gujarat Police and fools the like thereof! You are the most foolish enemies the Mujahideen of Islam have ever fought against! Look! We are directly challenging you that Insha Allah we will carry out our next attacks right under your "close vigil", your "critical surveillance" and yes, of course, in presence of all those confidential reports that you receive from your secret sources of the IB – the "Ignorance Bureau".

What you have yelled and panicked about the INDIAN MUJAHIDEEN being technologically advanced is absolutely true. Our forthcoming assaults shall verify your guesstimate once again and this time it will be terribly dreadful Insha Allah.

You boast of defusing our thirty bombs planted at Surat which your foren'sicks' claim to have failed due to defective IC's. But we know better! You are nothing but victims of our terrorizing plan that turns you helpless when the Wrath of Allah descends on you. Just think O numbskulls! How many microchips can be faulty? One? Or two? Or all thirty at the same time? This is yet another threat to those filthy Hindus of

Surat who have failed to take heed, and a reminder to Narendra Modi that it is not over, by Allah in whose hands rest our lives! It is just the beginning.

The INDIAN MUJAHIDEEN are now much more determined, resolute and organized than before towards their oath which they have pledged to Allah, and with His Will, we shall fulfill it thoroughly. Our "homegrown" unit is steadily multiplying, silencing all the noise that you make about eradication of the "radical elements". Your tyranny and oppression against Muslims will no longer be left unchecked and we are warning you to be prepared for the deadliest strikes by our Fidayeen (martyrdom) attacks which are already on the move. Your efforts to suppress Jihad by means of harassment by police and anti-terrorist agencies, coupled with rigorous employment of hired spies and informers purchased at a bargain price to aid you against us are all going to be in vain. Your lot in future is nothing but a brutal and bloody slaughter.

Yes! We are vigilantly watching your investigations and probes and we are noticing the arrests that you have made in the last 20 odd days and to relieve you from the shocking trauma you are subject to right now, here comes a healing touch for you.

- The INDIAN MUJAHIDEEN on its full authority declares that by the Grace of Allah not even a single mujahid from our ranks who played even a minute role in the blasts, has been arrested to date. We are completely safe and in Allah, The Most Sublime, do the believers put their trust. Whatever Ashish Bhatia and P.C. Pandey have bragged about Mufti Abul Bashir, Sajid Mansuri, Zahid Shaikh and other innocent brothers like them is a big lie and just a clear proof of their miserable failure that has disgraced the entire anti-Islamic force.

- You are trying to save face by broadcasting the forgery of taking the "mastermind" in custody assuming that this might work for you. No! By Allah, your senses have badly failed and it is a challenge that Insha Allah, you cannot even imagine who our mastermind is. Let us notify you, especially the top officials of ATS like Hemant Karkare and allies that our line of attack has already been "masterminded" for you.

- To make it plainer to you, the INDIAN MUJAHIDEEN (IM only) is in no way associated with the Students Islamic Movement of India (SIMI). We are an absolutely self-reliant and self sufficient group with each and every individual committed only to the cause of Islam and Jihad, with our fundamentals of intense hostility to Kufr (disbelief) and utmost affection for Muslims. The more you harass us by your countrywide arrests and tortures in the name of SIMI, the more you assist us to accomplish our targets. This is only going to smooth the progress of our fight against you and add to your agony. Your oppression can by no means stop our advance.

- Our heartfelt gratitude to Mr. Ken Heywood and his associate for their complete cooperation and guidance to make our attack a huge success.

The Times of India, we warn again, that your untrue and deceptive propaganda against SIMI and your bogus bragging about ATS is definitely going to lead you to the bloodiest massacre ever witnessed by history. Just hold on! The countdown to your devastation has begun.

At last, we sum up, cautioning all the enemies of Mujahideen, specifically the Police, the ATS, the Crime Branch, the IB agents, their hypocrite informers, their media defenders, and the "conscious" public in general, to refrain from committing any sort of misconduct against us.

Yes! You are now forced to choose between only one of the following: beware of troubling us or wait to be annihilated.

So just await our comeback.

And All Praise be to Allah, Lord Of the Worlds, and peace be upon His Messenger Muhammad, and all those who follow the guidance.

AL-ARBI.

32
The Court verdict in Ahmedabad blasts

The Court of Special Nominated Judge Ambalal R. Patel announced its verdict in the Ahmedabad blasts on 18 February, 2022. The court awarded death sentence to 38 terrorists and life term to 11 terrorists. The 11 terrorists will be in jail till dead. It was for the first time in India that the penalty of death by hanging was announced for 38 accused. Prior to this, death sentence was awarded to 26 accused in the Rajiv Gandhi assassination case.

In the Ahmedabad blast case, there were 78 accused and those terrorists sentenced to death are:

1. Zahid Sheikh son of Kutubuddin Sheikh, Ahmedabad, Gujarat, 2. Iqbal Kasam son of Kasam Sheikh, Vadodara, Gujarat, 3. Shamsuddin Sheikh son of Shahabuddin Sheikh, Ahmedabad, 4. Gyasuddin Ansari son of Abdul Haleem Ansari, Ahmedabad, 5. Mohammad Arif Kagzi son of Mohammad Iqbal Kagzi, Shahpur, Ahmedabad, 6. Mohammad Usman son of Anis, Vadodara, 7. Yunus son of Mohammad Mansoori, Ahmedabad, 8. Abbas son of Umar Samoja, Bhuj, Gujarat, 9. Mohammad Ismail, Ahmedabad, 10. Javed Ahmad son of Sagir Ahmad Sheikh, Ahmedabad, 11. Mohammd Rafiq Afridi, Ahmedabad, 12. Taushif Khan Pathan, Juhapura, Ahmedabad, 13. Kayamuddin Kapadia son of Sarfuddin Kapadia, Vadodara, 14. Imran Ibrahim son of Ibrahim Sheikh, Vadodara, 15. Safdar Husain Nagouri alias Husain Bhai alias Iqbal Nagouri son of Zahrul Husain Nagouri, Ujjain, Madhya

Pradesh, 16. Kamruddin son of Chand Mohammad Nagouri, Ujjain, 17. Amil Parvaz son of Qazi Saifuddin Sheikh, Ujjain, 18. Amin Sheikh, Indore, Madhya Pradesh, 19. Mohammad Mobin, Indore, 20. Mufti Abu Bashar Sheikh alias Abdullah son of Abu Baqar Sheikh, Binapar, Sarai Mir, Azamgarh, U.P., 21. Mohammad Shakeel Lohar son of Yameen Khan Lohar, village Loharka Aurangabad, district Bulandshahar, U.P., 22. Zeeshan Ahmad Sheikh, house number 311, Mohalla Baz Bahadur, Azamgarh, 23. Ziaur Rahman Teli, Agwanpur, police station Parikshitgarh, Meerut, U.P., 24. Mohammad Tanvir, Najibabad, Pathanpura, Bijnore, U.P., 25. Mohammad Arif Naseem Ahmad Mirza, Sanjarpur, Sarai Mir, Azamgarh, 26. Mohammad Shadab Ahmad, village Sanjarpur, Azamgarh, 27. Saifur Rahman alias Saifu, Azamgarh, 28. Afzal son of Mutalib Usmani, Mumbai (original resident of Madhuban, Mau, U.P.), 29. Asif Sheikh son of Basheeruddin Sheikh, Pune, Maharashtra, 30. Mohammad Arif alias Arif Badr alias Laden son of Badruddin alias Jumman Sheikh, Mumbai, 31. Mohammad Akbar alias Saeed alias Yaqub son of Ismail Chaudhary, Pune, 32. Fazle Rahman alias Rafiq alias Salauddin son of Musadiq Khan Durrani, Pune, 33. Sarfuddin Salim, Hyderabad, Telangana, 34. Ahmad Bawa, Karnataka, 35. Hafiz Husain alias Adnan, son of Tajuddin Mulla, Bijapur, Karnataka, 36. Sibli Ahmad alias Sabit son of Abdul Kareem, Kerala, 37. Saduli Abdul Kareem, Kerala, 38. Mohammad Sajid alias Saleem son of Ghulam Khwaja Mansoori.

Among those sentenced to death, Mufti Abu Bashar Sheikh, Saifur Rahman, Mohammad Arif Naseem Ahmad, Mohammad Shadab Ahmad, Zeeshan Ahmad Sheikh, Ziaur Rahman Teli, Mohammad Shakeel Lohar, and Mohammad Tanvir are residents of Uttar Pradesh.

Among the key terrorists involved in the Ahmedabad blasts, Mohammad Atif Amin, the North India commander of IM, and a resident of Sanjarpur in Azamgarh, was killed in the Batala House police encounter on 19 September, 2008. Also killed with him was Mohammad Sajid of Sanjarpur.

Imprisoned for life (to be in jail till dead)

1. Mehndi Hasan Ansari, 2. Mohammad Naushad Syed, 3. Rafiuddin Kapadia, 4. Atiqur Rahman, 5. Mohammad Ansar Nadvi, 6. Imran Ahmad Pathan, 7. Aniq Syed, 8. Mohammad Ali Ansari, 9. Mohammad Abrar, 10. Mohammad Sadiq Sheikh, 11. Mohammad Shafiq Ansari.

□

33

Important points of the ruling of Ahmedabad Court

1. Thirty (30) accused are members of SIMI. SIMI was declared to be a terrorist organisation and banned in 2001 and is banned up to 2023.
2. After SIMI was banned, terrorist activities were being conducted under the name of Indian Mujahideen.
3. SIMI was established in 1977. The objective of SIMI is to conduct terrorist activities in India and establish India as an Islamic country.
4. The terrorist activities posed a challenge to the constitutionally-elected Government in India.
5. A Government is not a robot, it is not a machine. It is a group of Constitutionally-elected people who control the country/states and are known as the Government. These include Members of Rajya Sabha, Lok Sabha, Vidhan Sabha and Vidhan Parishad.
6. Narendra Modi was the Chief Minister of Gujarat State, elected by the Constitutional system of India, and was heading the Gujarat Government, and a conspiracy was hatched to assassinate him.
7. A plot was hatched to conduct explosions by giving jihadi speeches to seek revenge for Gujarat riots that took place after the Godhra incident.
8. The objective of establishing Islamic rule in India, toppling the anti-Muslim government and creating

acrimony between Hindu and Muslim communities was to pose a challenge to the Government.

9. Meetings of SIMI were held in Ahmedabad, Vadodara, Surat, etc. between year 2006 and 2008. People of the Muslim community were trained in the terrorist training camps.
10. Those injured in the explosions were taken to the LG Hospital and Civil Hospital, where a large crowd had collected. In both hospitals, explosions were conducted in Maruti cars laden with explosives and gas cylinders, between 7.30 a.m. and 7.45 p.m., leading to widespread loss of life and property.
11. A conspiracy was hatched to murder Chief Minister Narendra Modi, Amit Shah, local Legislator Pradeep Singh Jadeja and social activist Pradeep Parmar, who were scheduled to visit the hospital after the explosion, but they were safe.
12. Pradeep Parmar along with his friends was helping the injured. He was injured in his right leg in the explosion.
13. With an intention of causing extensive damage in Surat city, bombs were planted at 29 places. The explosion could not take place because of failure in the bomb circuit in Surat.
14. In Ahmedabad, 56 persons were killed and 240 persons were injured. The accused are responsible for this.
15. The accused had hatched a criminal conspiracy and caused a terrorist incident in order to achieve a goal, for which all of them are equally responsible.
16. The accused resorted to many ploys in order to deter the witnesses from identifying the accused during the trial.
17. These are not ordinary criminals but habitual criminals.
18. They commit a crime by planning to save themselves from the charge before actually committing a crime,

during the investigation and during the judicial proceedings.

19. The argument of the accused is dismissed that the word jihad has been misinterpreted by political parties as well as by the media.
20. Jihad is a revered term but the word jihad has been misused by the Muslim terrorist organisations, who conduct terrorist activities against the laws of India as well as against the country.
21. By involving innocent Muslim youths in illegal activities in the name of jihad, the Muslim terrorist organisations engage in conducting terrorist activities against the country and also disintegrating the society.
22. Genuine Muslim organisations who believe in the Holy Quran should spread the real meaning of the term jihad and stop its misuse.
23. Genuine Muslim organisations which follow the Holy Quran must boycott Muslim terrorist organisations.
24. There should be discussion on the term jihad as based on *jihad* mentioned in the *ayats* of Quran and terrorism.
25. These accused have converted the peace in society to unrest and created fear and an atmosphere of fear in the society, for which they are not fit to be included in society.
26. There is no need to keep them in jail for conducting terrorist activities against the country. However, if they are retained in society, then they would be treated as separate entities, like cannibals.
27. Even the shadow of such persons is considered extremely dangerous for the society.
28. The court does not need to have mercy on the accused, because the accused do not have mercy towards innocent members of the society.
29. The death penalty is the only and last alternative for those engaged in terrorist activities.

30. The history of the accused is full of criminal acts.
31. Such accused should be given the maximum punishment under the law to ensure security and peace in the country and its people.
32. The Government should start a separate Department for the help and monitoring of the families of those having lost their lives in the riots or terrorist activities, so that the victims and their families can have trust on the Government and the law.

□

34

Terrorist act by Indian Mujahideen near Delhi Jama Masjid on the Second Anniversary of Batala House incident (19 September, 2010)

Yasin Bhatkal wanted to commit a big terrorist incident in Delhi on the second anniversary of the Batala House incident. The boat-shaped IEDs made by him had already proved to be lethal in blasts in Jaipur, Ahmedabad, Delhi (13 September, 2008), Gokul Chat Centre and Lumbini Park in Hyderabad, having caused massive casualties. Next to Arif Badr of Azamgarh, Yasin Bhatkal was supposed to be the second-best explosives expert among IM terrorists. He had created the boat-shaped bombs after cutting and carving wooden boards, a picture of which had also been placed in the second E-mail sent after the Ahmedabad blasts. This IED had earned the praise of the IM founders including Riaz Bhatkal, Iqbal Bhatkal and Amir Raza Khan.

The Batala House encounter had shaken the IM as, on one hand, its North India commander Atif Amin of Azamgarh had been killed and on the other, a large number of IM operatives were being arrested all over India. Riaz Bhatkal, Iqbal Bhatkal, Amir Raza Khan, Mohsin Chaudhary, Dr. Shahnawaz Alam, Ariz Junaid etc had fled to Pakistan and questions were being raised on the very existence and future of IM. Yasin Bhatkal alias Mohammad Ahmad Siddhi Bappa was living in Nepal with Asadullah Haddi and Pakistani terrorist Waqas Ahmad. Riaz Bhatkal, Iqbal Bhatkal and Amir Raza Khan had meetings with other terrorist organisations in Pakistan and planned a huge explosion in Delhi on the second anniversary of Batala House encounter.

Under this plan, Yasin came to Delhi and conducted a recce of many places in Delhi. He chose a crowded area near the Jama Masjid so that the casualties could be high. Yasin then arranged a Maruti-800 car and himself planted several boat-shaped bombs in the car. He also asked Asadullah Haddi and Waqas Ahmad to open fire with guns and involved many more men in the proposed operation.

Yasin Bhatkal was confident that the toll in this explosion would at least be 100 and its impact would be felt not only in India, but also abroad. Preparations were on for the scheduled Commonwealth Games in Delhi between 3 and 14 October, 2010. Tight security was being enforced as the Games were expected to attract players as well as sports-lovers and foreign tourists. Also, the verdict in the Babri Mosque-Ram Janmbhumi case was expected to be announced in the Allahabad High Court on 30 September.

For Yasin, it was just the right time to execute his plan. If successful, it would mark the second anniversary of the Batala House encounter and the claims of tight security for Commonwealth Games would be exposed in India and abroad. In view of the proposed court verdict on Ayodhya case, the communal environment was charged and security was tight in U.P. I was then posted as ADG (Law and Order). Besides me, the then DGP Karmavir Singh and Principal Secretary Home Kunwar Fateh Bahadur Singh were touring the entire State by helicopter and ensuring proper security everywhere. A big terrorist incident in Delhi could ignite the sensitive environment in U.P.

The terrorists prepared the IEDs on the night of 18 September and ensured that it would cause huge devastation. Yasin Bhatkal himself took the responsibility of causing the car bomb blasts. He had a sleepless night and he kept discussing the impending incident with Asadullah Haddi and Waqas Ahmad. At 4.59 a.m., the *azan* for the *fazr namaz* was heard; Yasin and his associates also offered the *namaz* and sought blessings for the success of the operation.

The trio took a quick breakfast and went to the Jama Masjid area to see the crowd. They decided to cause the explosions at 2 p.m. Coming back to their room at 10 a.m., they went out again on motor-cycles to make other arrangements. Yasin had parked the Maruti-800 car near a transformer near the Jama Masjid with the bomb timer set for 2 p.m. A tourist bus packed with foreigners was parked near the gate number 3 of Jama Masjid. Moments later, two persons on a motor-cycle came rushing towards the bus and fled after firing indiscriminately on it. Two tourists from Taiwan were injured in the firing which caused panic in the area. Two hours later, the Maruti-8 car parked near the transformer suddenly caught fire. It looked like an ordinary accidental fire in the car but it was later found that it was laden with boat-shaped bombs which could not detonate because of some technical fault. Thus, the lives of thousands of people were saved.

These boat-shaped IEDs had caused massive destruction in Ahmedabad on 26 July, 2008 but these could not detonate because of some fault in Surat the same day. The failure had caused huge disappointment to Yasin Bhatkal, Riaz Bhatkal and Amir Raza Khan.

The failure of the Batala House anniversary blast also caused big disappointment to Yasin and his accomplices. Even though they could not project the message they desired, a 5-page E-mail was sent to a media house in this regard – in a similar manner to the previous incidents. The idea was that the terrorist incident would attract a lot of media attention and an adverse image of India would be created in other countries.

□

35
E-mail sent by Indian Mujahideen after the terrorist incident near Jama Masjid

An E-mail message was sent by IM on the terrorist incident near Jama Masjid on 19 September, 2010 as follows:

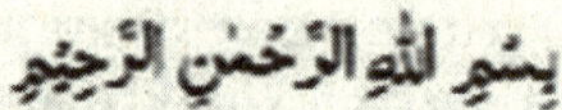

In the name of Allah The Most Beneficent The Most Merciful

As We Bleed, So Will You Seep

All the praises and thanks be to Allah, the Lord of the 'Alamin (mankind, jinn and all that exists). May Peace and Salutations be on the Commander of the Mujahideen Muhammad the Messenger (PBUH), his household, all his companions and all those who followed him until the Day of Judgment.

وَمَا لَكُمْ لَا تُقَاتِلُونَ فِي سَبِيلِ اللَّهِ وَالْمُسْتَضْعَفِينَ مِنَ الرِّجَالِ وَالنِّسَاءِ وَالْوِلْدَانِ الَّذِينَ يَقُولُونَ رَبَّنَا

أَخْرِجْنَا مِنْ هَٰذِهِ الْقَرْيَةِ الظَّالِمِ أَهْلُهَا وَاجْعَل لَّنَا مِن لَّدُنكَ وَلِيًّا وَاجْعَل لَّنَا مِن لَّدُنكَ نَصِيرًا ﴿٧٥﴾

And what is wrong with you that you fight not in the cause of Allah, and for those weak, ill-treated and oppressed among men, women and children, whose cry is: "Our Lord! Rescue us from this town whose people are oppressors; and raise for us from You one who will protect, and raise for us from You one who will help". Those who believe fight in the cause of Allah, and those who disbelieve, fight in the cause of Taghut (Satan). So fight you against the friends of Shaitan (Satan); Ever feeble indeed is the plot of Shaitan (Satan). (Quran 4:75)

Since July, the Paradise on earth, 'Kashmir' is being soaked with the blood of its sons. The Indian occupying forces have not spared the life of 8 years old boys to 80 years old elderly person or hapless Muslim women either. The death toll has already surpassed a hundred innocents.

فَتَقَطَّعُوا أَمْرَهُم بَيْنَهُمْ زُبُرًا ۖ كُلُّ حِزْبٍ بِمَا لَدَيْهِمْ فَرِحُونَ ﴿٥٣﴾

"And verify this Ummah of yours IS A SINGLE UMMAH and I am your Lord and Cherisher: Therefore Fear Me (and not other)." (Quran 23:53)

The Messenger of Allah (saw) also said, "The believers, in their love, mutual kindness, and close ties, are like one (human) body; when any part complains, the whole body responds to it with wakefulness and fever." [Saheeh Muslim]

The idol worshippers' Indian army has created **mayhem** this Eid by **ruthlessly killing 22 stone-pelting** youth. Muslim life is cheaper than vegetables in Kashmir. The criminal silence of the International community is far more dangerous than the oppression perpetuated on the helpless Kashmiri Muslims by the imperialist and expansionist attitude of the Indian state. Those who have chosen to remain silent are not just lending outright support for Indian idol worshippers' massacres of the innocent people but are also guilty of purposefully and deliberately committing the crime. They are all dumb and mute creatures. The peace loving Kashmiri Muslims who consider even undue cutting of trees as evil have been pushed against the wall since 1947 and are forced to take up arms out of desperation against Indian selfishness and illegal occupation. Killing a single innocent is equivalent to killing the whole humanity. But when injustice, oppression, tyranny and evil fill the land, killing becomes a necessity so as to establish the rule of (Supreme) Law and Justice.

In the given situation we are left with no other option and moreover it is the fareedha (obligation) on us from 'The Most Beneficent' and 'The Most Merciful' to contain and curtail the evil and vicious designs of the 'Real Terrorists'.

وَلَوْلَا دَفْعُ اللَّهِ النَّاسَ بَعْضَهُمْ بِبَعْضٍ لَّفَسَدَتِ الْأَرْضُ وَلَٰكِنَّ اللَّهَ ذُو فَضْلٍ عَلَى الْعَٰلَمِينَ ﴿٢٥١﴾

....And if Allah did not check one set of people by means of another, the earth would indeed be full of mischief. But Allah is full of bounty to the Alamin (mankind, jinns and all that exists). (Quran 2:251)

The Indian Mujahideen has finally decided to avenge the blood of each and every brother and sister as its topmost priority and duty towards the Ummah and Allah above all. Remember! As we bleed, so will you seep. As and when our innocents are butchered so will we mince you. As our children face the horrors so will your kids enjoy the same. We hereby congratulate you on this occasion and henceforth we bring you the agony of our Kashmiri brothers and sisters outside Kashmir, this time right at your seat-of-governance. All those culprits who are mum over our plight and lend open or silent support to the enemy of Freedom and Humanity are our rightful targets. When our people are mowed down, aren't they innocents? At least this one should explain the meaning of 'innocent. You have been fooling the masses with this silly catchword i.e. 'innocent'. We will teach you the real meaning of the word with all its 'grammar and thesaurus' until you grasp the correct understanding. We cannot simply forget lakhs of our martyrs until we provide you a sizeable compliment of the same kind. For the first time in 63 years we bring the screams and cries of our Kashmiri Muslims to your cities and we promise you more and better in series to be delivered right at your doorsteps, InshaAllah.

Rejoice! We will now rightfully play Holi with your blood in your own cities. Scores of fidayeen are restless to drop the Evil ones into the hellfire. On the one hand Muslim blood is flowing like water while on the other hand you are preparing for the festival of games. This is surely not a Childs' play; Mind you this is the initiative from the Lions of Allah and we Warn you to host the Commonwealth games if you have a grain of salt. We know that preparations for the games are at its peak; Beware!! We too are preparing in full swing for a Great Surprise! The participants will be solely responsible for the outcome, as our bands of Mujahideen love death more than you love life. In Kashmir you have succeeded in usurping our Right of self-determination with all your Chanakya policies but it will all be futile. Seems most of the foolish people have a very short memory. Don't you remember the COMMITMENT of your own Prime Minister Pandit Nehru?

On 27 October 1947, the day the Indian Army officially intervened in the Kashmir dispute; Jawaharlal Nehru sent the following telegram to Liaquat Ali Khan, the Prime Minister of Pakistan: *"I should like to make it clear that the question of aiding Kashmir in this emergency is not designed in any way to influence the State to accede to India. Our view which we have repeatedly made public is that the question of accession in any disputed territory or State must be decided in accordance with the wishes of people and we adhere to this view."* FOUR DAYS LATER JAWAHARLAL NEHRU DECLARED THAT: *"our assurance that we shall withdraw our troops from Kashmir as soon as peace and order are restored and leave the decision regarding the future of the State to the people not merely a pledge to your Government but also to the people of Kashmir and to the world."* Ref: A DISPUTED LEGACY (ALASTAIR LAMB p.182]

One fine day out of nowhere, East Timor suddenly appears on the world map ending Indonesian rule but the **hypocrite United Nations and the world community** turns a blind eye towards more than a half-century old Indian occupation on Kashmir. **UN resolutions on Kashmir's Right to self determination and Plebiscite are just paper-work and documentation which has resulted in acute procrastination of all concerned.**

Not only have lakhs laid down their lives, but innocent chaste women have paid with their honour, entire localities have been laid waste, tens of thousands of persons have disappeared and thousands have been buried in unnamed graves. Incidents like **Shopian, Kunan, Poshpora, Bommai, Kahigam, Pakhrpora, Kupwara and Bandipur** are no more news. These cannot be forgotten and forgiven at all.

On one hand more than 7 lakhs soldiers have seized every portion of Kashmir while on the other hand the Indian government is now busy in weaning away Kashmiri Muslims from all their sacrifices and trying to attract them towards demands like roads, jobs and sops, but **people will not allow a great mission to be sacrificed for petty gains, inshaAllah.** This arson, injustice, tyranny and highhandedness will have its echoes for sure across the country. In short, State-Terrorism has a heavy price to be paid.

O Kashmiri Muslims! We will not let you alone at this critical juncture. We assure you that the Indian Mujahideen will be at your sides to avenge the tyranny and oppression of these Hindus. We salute your greatness and valor affronting the great Shaitan.

O Muslim Ummah! Awake from the slumber, these Hindus are recklessly killing your brothers and sisters. Where are those Ulema and so-called Islamic scholars who waste their energies designing fatwas against us? Why are they **lip-locked over the genocide** of Kashmiri brothers and sisters? Remember! If you don't stand up and support your brethren at this hour you will find none to weep at your graves.

﴿وَقَاتِلُوهُمْ حَتَّىٰ لَا تَكُونَ فِتْنَةٌ وَيَكُونَ الدِّينُ لِلَّهِ فَإِنِ انتَهَوْا فَلَا عُدْوَانَ إِلَّا عَلَى الظَّالِمِينَ﴾ (١٩٣)

And fight them until there is no more Fitnah (disbelief & worshipping of others along with Allah) and all and every kind of worship (including rules and regulations in day to day affairs) is for Allah Alone. But if they cease let there be no transgression except against Az-Zalimun (polytheist wrongdoers and those who don't submit to Allah and His Messenger etc.) (Quran 2:193)

In the name of Allah we dedicate this attack of retribution to martyrs, **Shaheed Atif Amin** and **Shaheed Muhammad Sajid** (may Allah bestow mercy upon them) who proudly laid down their lives valiantly fighting the idol worshippers Delhi police on this day. Surely each and every drop of their blood has brought a new **life in the Muslim community** and this is confirmed from the fact that Indian Mujahideen ranks have **swelled unexpectedly manifold,** Alhamdulillah. In the Holy month of Ramadan teenaged Salman was brutally beaten up repeatedly by the Delhi Police and was hospitalized. Here comes our unique reply for this and we are always on toes for a Tit-for-Tat response.

We feel sorry to say that **Rakesh Maria** has shattered the myth of being an intelligent officer by arresting innocent youth who are totally unconcerned in the German Bakery case. The ceaseless urge to show performance has **bitten the top-cop mad** and **driven him out of his mind** as every other day he pops up with fake accused, **thanks to his acumen.** Why are you bent upon to destroy your career for the sake of this anti-muslim and ignorant R. R. Patil. Remember! We will once again come upon Bombay if you do not desist. And you know it very well that we @ Indian Mujahideen act as we speak.

The incident of our sister wearing Hijab who was insulted and humiliated at the KEM hospital in Bombay on orders of Bombay Police will not be forgiven. It seems Bombayites have very poor memory and they deserve a fresh bloodbath. We hereby warn that the Bombay Police Commissioner's office will be squarely responsible for the outcome.

The state-terrorism in Ratlam during Eid is an open invitation to the Indian Mujahideen. While the *'Najis'* (filthy) hindu idol worshippers desecrated the Masjid by throwing cow dung, all hell broke on innocent Muslim populace. This unfathered Superintendent of Police Mayank Jain himself and the District Collector spearheaded the brutality, the molestation of our mothers and sisters, the detention and torture of more than 700 Muslim youth, insults of our elders and ransacking and looting of our properties. These will never be left unaccounted. We urge the Muslims to be steadfast in this tough situation and supplicate to Allah so that we teach a befitting lesson to these idolaters. We promise you a sure shot response, inshaAllah. And remember that, those who transgress will know their end for sure.

وَلَمَنِ انْتَصَرَ بَعْدَ ظُلْمِهِ فَأُولَٰئِكَ مَا عَلَيْهِم مِّن سَبِيلٍ ﴿٤١﴾ إِنَّمَا السَّبِيلُ عَلَى الَّذِينَ يَظْلِمُونَ النَّاسَ
وَيَبْغُونَ فِي الْأَرْضِ بِغَيْرِ الْحَقِّ أُولَٰئِكَ لَهُمْ عَذَابٌ أَلِيمٌ ﴿٤٢﴾

And indeed whosoever takes revenge after he has suffered wrong, for such there is no way (of blame) against them. The way (of blame) is only against those who oppress men and rebel in the earth without justification; for such there will be a painful torment. (Quran 42:41-42)

قَاتِلُوهُمْ يُعَذِّبْهُمُ اللَّهُ بِأَيْدِيكُمْ وَيُخْزِهِمْ وَيَنصُرْكُمْ عَلَيْهِمْ وَيَشْفِ صُدُورَ قَوْمٍ مُّؤْمِنِينَ ﴿١٤﴾
وَيُذْهِبْ غَيْظَ قُلُوبِهِمْ وَيَتُوبُ اللَّهُ عَلَىٰ مَن يَشَاءُ وَاللَّهُ عَلِيمٌ حَكِيمٌ ﴿١٥﴾

Fight against them so that Allah will punish them by your hands and disgrace them and give you victory over them and heal the breasts of a believing people; And remove the anger of their (believers) hearts. Allâh accepts the repentance of whom He wills. Alláh is All-Knowing, All-Wise. (Quran 9: 14-15)

O Allah, deface them, break their backs and heads, split them up and destroy their unity; O Allah, afflict them with the loss of their near and dear ones as they have afflicted us with the loss of our near and dear ones; O Allah, we seek refuge in You from their evilness and we place You at their throats; O Allah, make their plotting their destruction; O Allah, suffice for us against them with whatever You wish; O Allah, destroy them, for they cannot escape You; O Allah, count them, kill them, and leave not even one of them.

Thank you very much O Allah; we love you so much O Allah.

9th Sha'wwal 1431; 19th September 2010

AL-ARBI.

□

36
Sheetala Ghat blast (7 December, 2010)

Blast at Sheetala Ghat, Varanasi – 2-year-old child killed (7 December, 2010)

The Sheetala Ghat blast was Yasin Bhatkal's idea. His plan to cause a big incident on the second anniversary of Batala House encounter had flopped. An IM module had been formed in Darbhanga. Now Yasin and Asadullah Haddi conspired to cause explosions in Varanasi on the 18th anniversary of the demolition of Babri mosque. They decided to use hydrogen peroxide as explosive instead of the usual boat-shaped bombs. But this plan too flopped. The terrorists failed to cause an explosion on 6 December, 2010 – the 18th anniversary of the mosque demolition; therefore, they caused an explosion the next day, 7 December, 2010. A two-year-old girl was killed in this blast and a few people were injured.

The Allahabad High Court had announced its ruling on the Babri mosque/Ram Janmbhumi dispute on 30 September, 2010 and the IM terrorists were not pleased with it and wanted to cause explosions in U.P. as a mark of protest. It was decided to cause a blast on 6 December, 2010 on the anniversary of the mosque demolition. At that time, Pakistani terrorist Waqas Ahmad along with Asadullah Haddi came from Karachi to Nepal and then arrived in Darbhanga. There they decided that a bomb blast in the religious city of Varanasi will send a tough message. Yasin Bhatkal, Waqas Ahmad, Asadullah

Haddi and Tara Babu from Darbhanga came to Varanasi to conduct a recce, covering Kashi Vishwanath temple, Sheetala Ghat, Dashashwamedh Ghat and Godaulia market. They went around all *ghats* and also ate their meals at a local eatery, and saw the Ganga *arti* in the evening where a large number of pilgrims and foreign tourists had gathered.

Then they took a taxi to Mughalsarai and boarded a train for Patna. Yasin Bhatkal and Asadullah Haddi then went to Kolkata to buy material for bomb making. They bought 200 litres of hydrogen peroxide from the chemical market in Bara Bazar and this was supplied in cans of 50 litres each. Then it was transported to Darbhanga where Yasin Bhatkal, Waqas Ahmad, Asadullah Haddi and Tahseen Akhtar alias Monu of Bihar made bombs with the ingredients. Two dozen digital clocks had been provided by Yasin Bhatkal from Delhi. Waqas Ahmad, who had received bomb making training in LeT training camps at Muzaffarabad in PoK, created bombs with explosives, detonators and the clock. On 6 December, 2010 all these terrorists came from Darbhanga to Patna by bus and then went to Mughalsarai and finally by taxi to Varanasi. While conducting a final recce in Varanasi, Asadullah Haddi and Yasin Bhatkal saw a *chabutara* (platform) on the right side while coming down the stairs at Sheetala Ghat. Asadullah Haddi was told that this was the right place to plant a bomb. The men were divided into two groups, comprising Yasin Bhatkal and Waqas Ahamad in one, and Asadullah Haddi and Tehseen Akhtar alias Monu in the other. They created the IEDs by mixing hydrogen peroxide, acetone and sugar in two white jerrycans of 10 litres each. This time they had used hydrogen peroxide because despite the successful blasts caused by the boat-shaped bombs in Hyderabad, Jaipur, Ahmedabad and Delhi, these bombs had failed to explode in Surat and near Delhi's Jama Masjid.

Aftab Alam alias Farukh alias Sheikh Chilli of Purnea, Bihar, had brought detonators from Bangalore. All of them reached the *ghats* of Ganga much before the Ganga *arti* was scheduled and went to a secluded corner to plant the bombs. Waqas Ahmad was setting the detonators when it exploded, injuring him in his hand. The others bandaged his hand and then the two jerrycans were placed before the Ganga *arti*. One blast took place in the hydrogen peroxide-based explosive on the upper stairs of the Sheetala Ghat.

A two-year-old girl sitting in her mother's lap was killed in the blast. Since the blast had taken place on the upper stairs, its impact was not felt on the lower steps where a large number of pilgrims and foreign tourists had gathered to watch the *arti*. I had reached the place along with my team from ATS to inspect the explosion site. IM had claimed responsibility for this incident by sending an E-mail.

□

37

E-mail sent by Indian Mujahideen on Sheetala Ghat blast

An E-mail was sent by IM after the Sheetala Ghat blast. The date mentioned on the E-mail was 6 December, 2010 but since the blast did not take place on 6 December, the E-mail was sent on 8 December, 2010. Following is the E-mail:

In the name of Allah The Most Beneficent The Most Merciful

Let's feel the pain together!

All Praise is for Allah (سبحانه وتعالى), The Lord and The Sustainer of the Worlds. And Peace and Salutations be upon the Prophet Muhammad (ﷺ).

وَمَنْ أَظْلَمُ مِمَّن مَّنَعَ مَسَاجِدَ اللَّهِ أَن يُذْكَرَ فِيهَا اسْمُهُ وَسَعَىٰ فِي خَرَابِهَا ۚ أُولَٰئِكَ مَا كَانَ لَهُمْ أَن
يَدْخُلُوهَا إِلَّا خَائِفِينَ ۚ لَهُمْ فِي الدُّنْيَا خِزْيٌ وَلَهُمْ فِي الْآخِرَةِ عَذَابٌ عَظِيمٌ ﴿١١٤﴾

And who are more unjust than those who forbid that Allah's Name be glorified and mentioned much (i.e. prayers and invocations, etc.) in Allah's mosques and strive for their ruin? It was not fitting that such should themselves enter them (Allah's Mosques) except in fear. For them there is disgrace in this world, and they will have a great torment in the Hereafter. **(Al Baqara:114)**

Indian Mujahideen attribute this attack to the 6th of December that will haunt your nation of world's *'Greatest DemoNcracy'* until Muslims are paid back justly and fairly for the loss of their beloved Babri Masjid, the precious lives of their near and dear ones, their pride, dignity and self-respect. O you lowliest, stupid worshippers of Shiva and Parvati's **'sexual organs'!** Be assured that **Indian Mujahideen,** the sons of Mahmud Ghazni, Muhammad Ghori, Qutb-ud-din Aibak, Firuz Shah Tughlaq and Aurangzeb **(may Allah bestow His mercy upon them)** have resolved that none of your Mandirs **will remain safe until and unless** all our occupied Masjids throughout with heregt JAHIDEEN India are returned back to the Muslims with honour.

Allah(سبحانه وتعالى) and Prophet's(ﷺ) Verdict about a Masjid:

Once a *masjid* is erected, it always remains a *masjid* **and the** 'property of Allah(سبحانه وتعالى) **until the Last Day.** It cannot return to being the property of any person or community even those who may have paid for establishing it. Neither above it nor below it on any floor can be used for anything but as a *masjid*. Hence, all rulings that apply to a *masjid* will now apply to the exact same area directly below it on each of the lower floors (including the basement); and likewise on all floors above it because **it is a *masjid* to the peaks of the heavens and likewise to the recesses of the earth below.**

O Muslims! For the sake of Allah(عزوجل) **STOP** trusting the Taghut Judiciary and the Taghut Parliament and mend ways to 'please' Allah(عزوجل) alone. Technically speaking even the so called 'supreme court' stands inefficient against legislations approved on the floor of the House. It needs no mention that time and again the Congress party with its hidden agenda has shown its true colors. Be it the inaction over the planting of the idol in 1949 or the shilanyaas, the ground-breaking ceremony of 1989 and finally the demolition of the Babri Masjid in 1992. **For all practical reasons the Masjid site has since been transformed into a Mandir, thanks to the Supreme Court order to maintain Status-quo.** The Allahabad High court's verdict of 'Aastha over Facts" is exemplary of the <u>bias judiciary</u> although Ram is purely a mythical figure. **The Supreme Court, the high courts, the lower courts and all the Commissions have utterly failed to play an impartial role regarding Muslim issues.** Narendra Modi who presided over the 2002 massacres of muslims in Gujarat is given a clean chit whereas the victims still run from pillar to post for justice. Even the 92 Mumbai culprits roam freely and enjoy government security. All the anti-Muslim pre-planned riots, arson, rapes, losses of lives and properties are still awaiting justice. The list is endless!

أَلَمْ تَرَ إِلَى الَّذِينَ يَزْعُمُونَ أَنَّهُمْ آمَنُوا بِمَا أُنزِلَ إِلَيْكَ وَمَا أُنزِلَ مِن قَبْلِكَ يُرِيدُونَ أَن يَتَحَاكَمُوا
إِلَى الطَّاغُوتِ وَقَدْ أُمِرُوا أَن يَكْفُرُوا بِهِ وَيُرِيدُ الشَّيْطَانُ أَن يُضِلَّهُمْ ضَلَالًا بَعِيدًا ﴿٦٠﴾

Have you seen those (hyprocrites) who claim that they believe in that which has been sent down to you, and that which was sent down before you, and they wish to go for judgement (in their disputes) to the Tâghût (faise judges) while they have been ordered to reject them. But Shaitân (Satan) wishes to lead them far astray. **(AlNisa 4:60)**

Also Quran explicitly hammers thrice:

وَمَن لَّمْ يَحْكُم بِمَا أَنزَلَ اللَّهُ فَأُولَٰئِكَ هُمُ الْكَافِرُونَ ﴿٤٤﴾

...And whosoever does not judge by what Allâh has revealed, such are the Kâfirûn (I.e. disbelievers - as they do not act on Allâh's Laws.) (Al-Maeda:44)

وَمَن لَّمْ يَحْكُم بِمَا أَنزَلَ اللَّهُ فَأُولَٰئِكَ هُمُ الظَّالِمُونَ ﴿٤٥﴾

...And whosoever does not judge by that which Allâh has revealed, such are the Zâlimûn (polytheists and wrongdoers-of a lesser degree). (Al-Maeda:45)

وَلْيَحْكُمْ أَهْلُ الْإِنجِيلِ بِمَا أَنزَلَ اللَّهُ فِيهِ ۚ وَمَن لَّمْ يَحْكُم بِمَا أَنزَلَ اللَّهُ فَأُولَٰئِكَ هُمُ الْفَاسِقُونَ ﴿٤٧﴾

...And whosoever does not judge by what Allâh has revealed (then) such (people) are the Fâsiqûn (the rebellious i.e. disobedient (of a lesser degree) to Alláh. (Al-Maeda:47)

O Muslims! We hereby declare that even if **all the ulema, scholars and muslim leaders** collectively deviate from or refuse **Allah(سبحانه وتعالى) and Prophet's(ﷺ) Verdict,** their decision will be right beneath our feet. Ultimately, Allah(سبحانه وتعالى) is Most Supreme. Any argument against the Quran and Sahih Hadith is totally unacceptable to us. Neither the All India Muslim Personal Law Board nor the Babri Masjid Action Committee nor the Sunni Waqf Board nor any litigant has any right to alter or compromise on any of these aspects whatsoever regarding the Babri Masjid. All sorts of bartering and bargaining is totally unacceptable to Allah(سبحانه وتعالى) and thus to the Muslims.

Our Ulema ought to be those who fear Allah(سبحانه وتعالى) the most as they are the most knowledgeable but today it seems inversely true. They were to be more responsible and be at the forefront like the Huffaaz (Quran scholars) companions of Prophet (ﷺ), several of whom were martyred in the cause of Allah (سبحانه وتعالى). They never sat back and were never content with giving lectures alone dying to join the good-books of the Kuffar. It won't be surprising if most scholars of our times fill the Hellfire.

We urge those ulema to behave sensibly, change their attitude towards this Holy Cause, fear Allah(عز وجل) alone, come forward, inspire and motivate the people and thus appease none but Allah (عز وجل) alone.

The Indian Mujahideen has time and again warned these infidel kuffars and idol worshippers and their rulers to desist from their repressive designs and injustices aimed at the Muslim community. These Pharaohs of India have themselves provided us the opportunity to once again strike at their throats.

O you nasty, rotten Hindus! We are fully aware of your preparations at the Babri Masjid site for the construction of a 'grand temple' over the corpses of our martyrs all over the country. The Indian Mujahideen warn these filthy Hindu zealots that even if a Grand Temple of Gold is built over the Babri Masjid we will destroy it at all costs. Remember! It was a Masjid, It is a Masjid and It will always remain a Masjid. At this juncture Muslims are silent due to their state of affairs. We hereby invite all our Muslim brethren to never be weak-hearted over the designs of these idolators and urge them to strengthen their faith in Allah(عز وجل) and unite for the cause of Islam. Surely, victory is awaiting us, *InshaAllah*. Our memories are still fresh and our hearts still bleeding over every muslim brother and sister who was hacked to death after the demolition of Babri masjid. Indian history is decorated with countless state-sponsored terror and state-managed riots. ***Shaheed kii jo maut hai wo qaum ki hayaat hai.*** Indeed every martyr enlivens the ummah. By Allah (عز وجل)! We will not budge until every inch of the Masjid is regained and lives of our martyrs avenged. By the grace of Allah (عز وجل) we will strike terror in the hearts and minds of these idol worshippers until the mountain of injustice is undone. *InshaAllah,* we will leave no stone unturned come what may till the anger of believer's hearts is removed and a Magnificent Masjid is built at the same spot. We have now achieved skills to teach Newtons'

3rd law in 'their own' terms. Our youth have all reasons to be proud and pompous to shoulder our responsibilities towards the Ummah, while our elderly can be content. *Alhamdulillah!* We seek their Duas and supplications for our cause.

وَلَا يَحْسَبَنَّ الَّذِينَ كَفَرُوا سَبَقُوا ۚ إِنَّهُمْ لَا يُعْجِزُونَ ﴿٥٩﴾ وَأَعِدُّوا لَهُم مَّا اسْتَطَعْتُم مِّن قُوَّةٍ وَمِن
رِّبَاطِ الْخَيْلِ تُرْهِبُونَ بِهِ عَدُوَّ اللَّهِ وَعَدُوَّكُمْ وَآخَرِينَ مِن دُونِهِمْ لَا تَعْلَمُونَهُمُ اللَّهُ يَعْلَمُهُمْ ۚ وَمَا
تُنفِقُوا مِن شَيْءٍ فِي سَبِيلِ اللَّهِ يُوَفَّ إِلَيْكُمْ وَأَنتُمْ لَا تُظْلَمُونَ ﴿٦٠﴾

And let not those who disbelieve think that they can outstrip (escape from the punishment). Verily, they will never be able to save themselves (from Allah's Punishment). And make ready against them all you can of power, including steeds of war (tanks, planes, missiles, artillery) to threaten the enemy of Alláh and your enemy, and others besides whom, you may not know but whom Allah does know. And whatever you shall spend in the Cause of Allah shall be repaid unto you, and you shall not be treated unjustly. [Al-Anfal: 59-60]

The manhandling and heckling of Kashmiri leadership in Indian cities is not at all a minor issue. These insane and cowardly Saffron Hindus on the behest of the IB and the administration pounce upon weak people. As usual we are going through minute details of the matter and have obtained vital clues of the mischief which we presume to be inappropriate to be divulged at this point of time. **Meanwhile we request the respected Syed Ali Shah Geelani Saheb and the Mirwaiz to maintain their self-respect and dignity.** These sons of monkeys and snakes will never heed to sensible arguments and historical facts. Please don't waste your time with these lowly creatures as they will never understand!

وَلَقَدْ ذَرَأْنَا لِجَهَنَّمَ كَثِيرًا مِّنَ الْجِنِّ وَالْإِنسِ ۖ لَهُمْ قُلُوبٌ لَّا يَفْقَهُونَ بِهَا وَلَهُمْ أَعْيُنٌ لَّا يُبْصِرُونَ بِهَا
وَلَهُمْ آذَانٌ لَّا يَسْمَعُونَ بِهَا ۚ أُولَٰئِكَ كَالْأَنْعَامِ بَلْ هُمْ أَضَلُّ ۚ أُولَٰئِكَ هُمُ الْغَافِلُونَ ﴿١٧٩﴾

Already have We urged unto hell many of the jinn and humankind, having hearts wherewith they understand not, and having eyes wherewith they see not, and having ears wherewith they hear not. These are as the cattle - nay, but they are worse! These are the neglectful. **(Al-Araaf:179)**

It's really useless to expect anything good from these ugly creatures. Indeed to cure some, force is the only option.

O dirty Hindu idolaters! **If you continue with these** 'injustices' **then we** promise **that we will continue our** war against **you. In the name of Allah(سبحانه) we are preparing for you since years and we will continue on this path.** Hope you will appreciate and relish this deadly slap in your face **for the reason that our brothers, sisters, elderly and kids have been subjugated to piles of humiliation at your hands. Remember they were also someone's father and someone's mother and also someone's child.**

And there is little doubt that 'wisdom comes with pain!'

وَلَكُمْ فِي الْقِصَاصِ حَيٰوةٌ يَّاُولِي الْأَلْبَابِ لَعَلَّكُمْ تَتَّقُونَ ﴿١٧٩﴾

And there is (a saving of life for you in Al-Qisâs (the Law of Equality in punishment), O men of understanding, that you may become Al-Muttaqûn (the pious-see V.2:2). **(Al-Baqarah:179)**

Lastly we appeal to all the Muslim countries to voice their concerns regarding oppression and injustice done by India upon their fellow brethren. It is their duty **to pressurize this 'Empire of Falsehood and Tyranny' regarding the longstanding Kashmir issue where** world's largest concentration of armed forces in an occupied territory **stands. This 'Hollow superpower', needs to be told loudly and clearly that it should get over its obsession with Muslims in India and that the Global Muslim Ummah is seriously concerned about the issues like Babri Masjid and Kashmir.**

That is all for now. InshaAllah we will get back to you very soon!

May Allah([illegible]) pardon us all our sins however huge they are and accept all our good deeds however tiny they might be. Ameen.

Thank you very much O Allah; we love you so much O Allah.

29th Zul Hijjah 1431; 6th Dec 2010

□

38

Blasts caused by Indian Mujahideen in Delhi High Court, Mumbai, Bodhgaya, German Bakery, Pune and Patna

1. Delhi High Court blast (7 September, 2011) - 15 killed, 79 injured

Explosions were caused in Delhi High Court premises on 7 September, 2011 in which ammonium nitrate and RDX were used. It killed 15 people and 79 were injured. The responsibility for this blast was claimed by HUJI. The NIA prepared a chargesheet against six persons who were – Wasim, Akram Malik, Junaid Akram Malik, Amir Abbas, Shakir Husain Sheikh alias Chhota Hafiz and Amir Kamal. This group belonged to Kishtwar in Kashmir. Wasim and Akram Malik had studied Unani medicine in Bangladesh and were associated with HUJI. Its supreme commander Iliyas Kashmiri was killed in a US drone attack in north-west Pakistan on 3 June, 2011. He belonged to Bhimber in PoK and was an active member of HUJI in Jammu & Kashmir. It is noteworthy that IM had been formed with help from HUJI and LeT, but IM terrorists always wrote in their E-mails that they were not related to these organisations or ISI. It was done to hide any involvement of Pakistan in the blasts.

2. Jhaveri Bazar, Opera House, Dadar Blasts in Mumbai (13 July, 2011) – 26 killed, 150 injured

IM faced tremendous pressure from security forces after

the Batala House encounter. Its North India commander Atif Amin had been killed in the Batala House encounter on 19 September 2008 and many other operatives had been arrested. However, the Pakistan-based IM terrorists Riaz Bhatkal, Iqbal Bhatkal and Amir Raza Khan wanted to reinforce that they were still in a position to cause blasts.

Riaz Bhatkal then planned to cause blasts in Mumbai and this task was given to Yasin Bhatkal alias Mohammad Ahmad Siddhi Bappa. Yasin had already created an IM module in Darbhanga. On 1 July, 2011, Yasin received a message from Riaz Bhatkal that explosives were ready for a big explosion in Mumbai. He was given 10-12 targets, such as Nariman Point, Gateway of India, Jhaveri Bazar, Opera House, Dadar and adjacent areas, Borivali and Dombivali – where a large number of Gujaratis live.

Riaz Bhatkal sent explosives from Bangalore. The delivery was made near the Hampan Katta, Mangalore, Noor Masjid. The deadly material delivered in Mumbai on 8 July, 2011 included 10-12 kg of gelatine in a blue bag, 10 kg ammonium nitrate and 25-30 detonators. Four cookers were bought from Byculla in Mumbai and IEDs were made in them. Yasin Bhatkal did the first recce and the rest were done by his associates. The final recce was done by Pakistani Waqas Ahmad in Opera House, Tabrez alias Daniel in Jhaveri Bazar and Tahseen Akhtar alias Monu and Yasin Bhatkal in Dadar. Finally, Opera House, Jhaveri Bazar and Bandra were chosen for the blasts. The serial blasts took place on 13 July, 2011 between 6.54 p.m. and 7.06 p.m., in which 26 persons were killed and 130 were injured.

After the blasts, its mastermind Yasin came by train to Jhansi and then to Delhi. He then went to Bangarmau, Unnao to the house of Basheer Hasan alias Talha alias Maulvi Sahab alias Master Saheb son of Abrar Husain, who was originally a resident of Karbala Maidan in Barabanki. Basheer Hasan used to teach Quran in Dabatul Haq *madarsa* in Khambauli Kasba in Bangarmau. He had received training along with two Bangladeshi terrorists in Pakistan in 2004. Master Basheer

Hasan joined HUJI after getting trained in Pakistan and then moved to Banihal in Kashmir in December, 1993 when he met Nasrullah of Pakistan. The latter had given him the code name 'Talha'. This HUJI group comprised 14-15 terrorists, mostly Pakistanis and he also received arms and grenade training there. He had launched an attack by AK-47 rifles on a convoy at the Doda dispensary picket in Banihal and had also launched a grenade attack on CRPF camp at Lal Bazar in Srinagar in December, 1994.

He joined IM through HUJI and got further training in Pakistan. Basheer Hasan alias Talha also wanted to open a *madarsa* in Sitapur where he could teach about *jihad* to children from a young age to turn them into *mujahideen*. Basheer Hasan also used to provide shelter to Yasin Bhatkal and other IM terrorists to Barabanki, Unnao, Lakhimpur Kheri and Sitapur in Uttar Pradesh.

3. Bodhgaya Blast (7 July, 2013) - 5 killed, 5 injured

Several IEDs were planted in Mahabodhi temple at Bodhgaya on 7 July, 2013, of which 10 IEDs exploded while three failed to explode. Five persons were killed in this incident, including two Buddhist monks and five were injured. The terrorists wanted to damage the idol of Bhagwan Buddha by causing the blast in Mahabodhi temple. At that time, clashes were common between the Armed Forces and Rohingya terrorists in Myanmar (Burma) and several Rohingya Muslims had escaped to Bangladesh and had taken shelter there. Some of them had illegally entered India and had settled here as well. Myanmar is a country of Buddhism followers and the people from there have deep faith in Buddhist shrines at Bodhgaya, Sarnath, Kushinagar, Vaishali, Shravasti and Kapilvastu. The plan to destroy the ancient idol of Lord Buddha in Bodhgaya was prepared by LeT in Pakistan and the terrorists had made a video of the place after doing its recce. **These facts were also narrated by David Headley to the NIA in 2010 after his arrest in US.**

Pakistan-based IM terrorist Riaz Bhatkal was the mastermind of this incident. The terrorists, wearing monks' attire, entered the *mandir* and got divided in groups of two. Six terrorists including Imtiaz Ansari, Tariq alias Ainul, Taufeeq and Mujibul Ansari had planted the bombs. Tahseen Akhtar, who headed the Ranchi module of IM, supervised the entire activity. The incident was probed by NIA. Later, an NIA court on 1 June, 2018 awarded life sentence to Haider Ali, Imtiaz Ansari, Tariq alias Ainul, Taufeeq and Mujibul Ansari.

4. Blast in German Bakery, Pune (13 February, 2010) – 18 killed, 60 injured

German Bakery in Pune is a favourite spot for Indian as well as foreign tourists. Situated closeby is the Osho Ashram where several foreigners live, as also a Jewish temple (synagogue).

A blast took place inside the German Bakery on 13 February, 2010 in which 13 persons were killed and 60 were injured. These included one woman from Italy, one Iranian and two Sudanese students. **The Pakistani-American terrorist David Headley had termed this incident as part of the 'Karachi Project'. The entire plot was hatched in Pakistan and executed by terrorists associated with IM, LeT and SIMI.**

On 4 December, 2010, a chargesheet was submitted in court by Maharashtra ATS against IM terrorists Mohammad Ahmad Siddhi Bappa alias Yasin Bhatkal, Mohsin Chaudhary, Riaz Bhatkal, Iqbal Bhatkal, Zabiuddin Ansari alias Jundal, Mirza Himayat Inayat Beg and Faiyaz Kagzi.

5. Pune blast (1 August, 2012) – 1 injured

A terrorist named Kateel Siddiqui was strangled to death in Pune's Yervada Jail by two inmates Sharad Mohol and Amol Bhalerao. These two were part of a criminal' gang of Pune and were angry with the anti-national activities of Kateel Siddiqui. To protest against Siddiqui's killing, bomb blasts were caused at the Tilak Smarak Ganga Mandir on 1 August, 2012 between 7.22 p.m. and 8.15 p.m. A senior Congress leader Sushil Kumar Shinde was scheduled to visit the temple on that day. However, no one was killed in this blast and only one person was injured. The explosive used in the blast was the signature material of IM – ammonium nitrate filled in a milk can, which exploded with a 9-volt battery. The case was unravelled and eight terrorists – Langde Irfan, Asad Khan, Imran Khan, Syed Firoz, Syed Maqbool alias Jubaid, Syed Arif alias Kasif, Munib Iqbal Memon and farukh Baghban – were arrested after their involvement was established.

6. Patna blast (27 October, 2013) – 6 killed, 85 injured

This was the time when the Country was caught in the run-up to the 2014 General Elections. Gujarat Chief Minister Narendra Modi had been named the Prime Ministerial candidate by the Bharatiya Janata Party. On 27 October, 2013, a 'Hunkar Rally' was organised in Patna in which 3 lakh people had collected. Serial blasts took place in Patna on that day between 10 a.m. and 5.15 p.m. in which six persons were killed and 85 were injured.

The first bomb exploded near Patna Junction railway station at 10 a.m., followed by blasts at the rally venue Gandhi Maidan, near Gandhi Maidan, near a cinema hall close to the Gandhi Maidan, Twin Tower building, a public toilet, Udyog Bhawan, east of Regent Cinema, near the Gandhi statue, south of Gandhi Maidan, near State Bank on west of Gandhi Maidan, children's park and inside Gandhi maidan. Blasts also took place when Narendra Modi was addressing the rally. All the bombs were of low capacity and the intention of terrorists was to cause a stampede after the blasts, which would lead to a large number of casualties.

One terrorist Tariq alias Ainul was injured (he later died) when he was planting a bomb at the Patna Junction railway station. His accomplice Imtiaz was caught while trying to flee from the spot and the entire conspiracy came to light. At the time the low-density blasts were taking place at the rally venue, the BJP leaders kept the situation under control by saying that it was cracker blasts so that there was no stampede, otherwise there would have been huge casualties.

This incident was also executed by the Ranchi module of IM, with Tahseen Akhtar alias Monu as the mastermind. Tahseen Akhtar was the nephew of the Janata Dal (United) leader Tauqeer Akhtar, and had turned a terrorist while studying in a *madarsa* at Chikmagalur in Karnataka. During the investigation, nine live bombs were recovered from a room of a small hotel in Ranchi on 5 November, 2013. These bombs were quite similar to those used in Patna blasts. It was found that the main role in this incident was played by Imtiaz Ali, Mujibullah, Haider Ali, Nauman and Taufeeq Ansari and a reward of Rs. 5 lakhs to Rs. 10 lakh was announced on their heads. The involvement of eight other terrorists was also revealed. These were – Noman Ansari, Mujibullah Ansari, Umar Siddiq, Azharuddin Qureshi, Ahmad Husain, Fakhruddin, Firoz Aslam, Iftekhar Alam and Alam (minor). All were members of the banned organisation SIMI and were recruiting young boys by showing them provocative *jihadi* videos.

The plan was hatched by Haider Ali, the Jharkhand incharge of SIMI, and this group was also responsible for the blasts in Mahabodhi Mandir at Bodhgaya. The gang members had learnt bomb-making from the Al-Qaeda magazine named *Inspire*.

□

39

Structure of Indian Mujahideen

The structure of the Indian Mujahideen terrorist group is as follows:

1. Chief Commander – Riaz Bhatkal, Iqbal Bhatkal and Amir Raza Khan
2. North Indian Azamgarh module – Commander Atif Amin, Sanjarpur, Azmgarh

No.	Members	Terrorist incidents
1.	Sadiq Sheikh	Dashashwamedh Ghat blast
2.	Mohammad Atif Amin	Shramjivi Express train blast
3.	Dr. Shahnawaz Alam	Delhi market blast
4.	Mohammad Arif	Sankat Mochan blast
5.	Mohammad Shadab	Mumbai local train blast
6.	Ariz alias Junaid	Golghar Gorakhpur blast
7.	Bada Sajid	UP Courts blast
8.	Abu Rashid	Jaipur blast
9.	Khalid	Ahmedabad blast
10.	Mohammad Saif	Delhi blast
11.	Chhota Sajid	Batala House police encounter
12.	Shakeel	
13.	Zia	
14.	Zeeshan	
15.	Shahzad alias Pappu	

16.	Mohammad Salman	
17.	Arif Badr	
18.	Saifur Rahman	
19.	Shadab (Doosra)	
20.	Asadullah alias Haddi	
21.	Shaqib	
22.	Mohammad Sarwar	
23.	Sarfuddin	

All these terrorists were residents of Azamgarh. They were initiated by Mohammad Sadiq Sheikh, the programming engineer of Cheeta Camp in Mumbai. Most of these terrorists had received their training in the LeT Muzaffarabad training centre in PoK. Sadiq Sheikh had brought along Atif Amin who later became the commander of IM's Azamgarh module. Atif Amin and Chhota Sajid had been killed in the Batala House police encounter in Delhi on 19 September 2008.

3. South India / Surat/ Pune Group

No.	Members	Terrorist incidents
1.	Mohammad Ahmad Siddhi Bappa alias Yasin Bhatkal	Bombs were planted in Surat on 26 July, 2008 but the blasts could not take place because of a circuit failure. If this explosion had indeed taken place, then many more people would have been killed than the number killed in Ahmedabad blasts. Yasin Bhatkal was the most ferocious terrorist of IM after Riaz Bhatkal and Iqbal Bhatkal. He was an expert in making boat-shaped bombs. It was the most effective explosive device by IM that had been used to cause vast devastation in Jaipur, Ahmedabad, Hyderabad Gokul Chat Centre and Lumbini Park and Delhi blasts. After the demolition of the Azamgarh module, he set up the Darbhanga module. He played a major role in many terrorist incidents in south India, Mumbai and north India locations.
2.	Akbar	
3.	Aniq	
4.	Fazal	
5.	Afzal	
6.	Kayamuddin Kapadia	
7.	Asif	
8.	Tanvir	
9.	Waseem	
10.	Naushad	
11.	Abu Baqar	

4. Publicity and E-mail Group

No.	Members	Role	Blasts in which E-mails were sent
1.	Iqbal Bhatkal	Planning	UP Court blasts
2.	Riaz Bhatkal	Planning	Jaipur blast
3.	Akbar	Driver	Ahmedabad blasts
4.	Mansoor Asghar Peer-bhoy	PDF setting	Delhi blasts
5.	Asif Sheikh	Writer of e-mail	Attack on foreigners at Jama Masjid
6.	Salman	Computer feeding/ formating	
7.	Majeed	Urdu/Arabic writing	
8.	Mohsin	Sender of e-mail	

Darbhanga module of Indian Mujahideen

1. Mastermind – Riaz Bhatkal
2. Mohammad Ahmad Siddhi Bappa alias Yasin Bhatkal
3. Asadullah alias Haddi, Azamgarh

No.	Members	Terrorist incidents
1.	Tahseen Akhtar 'Monu', local commander, Ranchi / Darbhanga	Bodhgaya blast
2.	Tariq alias Ainul	Blast at Narendra Modi's Hunkar Rally in Patna on 23 October, 2013
3.	Imtiaz Ali	Sheetala Ghat blast, Varanasi on 7 December, 2010
4.	Mujibullah	
5.	Haider Ali, head of SIMI Ranchi	
6.	Nauman	

7.	Taufeeq Ansari	
8.	Fasih Mohammad	
9.	Mohsin Chaudhary	
10.	Gauhar Siddiqui alias Qateel	
11.	Waqas Ahmad 'Pakistan'	

□

40
Brief description of E-mails sent by terrorists

Indian Mujahideen was formed by the Pakistani intelligence agency ISI in association with Pakistani terrorist organisations - Lashkar-e-Tayyaba and HUJI. Members of the banned organisation, Students' Islamic Movement of India (SIMI), had a major role in this terrorist organisation. Otherwise also, the cadre of SIMI had formed many extremist organisations, such as Usaba Committee, Asif Raza Commando Force, Karnataka Forum of Dignity, etc., and had conducted disruptive activities. All these outfits had come together to form IM and its terrorists were mainly trained by the Pakistani terror organisation LeT, run by global terrorist Hafiz Sayeed.

IM is actually the Indian version of LeT. The activities of IM had started in 2003 itself, but it revealed itself in the E-mail sent to media houses on 23 November, 2007 after the serial explosions in Courts at Lucknow, Faizabad (Ayodhya) and Varanasi. After this, provocative E-mails were sent to media houses by these terrorists a few minutes before the bomb blasts. Such E-mails were sent by IM before the court blasts on 23 November, 2007, Ahmedabad blasts (26 July, 2008) and the terror attack near Jama Masjid in Delhi on 19 September, 2010 to mark the second anniversary of the Batala House encounter. A terror E-mail was also sent by IM a day after the 18th anniversary of the demolition of the Babri mosque on 7 December, 2010. The five E-mails sent by IM have been given in original in this book, but their brief description is as follows:

1. Mail sent on blasts in three Courts in Uttar Pradesh (23 November, 2007)

"Bismillah-ar-Rahmanir-Rahim

Allah says: O faithful, fight these *kafirs* (non-believers) who live near you and they must see the strength within you." After that, the Quran *ayat* 122 from Surah Taubah is mentioned. After this, the IM mentions the Delhi 29/10, Varanasi March, 7/11 Mumbai local train blast and Hyderabad Gokul Chat and Park as their big successful attacks in India. They have also mentioned they have not executed the Malegaon, '*Samjhauta Express*' and Makka Masjid blasts in Hyderabad. Then it is mentioned that within a few minutes bomb blasts are going to take place in two cities of U.P.

Introducing themselves, they say that IM is not a foreign organisation and do not have any attachment with neighbouring country's agency, like ISI, LET, HUJI, etc. and that they are purely Indian.

They have mentioned that when Muslims were fleeing from India to Pakistan at the time of Partition, then Abdul Kalam Azad had stopped them and on behalf of Congress Party, (Gandhi, Nehru, Patel) had assured them that they could stay in India and they will be given full rights of rehabilitation. Then they have mentioned about the demolition of the Babri mosque and the riots thereafter, especially the communal riots in Maharashtra. Then they have mentioned the riots in Gujarat after the carnage in Godhra and written in provocative terms about the damages caused to Muslims.

In the end they have issued a warning that they are prepared enough to retaliate. This is not the war between two communities, but this is war for civilisation. They want to liberate the society from injustice, corruption, etc. According to them, only Islamic rule has the power to establish a civilised society and Islamic rule can be achieved by only the path of *jihad.*

Then they have written that now the Islamic raids are going to take place against lawyers within a few minutes. According to them, the police nabbed two innocent groups and framed them in fake charges of terrorism. A lawyer of these places had beaten those group members and refused to take their cases and did not allow others to take up their case. In the end they have said that you have seen our patience, now feel the aggression. *Allah-o-Akbar*

2. First E-mail on Ahmedabad blast (26 July, 2008)

In the first terror E-mail sent on Ahmedabad blast, a visual of the blast was posted along with the words 'The Rise of Jihad, Revenge of Gujarat' and 'Released by Indian Mujahideen in the land of Hind'. The logo of IM was also posted for the first time in this terror E-mail. In this 14-page mail, the IM mentioned five *ayats* of the Quran and below is a comment in English. In the beginning it is written that "O *kafirs* (non-believers of Islam), if you want justice, then you will get justice, and you will protest, then we shall come back and your security forces, howsoever large they are, will not be able to protect you. Allah is only with believers."

Then, it is written with reference to Quran that none should be worshipped other than Allah. "We have discarded you. The enmity and hatred between Muslims and you is forever, until you believe in Allah and only Allah. We shall keep fighting those till they accept that only the worship of Allah is acceptable and Muhammad is their messenger. You shall have to accept the loyalty towards Islam and Allah. O Hindus, your 33 crore dirty mud idols and idols of Ram, Krishna and Hanuman are not at all going to save your necks from the wrath of Allah. Your false belief will not save you from the wrath of Allah and you will get punishment. Only the acceptance of Islam and belief in Allah can stop you blood from flowing on the streets." In addition, they have also mentioned that "their *jihad* against Hindus and those who oppose us has started. The battle shall continue till you cease to exist."

They have written: "Wait, wait now only for five minutes. If you can stop the Mujahideen then do it, we shall make you face terror and give you grave punishment. Wait for five minutes and feel the terror of death."

The terror mail has also used objectionable and insulting comments against the leaders of Bharatiya Janata Party, RSS, Vishwa Hindu Parishad, Bajrang Dal, etc. They have also called upon "Muslims in Gujarat to rise, get organised and fight *kafirs* with courage. Remind them of the onslaught of Khalid bin Waleed, determination of Ali bin Abi Talib, the bravery of Saad bin Abi Waqqas, heroism of Abu Bakr and Umar, guts of Talhah and Zubair." In the end they have written, "Phrases like democracy, secularism, equality, integrity, peace, freedom, voting, election are a fraud."

Referring to Quran (9:123) it has been written that "the faithful must fight the *kafirs* who live near you and show them your strength." Muslims have been urged to join the IM and target Hindus, BJP, RSS, Bajrang Dal. Also kill policemen and their informants.

They have also warned some Muslim leaders. They also warned the Governments of Rajasthan, Uttar Pradesh, Madhya Pradesh, Andhra Pradesh, Karnataka, and Maharashtra that they should not harass Muslims. They have also written that "Muslims and members of SIMI are being arrested and persecuted in Indore, Ujjain, Mumbai and Karnataka. Release them; otherwise, be prepared to become the next target."

Lawyers of U.P. Bar Council who assaulted some Muslims have also been warned. In the end, newspapers, TV channels such as 'The Times of India' and 'Times Now' have also been threatened. In the end they have taken responsibility for the serial blasts in Ahmedabad. They have also written that Lashkar-e-Tayyaba and other organisations should not take responsibility for the Ahmedabad blasts. In the end they have announced that "those who fight against Allah, his messengers and the faith, will face more serious attacks."

3. Second E-mail on Ahmedabad blast (15 August, 2008)

This E-mail was sent 20 days after the first mail. It mentions an *ayat* of Quran and a comment in English. They had warned Hindus again that they will face more severe attacks. They had threatened ATS Gujarat, ATS Mumbai and Gujarat police that they are enemies of Islam and mujahideen and the next attack will be against them. They had termed the solving of the Ahmedabad case by Gujarat police as fake. They had also said that they are determined and organised, and their numbers are rising. According to them, none of the *mujahids* of IM had been arrested. They had termed the statement of Gujarat police officers Ashish Bhatia and P.C. Pandey on the arrest of Mufti Abu Bashar, Sajid Mansoori, Zahid Sheikh and others as a big lie. They had also written that they cannot even imagine who is the mastermind of Ahmedabad attacks, leave alone his arrest. They had threatened the Maharashtra ATS I.G. Hemant Karkare that they are on their target. They had also mentioned that they are not connected with SIMI.

In the end, they had expressed gratitude to Ken Heywood, an official of an American multinational company, whose computer was used for sending a terror E-mail in Navi Mumbai a few minutes before the Ahmedabad blasts. They had warned the police, ATS, Crime Branch, IB agents, informants and the media to desist from spreading misinformation against them.

4. Terror mail on the terror incident near Jama Masjid, Delhi (19 September, 2010)

In this E-mail, six *ayats* of the Quran are mentioned and there is mention of the so-called atrocities on Muslims in Kashmir. They write that the idol-worshipping Hindus have forced the Kashmiri Muslims to take up arms. The Mujahideen have decided that they will avenge the atrocities committed against them since 1947, as it is their sacred duty. Anyone who does not help Kashmiris will be on their target. They had also mentioned that they have played "Holi with your blood in your own cities." In the end they had written that this attack is in retaliation of the killing of Atif Amin and Mohammad Sajid in Batala House encounter. They had accused the Delhi police of harassing terrorist Salman Chhotu. They had questioned the solving of the German Bakery case by the then ATS chief Rakesh Maria and said that he had jailed the wrong persons. Some other officers of Maharashtra have been threatened.

5. Terror mail on Sheetala Ghat blast (7 December, 2010)

The Sheetala Ghat blast was a brainchild of Yasin Bhatkal. His plan to execute a big incident on the second anniversary of Batala House encounter had flopped and a Darbhanga module of IM had been formed. Then he and Asadullah Haddi planned to cause a blast in Varanasi on the 18th anniversary of Babri mosque demolition. This time they decided to use hydrogen peroxide instead of the boat-shaped bombs, but this plan also failed. Since the terrorists could not cause the blast on the 18th anniversary of demolition on 6 December, 2010, they executed it the next day, 7 December. In the blast at Sheetala Ghat, a two-year-old girl was killed and a few persons received simple injuries.

Yasin Bhatkal had sent a 5-page terror E-mail to media houses, in which he had mentioned Quran *ayats* at eight places with comments in English. In the beginning he wrote after the Quran *ayats* that these blasts were being done on the anniversary of the demolition of Babri mosque. The Babri Masjid was revered by them and they were hurt at its demolition. They have warned the Hindu devotees of Bhagwan Shiv and Mata Parvati that they are the descendants of Mahmood Ghajnavi, Mohammad Ghauri, Kutub-ud-Din Aibak, Firoz Shah Tughlaq and Aurangzeb, and they have decided that none of their temples will be spared until the mosques of Muslims captured by them are not returned.

"When a *masjid* is made, it remains a *masjid* and it is property of Allah and cannot be given to anyone and no one has the right to claim it." They have also written about the history of the Babri structure from 1949 as well as about court rulings.

They have threatened some Muslim leaders and Muslim leaders associated with All India Muslim Personal Law Board, Babri Masjid Action Committee, Sunni Waqf Board, etc. that they have no right to compromise on the Babri Masjid and it cannot be negotiated. They have termed Hindus as *kafirs* and threatened them that howsoever grand a temple is built on the site of Babri Masjid, they will demolish it and re-establish a mosque at that spot. No power would be able to stop them as Allah is with them.

They have advised Syed Ali Shah Geelani and Mirwaiz of Kashmir that they should not waste time and not compromise with Hindus (with derogatory terms). In the end they have said that they are fully prepared and had been preparing for this for a long time.

They have also appealed to Muslim countries that they should put international pressure on India.

□

41

Politics of appeasement on Godhra Carnage – 59 killed (27 February, 2002)

On 27 February, 2002, devotees of Lord Rama from Gujarat were returning to Gujarat from Ayodhya by the '*Sabarmati Express*' 'train. The train reached Godhra station in the morning. The extremist Muslims of Godhra had prepared a plan to kill these kar *sevaks*. At 7.43 a.m. in the morning of 27 February, 2002, a crowd of more than 1,000 rioters surrounded the coach number S-6 of the train and set fire to it after pouring petrol on it. This carnage led to the death of 59 *karsevaks* including many small children and women. The Godhra incident is considered the worst example of human cruelty. Extremist Muslims had committed a heinous crime, setting aside their humanity, in the manner of monsters. As a reaction to the Godhra incident, communal riots broke out at many places in Gujarat, including Ahmedabad, in which about 1,000 persons from both communities were killed. In the year 2004, a UPA government led by the Congress party was formed at the Centre and Lalu Prasad Yadav was made the Minister for Railways on 17 May, 2004. To strengthen his M-Y (Muslim-Yadav) vote-bank, Lalu Prasad Yadav tried to term the Godhra carnage as an accident. Assembly elections were scheduled in Bihar in 2005 and Lalu Prasad Yadav changed the narrative of the Godhra incident and through the U.C. Banerjee Commission, it was termed to be an accidental fire.

Politics of M-Y (Muslim-Yadav) Combination by Lalu Prasad Yadav

The M-Y combination was a brainchild of Lalu Prasad Yadav. He rode this combination to power in Bihar and formed the government for the first time in 1990 and remained the Chief Minister for 15 years. The script for this was written in the Bhagalpur riots (from 24 October, 1989 to 06 December, 1989). Muslims felt that in these riots, the Congress party had betrayed them. The then Chief Minister Satyendra Nath Sinha had failed to control the riots and this had angered the Muslims of Bihar, who constituted about 17 per cent of the state's population. After their resentment against the Congress, they were looking for a leader who could stand by them. Lalu Prasad Yadav grabbed this chance and became their voice, thus attracting Muslim voters towards his party. The Yadavs, constituting 14 per cent of Bihar's population, also stood behind Lalu Prasad Yadav and thus, the M-Y combination became his core vote-bank.

"BHURA-BAL saaf karo"

In the year 1990, the recommendations of the Mandal Commission were implemented, which tightened Lalu Prasad Yadav's grip on the backward castes. To strengthen this, he targeted the four main upper caste groups in Bihar – Bhumihar (BHU), Rajput (RA), Brahmin (B) and Kayastha or Lala (L) – and gave a slogan: *BHURA-BAL saaf karo*. He considered these four groups to be responsible for the economic, social and political backwardness of the backward castes, Dalits and Muslims in Bihar. His supporters lapped up this slogan and he became stronger in Bihar. A large number of upper caste officers in the IAS and IPS were marginalised.

On 23 October, 1990, Lalu Prasad Yadav stopped the Somnath to Ayodhya 'Rath yatra' of Bharatiya Janata Party leader Lal Krishna Advani in Samastipur in Bihar and took Advani into custody. This *yatra* led by Advani had started from Somnath in Gujarat and was scheduled to reach Ayodhya after travelling through many states. This was a huge effort to create awareness about the construction of a Ram temple in Ayodhya. The arrest of Advani and the stopping of the *yatra* made Lalu Prasad Yadav even more popular among the Muslims and Lalu himself never shied away from taking credit for this. In the initial years he did become politically strong but later, a separate and parallel power structure of criminals and gangsters came into being which included many elements from his own political party. Kidnapping for ransom became an industry. Extortion and seeking protection money from businessmen, traders, private hospitals and other commercial establishments became commonplace. Entire Bihar was in the grip of criminals and gangsters.

Even I am an eye-witness to this. For seven years, from 1996 to 2003, I was posted as the Chief Security Commissioner in North-Eastern Railway, in Gorakhpur. My jurisdiction included Uttar Pradesh and Bihar. Two officers of the SP rank in RPF were posted in Sonpur and Samastipur divisions of the Railways in Bihar. In my seven-year tenure, I worked with the then Minister for Railways Ram Vilas Paswan and Nitish Kumar. Both ministers were very efficient and used to visit Bihar almost every week and travel in the state. Whenever the Railway Ministers arrived, the senior officers of NER led by the General Manager accompanied him. All of us officers had to visit those places connected with the Railways where the minister travelled. These two ministers converted the metre-gauge Railway track in Bihar to broad gauge, and it was with their efforts that a new zonal Railway called East Central Railway was established with headquarters in Hajipur, Bihar. The foundation of the Hajipur Railway zone was to be laid by the then Prime Minister H.D. Deve Gowda, which became effective from 2002. The then Chief Minister of Bihar Lalu Prasad Yadav used to participate in all major programmes of the Railways and he used to be accompanied by a large number of his followers. These privileged followers included Shahabuddin, the then Member of Lok Sabha from

Siwan and a dreaded gangster. Shahabuddin and his followers' terror was at its peak. While returning from Patna, he and his accomplices often used to occupy all berths in the AC first-class compartment of '*Vaishali Express*' that ran from Barauni to Siwan, Gorakhpur and Lucknow to Delhi. The passengers with a valid reservation in the compartment were forced to slink in a corner and wait for the forcible occupants to get down at Siwan. Noted gangsters and criminals and their associates used to attend all government functions as well.

Charwaha Schools

Most of my official touring was during the Railway Minister's tours in North Bihar. I had seen the reality of Lalu Yadav's dream project 'Chawaha Schools' from close quarters. It was among the most talked-about projects of the Rashtriya Janata Dal chief Lalu Prasad Yadav. These schools were set up to cater to children aged five to 15 years and who were engaged in tending to cattle. Such children used to come to schools in the morning, leave their cattle for grazing and the teachers used to take their classes. In a corner of the school, women were trained in making *papad, bari, achar,* etc. These schools attracted a lot of attention and observers from US and Japan used to come to see them. When these schools were opened on 15 January, 1992, Lalu Prasad Yadav took a class in a school and, speaking in Bhojpuri, taught them how to count numbers. He had told this marginalised section of society to stop addressing the *zamindars* as *malik* (lords or owners). Up to March, 1992, 113 'Charwaha Schools' were opened in undivided Bihar. These functioned for the initial one year, but gradually the students and teachers stopped coming to school. Six government departments – Agriculture, Irrigation, Industries, Animal Husbandry, Rural Development and Education – were involved in running them and Agriculture Department was the nodal agency. These schools closed one by one and Lalu Prasad himself was embroiled in the fodder scam. It was probed by the CBI and 66 cases were registered in this connection. Courts sentenced him to jail in all cases for a total of 32 years and he was imprisoned for years. His jail term started when he surrendered in a special court on 30 July, 1997 during the CBI probe. A few days earlier, on 25 July, 1997, he had to resign as Chief Minister after a warrant for his arrest was issued by the Special Court and he handed over the post to his wife Rabri Devi. She was elected to the Vidhan Sabha and Vidhan Parishad many times and was Chief Minister thrice. She handled Lalu Prasad Yadav's political legacy while he was in jail.

U.C. Banerjee Commission (4 September, 2004)

Assembly elections in Bihar were scheduled in 2005. Lalu Yadav foresaw his defeat in view of the prevailing lawlessness and poor governance. He was made the Minister for Railways on 25 May, 2004 when the UPA Government took office. He then decided to win over the trust of Muslims and proceeded to change the narrative of the Godhra carnage. On his initiative, the Union Cabinet decided to institute a judicial investigation into the Godhra incident. A judicial commission was set up on 4 September, 2004 headed by retired judge of the Supreme Court, Justice U.C. Banerjee to probe the Godhra incident. There was a political motive behind setting up this commission. Lalu Prasad Yadav wanted to appease the Muslim community by setting up the commission and thus strengthen his vote-bank. He expected to benefit from this in the 2005 state election.

The Commission submitted its report on 17 January, 2005 and it said that the fire which caused the death of the Ram devotees was an accident. The Banerjee Commission totally rejected the facts that the fire was caused by rioters. Lalu Prasad Yadav immediately called a Press briefing to announce that Muslims had no role in the Godhra carnage. In his own *desi* style he said that the fire was caused by the *chillum* smoked by *sadhus* and *babas* returning from Ayodhya. He also targeted Nitish Kumar who was the Minister for Railways at the time of the Godhra incident, implying that Nitish Kumar had not stood by Muslims at that time and it was him (Lalu) who had brought relief to Muslims through the report of the judicial commission. In the 2005 Bihar Assembly election, Lalu Prasad highlighted the Banerjee Commission report during the 2005 election campaign and targeted Nitish Kumar, his political opponent. However, Lalu Prasad's party Rashtriya Janata Dal was ousted from power and Nitish Kumar became the Chief Minister of Bihar for the first time.

Railway Board – at the service of Justice U.C. Banerjee

The office of Justice U.C. Banerjee was allotted on the second floor of Rail Bhavan. Railway Minister Lalu Prasad Yadav also had an office on the same floor. Right in front of Railway Minister's office, his OSD. Sudhir Kumar (IAS, 1987) also had an office. Justice U.C. Banerjee was given an office adjacent to Sudhir Kumar's office. Justice Banerjee kept visiting many major cities during the tenure of Justice Banerjee Commission. He often used to come to Lucknow and used to party in the suite of the famous five-star hotel 'Taj'. R.V. Singh (IRTS, 1982) during 2003-2005, was posted as ADRM in Northern Railway, Lucknow. He once told me during a conversation that once Justice Banerjee was about to come to Lucknow. He wanted to stay in the suite of five-star hotel 'Taj'. As usual, the request for suite was made, but could not be arranged due to pre-occupancy. A day before his arrival, in the evening, with great difficulty, a suite could be arranged at the Taj Hotel. Due to lack of timely arrangements, Justice Banerjee got annoyed and cancelled his programme. No stone was left unturned by the

Ministry of Railways in the service of Justice Banerjee. Two persons from Bachhrawan (Rai Bareilly) used to come to meet R.V. Singh. They were demanding government jobs in the Railways for their sons. They had told R.V. Singh that they were also travelling in the '*Sabarmati Express*' on 27 February, 2002. His coach was also near the S-6 coach, which was burnt by the fundamentalists. 59 *Ram bhakts* were burnt alive in the

S-6 inferno. In the Banerjee Commission, affidavits were taken from both those persons and assurances were given that their children would be given government jobs in the Railways. It was written in the affidavit that they were also travelling on the '*Sabarmati Express*' that day. The fire broke out accidentally in coach number S-6. His sons were lured with government jobs in Railways to sign the false affidavit.

The drafting of the Banerjee Commission was done by Sudhir Kumar, OSD to Railway Minister Lalu Prasad Yadav and typed by Dilip Kumar. Dilip Kumar of Northern Railway was posted at Baroda House and was attached to the Railway Minister's office. Sudhir Kumar had given an application on 17 July, 2021, to lodge an FIR against the then Bihar Chief Minister Nitish Kumar and several senior officials at Gardnibagh police station in Patna, Bihar.

Sudhir Kumar, while posted in Bihar, was also the Chairman of the Bihar Staff Selection Commission (BSSC). In the year 2014, IAS Sudhir Kumar's name cropped up in connection with the question paper leak of SSC Combined Competitive Examination. To investigate this scam, Bihar government had constituted an SIT, which was headed by Manu Maharaj, the then SSP, Patna. During the investigation, Sudhir Kumar along with his brother Awadhesh Kumar, sister-in-law Manju Devi, nephews Ashish and Arun and a relative Rajan were arrested on 24 February, 2017. He remained in jail for about three-and-a-half years. Sudhir Kumar retired in February, 2022. Lalu Prasad Yadav continued to describe Sudhir Kumar as an honest officer. Sudhir Kumar was also posted with the then Deputy Chief Minister, Tejashwi Prasad Yadav, son of Lalu Prasad Yadav.

Banerjee Commission Report Rejected

The report of Banerjee Commission was challenged in the Gujarat High Court by Neelkanth Tulsidas Bhatia, who was among the injured in the Godhra incident. On 13 October, 2006, the Gujarat High Court ruled that the constitution of the

U.C. Banerjee Commission was illegal and unconstitutional, since the Nanavati-Shah Judicial Commission was already probing the Godhra incident and related cases. The High Court also said that the result of the investigation by the Banerjee Commission was unacceptable. The court also ruled that the Banerjee Commission's report should not be placed in the Lok Sabha and Rajya Sabha. Thus, the objective of Lalu Prasad to change the narrative of the Godhra carnage was defeated.

Obstacles in the Investigation of Godhra Carnage

There were several obstacles in the investigation of the carnage at Godhra. Some important facts related to the case are as follows:

1. 27 February, 2002 – Coach number S-6 of *'Sabarmati Express'* standing in Godhra was surrounded by a crowd comprising Muslims and it was set on fire, in which 56 pilgrims returning from Ayodhya were burnt alive.
2. 28 February, 2002 – Communal riots flared up in many places in Gujarat in which about 1,000 persons from both communities were killed.
3. 6 March, 2002 – Gujarat government set up the Nanavati Commission and it was entrusted the investigation into the Godhra carnage as well as other incidents in Gujarat.
4. 9 March, 2002 – The police slapped charges of murder, arson and criminal conspiracy against all accused.
5. 25 March, 2002 – Sections of POTA (Prevention of Terrorism Act, 2002) were withdrawn from the accused.
6. 18 February, 2003 – Bharatiya Janata Party government came into power in Gujarat and the Sections of POTA were slapped again on the accused.
7. 21 November, 2003 – The Supreme Court stayed the judicial hearing of the cases related to Godhra incident and subsequent riots.

8. 4 September, 2004 – Minister for Railways Lalu Prasad Yadav constituted a Commission headed by retired Supreme Court Judge, Justice U.C. Banerjee, to probe Godhra incident.
9. 21 September, 2004 – The newly-formed UPA government at the Centre repealed the POTA and decided to review the charges under POTA on the accused in the Godhra case.
10. **17 January, 2005 – U.C. Banerjee Commission submitted its report and said that the fire in Coach S-6 of *'Sabarmati Express'* was a mere accident. He also said that external elements had not started the fire in Coach S-6.**
11. 16 May, 2005 – The POTA Review Committee suggested that charges under POTA should not be slapped against the accused.
12. **13 October, 2006 – Gujarat High Court ruled that the constitution of the U.C. Banerjee Commission was illegal and unconstitutional because the Nanavati-Shah Judicial Inquiry Commission was already probing the Godhra incident and related cases. The High Court also said that the results of the inquiry by the U.C. Banerjee Commission were unacceptable.**
13. 26 March, 2008 – The Supreme Court set up a 'Special Inquiry Commission' to probe the fire in the Coach S-6 of *'Sabarmati Express'* at Godhra and eight other related cases.
14. **18 September, 2008 – The Nanavati Judicial Inquiry Commission submitted the report of inquiry into the Godhra carnage to the state government.**
15. 12 February, 2009 – The Gujarat High Court upheld the recommendations of the POTA Review Committee and said that this law could not be applied in this case.
16. 20 February, 2009 – A relative of one of the victims of the Godhra case challenged in Supreme Court the

decision of the High Court withdrawing POTA against the accused.

17. 1 May, 2009 – Supreme Court withdrew the restrictions on hearing the Godhra case and the special inquiry team headed by former CBI director R.K. Raghavan expedited its investigation into Godhra case and nine other sensitive cases related to the subsequent riots.
18. 1 June, 2009 – Judicial hearing on the Godhra case began in the Sabarmati Jail at Ahmedabad.
19. 6 May, 2010 – Supreme Court stayed the verdict by the court hearing the Godhra case and nine sensitive cases related to Gujarat riots.
20. **28 September, 2010 – The judicial hearing into the Godhra case was completed in Sabarmati Jail but the verdict could not be announced in view of the stay by the Supreme Court.**
21. **18 January, 2011 – Supreme Court withdrew the stay on announcing the verdict.**
22. 22 February, 2011 – The Special Court found 31 persons guilty in the Godhra carnage and acquitted 63 others for lack of evidence.
23. **1 March, 2011 – The Special Court announced death penalty for 11 accused and life imprisonment to 20 accused. Those sentenced to be hanged till death were: 1. Haji Bilal Ismail, 2. Abdul Majid Ramjani, 3. Razzaq Kurkur, 4. Salman alias Salman Zarda, 5. Zabeer Behra, 6. Mahboob Latika, 7. Irfan Papilya, 8. Sokut Lalu, 9. Irfan Bhopa, 10. Ismail Sujela, 11. Jubir Bimyani.**

□

42

Muslim appeasement by Mayawati Government – R.D. Nimesh Commission

Courts in Lucknow, Faizabad and Varanasi were rocked by serial blasts on 23 November, 2007, in which 15 lawyers and others were killed. It was a terrorist incident and subsequently on 26 November, 2007, the U.P. ATS was set up. I was made its first ADG. The court blasts had shocked the entire state but the U.P. ATS, STF cracked the case. On 22 December, 2007, two dreaded terrorists Khalid Mujahid (son of Jameer Mujahid, resident of Madiyahu in Jaunpur) and Hakim Tariq Kasim (son of Riaz Ahmad, resident of Azhar Unani dispensary, Shankarpur, Rani Ki Sarai, Azamgarh), were arrested from outside the Barabanki railway station. The case was investigated promptly and chargesheet submitted to Barabanki District and Sessions Court.

The arrests caused an uproar among the Samajwadi Party, Congress Party, Rashtravadi Congress Party (NCP) and Ulema Council. These organisations said the accused were innocent and staged protests in Azamgarh, Jaunpur and Lucknow.

As per her appeasement policy, the then Uttar Pradesh Chief Minister Mayawati set up a one-member inquiry commission on 14 March, 2007. As proposed by the then Principal Secretary Home Kunwar Fateh Bahadur Singh, retired District Judge R.D. Nimesh was appointed Chairman of this Commission. At that time, I had raised an objection with the state government, saying that this would weaken the morale of the officers who had arrested

the terrorists, and it will not be in the interest of the state and will have far-reaching consequences. I was told that the 2009 Lok Sabha election was nearing and the ruling Bahujan Samaj Party wanted to appease the Muslim community so as to keep the Muslim vote--bank happy. It was also assured that the Commission would be scrapped after the 2009 elections were over.

The General Elections were completed and the Bahujan Samaj Party was pushed to the third position in the state after winning a mere 19 seats. However, the term of the R.D. Nimesh Commission was extended at the behest of the Principal Secretary Home Kunwar Fateh Bahadur Singh.

Then the Bahujan Samaj party started to worry about the 2012 U.P. Assembly election, for which it was important to conserve the Muslim vote-bank. The election saw the Bahujan Samaj Party suffer a huge defeat and the Samajwadi Party formed the government with Akhilesh Yadav as the Chief Minister in March, 2012.

Akhilesh Yadav extended the term of Nimesh Commission

The then Chief Minister Akhilesh Yadav also extended the term of the Nimesh Commission as part of his Muslim appeasement policy. In a bid to seek a favourable report from him, Judge R.D. Nimesh was also made Chairman of the Tappal Commission. As I had anticipated that the Nimesh Commission was set up under vote-bank politics and will have far-reaching consequences, its report was predictable. It said in its report that no comment could be made on the case as it was pending in court, but the arrest of Khalid Mujahid and Tariq Kasmi appeared suspicious. Thus, the Nimesh Commission prepared the script for providing relief to the terrorists in the case. The Akhilesh Yadav government immediately decided to withdraw the cases against Khaild Mujahid and Hakim Tariq Kasmi in the court blasts case, but the Barabanki District and Sessions Court put a stay on the proposal.

In the meantime, Khalid Mujahid died from sunstroke in Barabanki district hospital while being transported from Ayodhya Court to Lucknow on 18 May, 2013. The Akhilesh Yadav government on 19 May, 2013 registered a fake case of murder against 42 police officers in Barabanki *kotwali.* **On a verbal submission by Khalid's uncle Zaheer Alam Falahi, son of Abdul Razzak, resident of Madiyahu in Jaunpur, a case was registered in the *kotwali* Barabanki at 3.30.a.m. on 19 May, 2013, as crime number 295/13, under Section 302/120B IPC, in which the following police officials were named:**

1. Brij Lal, the then Additional Director-General of Police, Uttar Pradesh
2. Chiranjeev Nath Sinha, Deputy SP
3. Manoj Kumar Jha, Additional Superintendent of Police
4. Vikram Singh, the then Director-General of Police, U.P.
5. S. Anand, Additional Superintendent of Police

In addition, some officials of the IB were also named, totalling 42 persons

The Uttar Pradesh Government promptly handed over the investigation in this case to the CBI, but the CBI refused to take up the case saying it was based on false claims. Then the Allahabad High Court (Lucknow Bench) handed over the investigation to the U.P. Crime Branch CID. Officers of the CID also faced pressure to frame charges against the officers named in this case. In 2017 there was a change of Government in U.P. and a Bharatiya Janata Party Government was formed led by Yogi Adityanath. In July, 2017, the matter came to an end after filing a final report.

The case against terrorist Tariq Kasmi was heard in the Court of Special Sessions Judge Barabanki, SP Arvind. The court on 24 April, 2015 sentenced him to life imprisonment for possessing detonators and RDX. Life term was also awarded to him for the Golghar, Gorakhpur blast, Lucknow and Ayodhya Courts blasts. Thus, the objective of withdrawing the cases against terrorists as per appeasement politics could not succeed. A detailed description of this case is given elsewhere in this book.

□

43

Withdrawal of 14 Chargesheets against terrorists by Samajwadi Party

Assembly elections were scheduled in Uttar Pradesh in 2012. The Samajwadi Party announced in its manifesto that in case it formed the government, Muslims jailed on terrorism charges would be released. The party came to power after securing majority and Akhilesh Yadav became the Chief Minister. As per the election promise, a decision was taken to withdraw the chargesheets submitted in courts by the police related to cases of terrorism. The cases withdrawn by the then Government are as follows:

Miscellaneous Bench No. 4683/2003, Ranjan Agnihotri and others Vs Union of India and list of other charges, for which orders were issued by the state government to withdraw the cases:

Number of districts-7, number of charges -14, number of accused-19

S. No.	District & PS	Case Crime No. and Sections	Name of accused	Resident	GO no and date of case withdrawal
1	Varanasi, Dashashwamedh Ghat	11/2006, Sec 3/4/5, Explosive Substances Act	1. Shamim alias Sarfaraz	Kaundha, PS Alinagar, Chandauli	07WC/ Seven-Nyay-5-2013-2854 WC/2012, dt 5-3-2013
2	Gorakhpur, Cantt	812/2007, Sec 307 IPC, 3/4/5, Explosive Substances Act, 7 Criminal Law Amendment Act, 16,18,23Unlawful Activities (Prevention) Act	1. Mohd Tariq Kasmi	Sammopur, PS Rani Ki Sarai, Azamgarh	389WC/ Seven-Nyay-5-2013-1401 WC/2012, dt 5-3-2013
3	Bijnore, Najibabad	290/2002, Sec 3(1)(1), Official Secrets Act-1923 IPC	1. Ahmad Hasan alias Babu	Nai Basti, Charbagh, Jabtaganj, Bijnore	816WC/ Seven-Nyay-5-2013-2836 WC/2012, dt 22-3-2013

S. No.	District & PS	Case Crime No. and Sections	Name of accused	Resident	GO no and date of case withdrawal
4	Wazirganj, Lucknow	380/2007, Sec 124A, 153A, 109, 114, IPC	1. Mukhtar Husain, 2. Mohammad Ali Akbar, 3. Azizur Rahman, 4. Naushad Hafiz, 5. Noorul Islam	1. Nandigram, Midnapur, 2. 24 Pargana, W Bengal 3. 24 Pargana, W Bengal 4. Baddapur, Bijnore 5. 24 Pargana, W Bengal	867WC/ Seven-Nyay-5-2013-2829 WC/2012, dt 15-4-2013
5	Husainganj, Lucknow	(1) 221/2007, Sec 115, 120B, 121, 121A, 122, 124A IPC	1. Yaqub	Tarapur, PS Badhapur, Bijnore	338WC/ Seven-Nyay-5-2013-2839 WC/2012, dt 18-4-2013
	Naka, Lucknow	(3) 220/2007 Sec 121, 121A, 122, 115, 120B, 124 IPC	1-Nasir Husain	Badhapur, Bijnore	

S. No.	District & PS	Case Crime No. and Sections	Name of accused	Resident	GO no and date of case withdrawal
	Naka, Luknow	(4) 221/2007, Sec 4/5 Explosive Substances Act and 16/18/20/23, Unlawful Activities (Prevention) Act	1. Nasir Husain	Badhapur, Bijnore 16S, Ikramul Haq Apartments, La-Touche Road, PS Aminabad, Lucknow	
	Kaiserbagh, Lucknow	(5) 213/2007, Sec 121, 121A, 122, 123, 124, 124A IPC and Sec 3, Explosive Substances Act	1. Mohd Kaleem 2. Syed Abdul Mobeen	Bagahva, PS Itwa Bazar, Dist Siddharthanagar	
6	Sachendi, Kanpur Nagar	(1) 332/2009, Sec 115, 120B, 419, 420, 467, 468, 471 IPC	1. Imtiaz Ali	31, Purani Vailai, Kasba and PS Mau Ranipur, Dist Jhansi	324WC/ Seven-Nyay-5-2013-2843 WC/2012, dt 18-4-2013
	Bithoor, Kanpur Nagar	(2) 176/2009, Sec 115, 121, 121A, 123 IPC	1. Sitara Begum		
	Swaroopnagar, Kanpur Nagar	(3) 124/2000, Sec 307, 324, 427, 120B, 121, 121A, 122, 123, 124A IPC and 3/5, Explosive Substances Act	1. Arshad	Kasba Khanpur, PS Auraiya, Dist Auraiya	

S. No.	District & PS	Case Crime No. and Sections	Name of accused	Resident	GO no and date of case withdrawal
7	Ganj, Rampur	506/2002 Sec 121/121A IPC and 1(A) Prevention of Terrorist Activities Act-2002 (POTA)	1. Maqsud 2. Javed alias Guddu 3. Taj Mohammad	Mohalla Nalapar, Akhara Malli Khan, PS Kotwali Nagar, Dist Rampur Astabal road, Mohalla Sarai Sahadat Kar Khan, PS Ganj, Dist Rampur Mohalla Chauki Teen, PS Ganj, Dist Rampur	294WC/ Seven-Nyay-5-2013-2828 WC/2012, dt 18-4-2013
8	Kotwali Nagar, Barabanki	1891/2007, Sec 121/121A/122/124A/ 332 IPC, 4/5, Explosive Substances Act and 16, 18, 20, 23 Unlawful Activities (Prevention) Act	1. Tariq Kasmi 2. Khalid Mujahid	Sammopur, Rani Ki Sarai, Dist Azamgarh House no 37, Mohalla Mahatwana, PS Madiyahu, Dist Jaunpur	93WC/ Seven-Nyay-5-2013-2837 WC/2012, dt 18-4-2013

Stay by Allahabad High Court on withdrawal of cases against Terrorists

The Allahabad High Court caused a huge setback to the decision of the Akhilesh Yadav Government to withdraw 14 cases against terrorists. The High Court made a strong observation in this case and asked why the Government wanted to withdraw the charges when the cases were in court. A Bench of Justice R.K. Agrawal and Justice R.S.R. Maurya of Allahabad High Court said: "Today you are releasing terrorists, tomorrow you can give them the Padma Bhushan as well." The Akhilesh Government was caught on the backfoot after the court's observation and said the cases against terrorists will not be withdrawn. The High Court Bench, hearing a public interest petition, asked whether this decision of the Government will not encourage terrorists. At the same time, the Court asked on what basis the cases were being withdrawn against the accused. It was mentioned that by withdrawing cases under IPC Sections 302, 307, 323, 427 and 120B, a wrong message would be sent to the society and it would encourage terrorism. It said that the Court will decide who is a terrorist and who is not, and not the Government.

Similarly, 19 persons were arrested in connection with serial blasts in Courts in Varanasi, Lucknow and Faizabad (Ayodhya) on 23 November 2007. The State Government decided to withdraw cases against these accused as well. The Court also nullified this decision of the Akhilesh Yadav government. The High Court Bench said that the Central Government could decide about the persons held on charges of terrorism since the law was enacted by the Centre, and therefore the state government had no right to take a decision. A full Bench comprising Justice DP Singh, Justice Ajay Lamba and Justice Ashok Pal of the Allahabad High Court announced this while ruling on the stay granted against the State Government's decision by a Bench of two judges.

Punishment to Hakim Tariq Kasmi in Barabanki case

A local Court in Barabanki district had quashed the State Government's decision to withdraw the case regarding arrest in Barabanki of Hakim Tariq Kasmi and Khalid Mujahid in the court blasts. The Court went ahead with the case and announced life imprisonment for Hakim Tariq Kasmi. The other terrorist Khalid Mujahid died from sunstroke on 13 May, 2013 while being brought from Ayodhya Court to Lucknow.

Punishment to the accused in attack on CRPF Group Centre in Rampur

Terrorists of Lashkar-e-Tayyaba had attacked the CRPF Group Centre in Rampur on the night of 31 December, 2007/1 January, 2008, in which seven CRPF personnel were killed. I was at that time posted as ADG (Law and Order), Crime, U.P. STF and U.P. ATS. The India commander of LeT Shabauddin (Madhubani, Bihar), Mohammad Sharif alias Sohail Ansari (Rampur), Jang Bahadur Khan (Moradabad), Mohammad Fahim Ansari (Goregaon, Maharashtra) and two Pakistani *fidayeen* Imran Shahzad and Mohammad Farukh had been arrested. AK-47 rifles, RDX and other explosives were recovered from their possession. Chargesheet against all the accused was submitted in the District and Sessions Court of Rampur and the Akhilesh Yadav government decided to withdraw the chargesheet.

Later, the court of ADJ Rampur, Sanjay Kumar, had on 2 November, 2019 announced the death penalty to the LeT India commander Shabauddin, Mohammad Sharif alias Sohail Ansari, two Pakistani *fidayeen* Imran Shahzad and Mohammad Farukh. Jang Bahadur alias Baba Khan was jailed for life while Faheem Ansari was jailed for 10 years.

The Akhilesh Yadav Government had withdrawn 14 cases against terrorists. After the court stayed the withdrawal of cases, proceedings were held in courts. In many cases the terrorists were given the death sentence while many others were jailed for life.

□

44
Mulayam Singh withdrew cases against terrorists

A Muslim politician Syed Shahabuddin had called upon Muslims in 1993 that they should not celebrate 26 January as Republic Day in protest against the demolition of the Babri mosque structure. Shahabuddin was a former IAS officer and also a member of the Babri Masjid Action Committee. However, Muslims in Meerut enthusiastically participated in the 26 January celebrations and I also participated in one such function in Chowk area. I had returned home and was putting away my uniform that around 6.45 p.m. there was the sound of a huge blast. The Police Control Room informed me that there was a bomb attack on a PAC picket at Imliyan Mohalla on Hapur Road in Meerut. I immediately rushed there.

A picket comprising about 10 Jawans of the 41st Battalion of PAC, Ghaziabad, had been posted at the main road in Imliyan area, considered communally-sensitive. Such pickets had also been deployed at some other points in Meerut. The men posted at the site told me that around 6.45 p.m., two young men came running towards the PAC post and the one in front threw a bomb at Constable Pramod who was on guard duty. Before the other men could react, the second man threw another bomb inside the tent at the picket. While the Guard, Pramod was seriously injured, Nayak, Mahendra Sharma who was standing near the tent, was critically injured and he died after being rushed to Meerut Medical College. Head Constable, Rohtash Singh and Deshraj Singh were also seriously injured and were rushed to the medical college.

The communal atmosphere in Meerut was seriously affected and a riot could somehow be averted. There was every possibility that miscreants could push entire Meerut city into a communal cauldron.

I immediately ordered imposition of curfew in Meerut city. I was told that the two attackers had fled towards the Muslim-dominated locality and were likely to be hiding inside a mosque. It was also felt that they could be arrested if an intensive search was conducted, but I desisted from doing so, as per a considered strategy. I recall that during the major communal riots in Meerut in March-June, 1987, inconsideratc search operations had caused a l ot of problems in riot control.

In the morning, blood spots were found near the picket that led to the Islamabad locality. The stains had remained on the ground because the immediate imposition of curfew had completely stopped movement of people. Within 12 hours of the incident, an injured man named Abdul Jabbar (son of Abdul Rashid, resident of house number 188 in lane number 1, Gola Kuan, Islamabad, Police Station Lisari Gate, Meerut) was arrested from Islamabad area. He later admitted to throwing a Chinese-made plastic grenade at the PAC picket and revealed the name of his accomplice as Ayub. Later the names of all terrorists involved in the incident came to light. Jabbar could not shelter himself while throwing the grenade and was therefore hit in his leg by thc shrapnel, hence the bloodstains. Besides Abdul Jabbar, the others involved in this terrorist incident were – 1. Mohammad Ayub (son of Haji Munshi, resident of 335, Islamabad), 2. Yunus (son of Haji Munshi, resident of 335, Islamabad), 3. Mohammad Yaqub (son of Haji Munshi, resident of 335, Islamabad), 4. Abdul malik (son of Abdul Waheed, resident of 269, Kidwai Nagar), 5. Amir Hamza (son of Mohammad Abdul Majeed, resident of 164, Kidwai Nagar), 6. Dr. M. Irfan (son of Salimuddin, resident of 164, Kidwai Nagar), 7. Saleem alias Saleem Patla (son of Abdul Rahman, resident of 197, Islamabad) and 8. Saleem Mota (resident of 48, South Islamabad).

Cases against all these terrorists were slapped for murder, treason, Explosives Act and provisions of TADA (Terrorist and Disruptive Activities Prevention Act). Under the TADA provisions, the confessional statement given by the accused in front of a Superintendent of Police was acceptable by law. I had to take these terrorists on police custody remand so that we could reach the bottom of the terrorists' network.

At that time, R.C. Chaturvedi was posted as District Judge, Meerut. He was known as a straightforward and honest Judge. We all respected him but there was doubt if we could get police remand of the arrested persons. It was not proper to directly request him. Then I, along with the then District Magistrate Jai Shankar Mishra (IAS, 1980) went to meet him and sought his guidance as to how we should record the terrorist's confession. The Judge immediately ordered coffee for us and asked for two or three TADA case files and described the procedure to me in detail. I did not want any technical error or lapse in recording the confession of the terrorist and while having coffee, told the Judge the entire sequence of events. However, out of hesitation, I did not talk about his police custody remand. As I rose to leave, the Judge himself commented that this was a serious matter and he would grant police custody remand of the arrested man. The chief terrorist Jabbar was produced before the District Judge. The Judge talked to him and questioned him for a long time. The terrorist admitted to having thrown the bomb and told the Judge the names of his accomplices. The Judge recorded this information on the remand sheet and granted police custody remand for 12 days. The then SP, City of Meerut, Vimal Kumar Vajpayee, recorded Jabbar's statement under the TADA provisions.

Attack on Nauchandi PAC Picket

This same group of terrorists had attacked the PAC camp in the premises of Nauchandi Police Station on 13 July, 1992. They had used Chinese stick grenades in which Head Constable, Tassavar Husain of 2nd Battalion PAC, Sitapur, was seriously injured. Later, one leg of Head Constable, Tassavar Husain had to be amputated. This incident was unravelled after Jabbar's arrest and he had played a role in this attack also. His accomplice in this attack was Saleem Mota, a resident of 48, South Islamabad in Lisari Gate Police Station Meerut, Ayub, son of Haji Munshi, a resident of Islamabad, and Saleem alias Patla of lane number 1, Islamabad. Some pieces of wood were recovered from the spot, but these were not taken seriously by the police. These pieces were of the Chinese stick grenade supplied from Pakistan and commonly used in terrorist incidents in Punjab and Jammu & Kashmir. This grenade had a wooden handle which closed like a bottle lid. The attacker had to open this lid, pull out a strong string and throw the grenade, which exploded after 4.5 seconds. It could be thrown up to a large distance as it was lightweight because of the wood. Many such grenades could be hidden inside clothing and thus taken anywhere.

Blast in Roadways Bus number U.P.-07-4326

A bus of U.P. Roadways, number U.P.-07-4326, was going from Delhi to Saharanpur on 23 January, 1993. At a stop, a man entered the bus, put a bag on the rear seat and got down. Soon thereafter, smoke arose from the rear seat, causing a commotion among passengers. The driver stopped the bus and all passengers got down. The conductor tried to remove the bag with a wooden stick when it suddenly exploded, destroying the entire bus. Vijay Vir Tyagi, a resident of GT Road, Khatauli, Muzaffarnagar, was killed in this incident and many others including the bus driver, were injured. This case too was unravelled after Jabbar's arrest. In this incident, RDX brought from Kashmir was used. Among those arrested were members of the same gang of terrorists, including Saleem Mota, Saleem Patla, Abdul Jabbar, Ayub and Zakir, son of Yaqub and Faiyyaz, son of Chanda, residents of Islamabad, Police Station Lisari Gate in Meerut. Charges under Sections of IPC and Section 3 and 4, TADA, were framed in this case.

Terrorist Jabbar had gone from Meerut to Kashmir in search of business and used to sell clothes there. He came into contact with *jihadi* groups there and became a terrorist. Later he came back to Meerut and formed his own gang. The RDX and Chinese grenades used in the attacks on PAC picket and the Roadways bus were brought from Pakistan to Kashmir and then Jabbar and Saleem Patla had carried the stuff to Meerut. Chinese plastic grenades and stick grenades had been used in the attack on PAC pickets in Nauchandi Police Station and Imliyan, while RDX brought from Kashmir was used in the attack on the bus. During the days of terrorism in Punjab, the terrorists used similar Chinese plastic and stick grenades obtained through Pakistan. With the arrests of terrorists in Meerut, it was for the first time that RDX and Chinese grenades were found to be used in Uttar Pradesh and these explosives were meant to be used in other incidents also. The Meerut Police had submitted a chargesheet in court with the terrorists being charged for murder, attempt to murder, Explosives Act and provisions of TADA.

Decision by U.P. Government to withdraw cases

In 1993, a Janata Dal Government was formed in Uttar Pradesh and Mulayam Singh Yadav became the state's Chief minister for the second time. After taking charge, he announced the withdrawal of chargesheet from courts in the case of attacks on two PAC pickets in Meerut and the blast in U.P. Roadways bus. He had taken this decision as part of his policy of appeasement of Muslim to gain votes. The case of such a terror attack was withdrawn in which a PAC personnel Sharma was killed and many others were injured. Terrorists had blown up a bus, a PAC picket had been attacked by grenades, a Police Head Constable was injured and lost a leg, becoming disabled for life. Terrorists had used deadly explosives such as RDX, grenades, etc.; they had been trained in Kashmir. Even then the Chief Minister Mulayam Singh Yadav had ignored the seriousness of the incidents and had withdrawn cases under TADA to satisfy his vote bank.

The District and Sessions Judge of Meerut rejected the decision of the Mulayam Singh Yadav Government to withdraw the cases and cases against all terrorists went ahead. In 1995-96, I was posted as DIG Agra Range and I had myself gone to record my statement as evidence. The Meerut Sessions Court had awarded life imprisonment to all the terrorists involved in this case.

□

45

When it was a crime even to talk about terrorism

Uttar Pradesh Police had been observing Police Week for decades. A grand parade is held in the Police Lines of Lucknow, in which personnel of U.P. Civil Police, PAC, Radio branch, GRP, STF, ATS, Fire Services, Dog Squad and Mounted Police participate with their arms and equipment. Traditionally, the State's Governor takes the salute in this parade and on this occasion, Medals awarded by the President of India are presented to police officers and personnel. It is a moment of great pride for those receiving this honour.

The Police Week was organised with enthusiasm in the third week of November, 2006. A grand Police Parade was held and the then Governor T.V. Rajeshwar took the salute. Prior to the Governor's arrival, the then Chief Minister Mulayam Singh Yadav had also taken the salute and before him, the then DGP, U, P, Police, Bua Singh, had taken the salute. All police officials had donned the traditional winter uniform. The IPS and PPS officers had worn tunic and cross belts, with medals shining on their chests. Chief Minister was accompanied by his colleagues and there was an air of festivity in Police Lines.

After the Police Parade, several meetings were held among senior police officers in which issues like crime control, police organisation, modernisation, demands of the police department, problems and welfare of police personnel are discussed. As a matter of tradition, the Governor and the

Chief Minister host a dinner for police officers. A Mess Night is organised in the Police Mess, Lucknow, in which a colourful cultural programme is held, followed by dinner. The Police Week had concluded on Sunday 26 November, 2006.

In the conference of Police Officers, a presentation was made on different subjects at the Police Radio Headquarters. The ADG Railways and Technical Services, B.K. Bhalla (IPS, 1974) had prepared a presentation on the problem of terrorism in India, with the title 'Scenario of Terrorism in India', which had been approved by the then DGP Bua Singh. B.K. Bhalla was considered a close and favoured officer of the then Chief Minister Mulayam Singh Yadav and had been entrusted with two important wings – Railway Police and Technical Services. In his presentation, he had described in detail the problem of terrorism in India, especially the terrorism cases on the railways. He had highlighted as important points issues like main reasons for terrorism in India, modus operandi of terrorists, bombs and explosives used in terrorist incidents, etc. He had presented the '*Shramjivi Express*' train blast (28 July, 2005) as a case study. In his presentation, he had also included cases of train blasts elsewhere in India. He had described in detail about the hideouts of terrorists, cities, etc. He had also written about the Imarat-e-Sharia situated near Patna in Bihar and mentioned that several terrorists visited this place, as had been revealed after interrogation of many terrorists. As soon as the mention of Imarat-e-Sharia in Phulwari Sharif in the presentation came to light, Muslim organisations created a ruckus. The presentations presented in the Police Officers' Conference are an internal matter of the police and not shared with the media. The presentations are supposed to alert the police officers as to how maintenance of law and order can be improved. The presentation of a case study is supposed to improve the working of the police. An officer present at the conference leaked the presentation made by B.K. Bhalla and it was published by reporters Pervez Iqbal Siddiqui in *The Times of India* and M. Hasan in *Hindustan*

Times and also in the 'Pioneer News Service' and some Hindi newspapers.

Mulayam Singh Yadav faced tremendous pressure from Muslim clerics. The then Railways Minister Lalu Prasad Yadav. Lalu even gave a statement on 30 November, 2006 that "the Uttar Pradesh government must immediately recall the IPS officer who gave a statement about the Imarat-e-Sharia building in Bihar being connected to terrorists." The issue was raised during Zero Hour in Parliament and Lalu Yadav said that the officer with whose reference the news was published in newspapers was in the Railways from the U.P. cadre. He also blamed the officer concerned as being communal and urged the State Government to recall him and not send such officers to the Railways. According to Muslim clerics, the building named Imarat-e-Sharia mentioned in B.K. Bhalla's presentation had been established in 1921 and was a centre providing religious education to Muslims.

Both Lalu Prasad Yadav and Mulayam Singh Yadav indulged in a politics based on Muslim vote-bank. Both these politicians feared that their Muslim support base could shift because of the anger of the Muslim clerics. Both these politicians could go to any extent to appease the Muslims. Mulayam Singh Yadav came back from New Delhi to Lucknow on 29 November, 2006 and put B.K. Bhalla under suspension (he could be reinstated only in February, 2007.) The ADG (Law and Order) Padman Singh (IPS, 1976) was transferred in this connection to Crime Branch, CID, and A.C. Sharma (IPS, 1977), a favoured officer of Mulayam Singh Yadav, was made the ADG (Law and Order).

B.K. Bhalla's presentation was based on facts. He had been suspended as per the policy of Muslim appeasement. In 1994, Mulayam Singh Yadav had withdrawn the chargesheets connected with the case of bomb blasts at PAC pickets and in the Roadways bus. Many years later in 2013, his son Akhilesh Yadav had withdrawn chargesheets in 14 cases involving terrorists. It was only because of the intervention of Courts that many terrorists had been punished with death and life imprisonment.

The presentation submitted by B.K. Bhalla is given here in its original form. He has mentioned towards the end of his presentation that in case a terrorist attack is directed by Pakistan in India, then Indian Armed Forces must cross the Line of Control and destroy centres of terrorism in Pakistan. This argument put forth by Bhalla was proved true when Indian Forces entered PoK in 2016 and 2019 and destroyed terrorists' hideouts.

The presentation:

SCENARIO OF TERRORISM IN INDIA
Main reason for terrorism in India

- KASHMIR PROBLEM – The root cause.
- Sponsored by Pakistan through ISI.

This fact confirmed by

- Investigation agencies of different states
- Human Rights Watch Group
- U.S. Government
- U.N. Security Council
- Survival of Government in Pakistan largely depends upon ensuring that KASHMIR problem remains on the forefront and thus hatred towards Indian Government remains the main focus and misdeeds of the rulers in Pakistan takes backstage.
- Indian foreign policy of Non Alignment does not suit America. Due to this and strategic location of Pakistan in Asia, America supports Pakistan to further its own interest in this region.
- Pakistan describes Kashmiri militants as 'freedom fighters' and accepts giving 'moral support' only.
- Three full-fledged wars by Pakistan in 1965, 1971 and 1999 in Kargil and creation of Bangladesh after 1971 war.

SPREAD OF TERRORISM

- Easy cross over at the porous border of Punjab, Nepal, W. Bengal, etc.

- In Kashmir – Pakistan sponsored terrorism since our independence.
- Local issues brought to limelight, e.g., 'Punjabi Suba'.
- Sikh terrorism in eighties.
- First major terrorist activity outside Kashmir.
- Supported by Pakistan/I.S.I.
- Now almost over.

Now Bangladesh/Nepal being used as entry/exit point for terrorists.

- Gradually whole of India affected now. Terrorist activities noticed in places where there is a sizeable Muslim population.
- Their poverty and religious sentiments exploited.

As a result, there are a number of such places in India where the activities of ISI and terrorist organisation have come to light such as

- WEST BENGAL – Calcutta, Murshidabad.
- BIHAR – Fulwari Sharif.
- JHARKHAND – Jamshedpur.
- U.P. – Aligarh, Varanasi, Jaunpur, etc.
- Delhi.
- GUJARAT – Ahmedabad.
- MAHARASHTRA – Mumbai, Malegaon
- KARNATAKA – Bangalore.
- ANDHRA PRADESH – Hyderabad.

MODUS OPERANDI

In the garb of SIMI and other Muslim fundamentalist organisiations—

- Poor Muslim youths given monetary help.
- Their religious sentiments in the name of ISLAM aroused.
- Some of them taken to Bangladesh and from there, to Pakistan to be trained in terrorist activities.
- Brought back to India via Bangladesh.
- Perform terrorist activities in India with the help of local recruits.

- After 9/11 and U.S. attack on Taliban-Afghan, Taliban terrorists have migrated to Pakistan and are also being used in terrorist activities in India.

OTHER SOURCES

- Terrorism in India also being supported by:
- Drug Syndicate (Dawood Ibrahim, etc.)
- Fake currency circulation (via Nepal/Bangladesh)
- Arms are freely available on Pakistan-Afghanistan border.
- Consignments of arms, RDX and fake currency was sent to India via sea and other routes.

Main Ingredients of Bombs at Present AMMONIUM NITRATE

- Used mainly as explosive in mining and also as fertiliser
- Bundelkhand area of U.P. has a lot of mining activities and Ammonium Nitrate is easily available.
- Big consignments seized at Jalaun/Agra.
- Known as fertiliser bomb.
- Easy availability throughout India.
- RDX.
- Fuel oil.
- Timer device.
- Bombs mainly made in pressure cookers currently.

CASE STUDY– '*SHRAMJEEVI EXPRESS*'. BLAST, 2005

- Material used in the blast contained Ammonium Nitrate, RDX and fuel oil.
- 22 Blast cases pertaining to G.R.P. between 1991 and 2005 were analysed.
- Several cases of bomb blasts in and around Varanasi were analysed. Bombs had identical ingredients, but cases were not investigated properly and were ignored, saying they were local incidents.
- Sketches of suspects were prepared and circulated.
- Detailed investigations brought to light a small place named Fulwari Sharif near Patna.
- Firdaus Raza of Godhra incident, Gulshan Sarvar Falahi

of Bombay blast case and Aftab Ansari of American Center, Calcutta shoot out were linked to Fulwari Sharif.

- Imarate Saria - an organisation is active in Fulwari Sharif whose dictate prevails among the hardliner Muslims of Bihar/Jharkhand/West Bengal/Orissa/ Bangladesh.
- Activists of ISI, Lashkar-e-Toiba, SIMI and HUJI from Pakistan and Bangladesh keep visiting Fulwari Sharif via Bangladesh border.
- West Bengal police had arrested (1) Md. Ainul r/o Howarh (2) Md Waqar r/o Bahawalpur, Pakistan (3) Tariq r/o Jamshedipur, Jharkhand in terrorist activities.
- Another hardcore SIMI activist Abdullah r/o Vaishali, Bihar who was comfortably staying in Varanasi was arrested by Calcutta police from Varanasi.
- GRP team went to Calcutta and interrogated above mentioned Abdullah and Tariq and learnt that Abdullah while studying in Delhi came in contact with Tariq through his brother-in-law in Okhla House, Delhi.
- In course of giving religious discourses, he participated in various jalsas in Jamshedpur, Patna, Bengal, etc. and in due course got entangled in terrorist activities. During this period, Abdullah came in contact with Obadur Rahman of Bangladesh who was –
- Active member of HUJI – a terrorist organisation of Bangladesh.
- Wanted in serial bomb blast case in Bangladesh.
- Later arrested by Bengal Police in Murshidabad under Foreigner's Act.
- GRP team interrogated Obadur Rahman in Behrampur Central Jail and learnt that he, along with following, had executed 'Shramjeevi' blast—
  1. HILAL r/o Rajshahi, Bangladesh.

2. NAFIKUL r/o Murshidabad, W. Bengal.
3. KANCHAN @SHARIF r/o Rajshai, Bangladesh.
4. Md. RONI r/o Rajshai, Bangladesh.
5. GULAM YAZDANI@YAHYA r/o Hyderabad.
6. (1) HILAL and (2) NAFIKUL were arrested by Maldah, West Bengal Police and were brought to Delhi by Special Cell, New Delhi and were later interrogated by GRP team.
7. Two other terrorists Anisul and Shahin of Bangladesh arrested by Delhi police also confirmed the above facts when interrogated by GRP team in N. Delhi.
8. Warrant 'B' of Obadur Rahman, Hilal and Nafikul was made and they were brought to Jaunpur and taken on police remand.
9. On interrogation, it was revealed that same gang was involved in Khushrupur blast near Patna in which 62 people died.
10. GULAM YAZDANI killed in Delhi police encounter and above three chargesheeted on 21.06.2006 and case is under trial where OBADUR RAHMAN has confessed before the court.
11. HUJI and ISI were behind the 'Shramjeevi' blast.

SOLUTION

- Presently there is lack of co-ordination between different investigation agencies investigating different terrorist related cases in India.
- During 'Shramjeevi' blast investigation in February, 2006 information regarding active SIMI activist and suspect ZIAUDDIN@JALALUDDIN of Phulwari Sharif, Patna was given to Maharashtra police by ADG Railways, U.P. that he is staying with his brother FARGUDDIN, @ a mechanic in Bhabha Atomic Research Centre.
- No action taken till 11 July, 2006 train bombings.
- Later both the brothers arrested by Maharashtra police.
- All terrorist-related cases should be investigated by one single agency throughout India.

ULTIMATE SOLUTION

Drastic but only solution to terrorism in India is—

"Next time Pakistan tries to repeat any activity like Kargil war, we should cross over L.O.C. (Line of Control) and destroy the terrorist camps there."

Reports appearing in major newspapers after the suspension of B.K. Bhalla (IPS, 1974) on 29 November, 2009:

Times of India Lucknow, 30 November 2006

Bhalla suspended for remarks against IeS

By Pervez Iqbal Siddiqui/TNN

Lucknow: Chief minister Mulayam Singh Yadav on Wednesday evening ordered suspension of additional director general of police (ADG), Railways, VK Bhalla, reportedly for his comments on India's foreign policy in his presentation during the recently concluded Police Week. Indications are that the unexpected suspension came only to preempt an uproar in Parliament on Thursday over the senior police officer's utterances.

The suspension orders were issued shortly after Mulayam returned from Delhi with a hint that Bhalla's comment on Imarat-e-Sharia may be taken up by the political rivals in Parliament on Thursday. Sources said that the issue was to be raised on Wednesday but was deferred as Greg Chappell's comment on MPs dominated the proceedings.

During the Police Week that concluded on Saturday, Bhalla presented a study on Shramjeevi Blasts in 2005 under the title of "Scenario of Terrorism in India". In his presentation, the senior IPS officer pointed out that the commands of Imarat-e-Sharia (IeS) in Phulwari Sharif (Bihar) was respected among hardliner Muslims in Bihar. The report also stated that ISI, Lashkar-e-Taiba, HuJI and SIMI activists use Bangladesh route to visit India from Pakistan and Bangladesh as well. Terrorists have been active in India as activists from Simi and other fundamentalist organisations, the report said.

The issue came to the notice of some Bihar MPs in Delhi during an informal chat with Maulana Nizamuddin, the general secretary of IeS who was in the national capital to attend the All India Muslim Personal Law Board's working committee meeting. ► P8

Bhalla suspended

By Pervez Iqbal Siddiqui/TNN

Lucknow: The parliamentarians took a serious view of the issue and had planned to corner Samajwadi Party in Parliament on Thursday. Believed to be in the good books of the present regime, Bhalla has been serving as ADG Railways for over two years now. In between he was also looking after technical services department. Fingers were pointed at his holding two important offices at a time when recruitments were underway in both the units.

The government move is also being seen as an attempt to placate Muslim sentiments hurt by the officer's comment. Clerics like Maulana Khalid Rasheed, the Naib Imam of Eidgah and member of AIMPLB termed, Bhalla's suspension as "better late than never" move of the government.

The IeS came into being in 1920s at a ceremony in Bihar that was presided over by Maualan Abul Kalam Azad and is believed to be the top body of Dar-ul-Qaza (Sharia courts) of Bihar, Orissa and Jharkhand. It's known for providing quality education to the minority community.

Pioneer Lucknow, 30 November 2006

Report on terror leads to ADG's suspension

Muslim clerics sore over reference to Patna outfit, govt says remarks on foreign policy unwarranted

[illegible]

Continued on Page 3

Report...

Pioneer that it was unanimously demanded that the erring official must be suspended and objectionable remarks withdrawn immediately.

According to him, the head of the Imarate Saria, Maulana Nizamuddin, is also the general secretary of the All India Muslim Personal Law Board. "Dignitaries like President APJ Abdul Kalam and UP Chief Minister Mulayam Singh Yadav have visited Phulwari Sharief, which is a prestigious centre known for academics," said Khalid Rasheed.

He said that in the Muleyam Singh Yadav government, several RSS-minded police officers were trying to paint Muslim clergy as anti-national which was unfortunate and alarming. "As the organisation is based in Bihar, UP Police unnecessarily dragged its feet in the matter," he said.

However, issuing the suspension orders, the state government made no mention of any pressure from any community but said that Bhalla's remarks regarding on the foreign policy were against service rules, so ha had been put under suspension. The state government also claimed that the statements of Bhalla would hurt India's relations with other countries.

Questions over why the government acted four days after the Presentation Book was circulated and why it spared those who had approved the draft, however, remain unanswered.

Hindustan Times Lucknow, 30 November 2006

UP police tarnishing image of Imarate Sharia: AIMPLB

M Hasan
Lucknow, November 26

THE ALL India Muslim Personal Law Board (AIMPLB) today condemned the UP police for tarnishing the image of renowned Imarate Sharia (Phulwari Sharif) in Bihar. The board said the UP police had mischievously prepared a report to damage reputation of the organisation.

The UP police at the officers' conference during the police week, which concluded on Sunday, presented a report "Scenario of terrorism in India". The document in possession of Hindustan Times was prepared by additional director general (Railways) VK Bhalla, who is close to present dispensation. While discussing 'Shramjeevi Blast 2005', the officer said, "Imarate Sharia — an organisation is active in Phulwari Sharif, whose dictate prevails among hardliner Muslims in Bihar, Jharkhand, West Bengal, Orissa and Bangladesh". The report further said, "Activists of ISI, Lashkare Tayyeba, SIMI, HUJI from Pakistan and Bangladesh keep visiting Phulwari Sharif via Bangladesh". The report also noted that terrorists had been working in the "garb of SIMI and other Muslim fundamentalist organisation".

Condemning the report, the AIMPLB general secretary and chief of 'Imarate Sharia', Maulana Nizamuddin told Hindustan Times that it was a conspiracy of the UP police to smear the image of an organisation, which had been rendering welfare services for the last 80 years. He said it was table draft by the same UP police officers who had been desperately trying to dub entire community as terrorist.

Nizamuddin said he would take up the issue at the next meeting of AIMPLB. He said 'Imarate Sharia' had played historical role in independence struggle and it was unfortunate that UP police had been making efforts to spoil its reputation.

COP'S REPORT ON PHULWARI SHARIF

He said the Muslims would not tolerate such behaviour of the UP police. He said the comment in the report amply indicated 'communal approach' of the officer who had prepared the document. He said there were desperate move to create trouble in the community by such reports. He also refuted the charge of Bhalla that it was hardliners' organisation.

Expressing anguish over the issue, Naib Imam Eidgah Maulana Khalid Rashid said it was unfortunate that a senior police officer had leveled such a baseless allegation against the institution. He said it was a conspiracy of the UP police against Muslims. Demanding apology from the officer, Rashid did not rule out the possibility that one day the UP police would dub AIMPLB as a 'terrorists organisation'. He said the officer had insulted the entire Muslim community.

The AIMPLB spokesman Qasim Rasool Ilyas said 'communal element in the UP police' had been painting the community in black lines. He said the institution had no influence in Bangladesh. *mhasan@hindustantimes.com*

हिन्दुस्तान दैनिक समाचार पत्र 1 दिसम्बर 2006
लखनऊ संस्करण

आतंकी पनाहगाह बताने की रिपोर्ट तो एसटीएफ की थी

इमारत-ए-शरिया के बारे में अपना पर्चा निलंबित एडीजी भल्ला ने तो पढ़ा ही नहीं था

प्रधानमंत्री व गृहमंत्री से हस्तक्षेप की माँग

आईपीएस को वापस बुलाए यूपी: लालू

राष्ट्रीय सहारा हिन्दी दैनिक लखनऊ संस्करण 1 दिसम्बर 2006

भल्ला के निलंबन से अफसरों में रोष

लखनऊ, 29 नवम्बर (एसएनबी)। अपर पुलिस महानिदेशक राजकीय रेलवे पुलिस एवं रेडियो वीके भल्ला के निलंबन से वरिष्ठ पुलिस अधिकारियों में रोष व्याप्त है।

श्री भल्ला 1974 बैच के तेज तर्रार आईपीएस अधिकारी हैं और एक ईमानदार छवि वाले अधिकारी के रूप में जाने जाते हैं। श्री भल्ला की ईमानदारी और प्रशासनिक कुशलता को देखते हुए ही शासन ने उन्हें बड़े एवं महत्वपूर्ण विभागों का प्रभार दे रखा था जिसे वह बहुत लम्बे समय से सफलतापूर्वक संभाले थे। श्री भल्ला ने एक ओर जहां रेलवे पुलिस की छवि सुधारी, वहीं दूसरी तरफ उन्होंने रेलवे अपराधों पर नियंत्रण कर अपनी धाक जमायी।

अपर पुलिस महानिदेशक श्री भल्ला रेडियो पुलिस के पूरे तंत्र के आधुनिकीकरण के सूत्रधार रहे हैं और शुरू के दिनों से ही पुलिस में अनुशासन के पक्षधर रहे। इसके साथ ही संवेदनशीलता के फलस्वरूप अपने मातहतों में भी वे अत्यंत लोकप्रिय हैं। वह मुख्यमंत्री के भी काफी प्रिय एवं विश्वसनीय अफसर जाने जाते रहे है। उनके निलंबन पर अनेक सवाल उठ रहे है और चर्चा है कि वह कुछ वरिष्ठ पुलिस एवं प्रशासनिक अधिकारियों की जलन व गुटबंदी का शिकार हुए हैं।

□

46

Politics on the Batala House encounter and action against Azamgarh module of Indian Mujahideen

On 22 May, 2004, a Congress-led UPA Government was formed at the Centre, headed by Dr. Manmohan Singh. During the tenure of this Government, major terror attacks had happened in the country. **The court blasts in U.P., Sankat Mochan blast, Dashashwamedh Ghat blast, Sheetala Ghat blast at Varanasi, '*Shramjeevi*' train blast at Jaunpur, terror attack on Rampur CRPF Group Centre, Golghar Gorakhpur blast, Jaipur blast, Ahmadabad blast, German Bakery Pune blast, Bangalore blast, Guwahati blast, Bodhgaya blast, blast in Narendra Modi's 'Hunkar Rally' in Patna, Mumbai local train blast, Gateway of India and Jhaveri Market, Mumbai blast, blasts in Delhi - Sarojani Nagar, Govindpuri, Paharganj, car blast near Jama Masjid and attack on bus of foreign tourists, Gokul Chat, Lumbini Garden, Hyderabad blast, Connaught Place, Central Park, Greater Kailash blast and well-known terror attack of Lashkar-e-Taiba in Mumbai on 26/11/2008, happened during this Government.**

In the Batala House encounter, the involvement of Indian Mujahideen was exposed. The Police of Delhi, Gujarat, Maharashtra and U.P. along with different states' security agencies were raiding the hideouts of IM and many persons along with IM supporters were arrested in this connection. Fearing a loss of its Muslim vote-bank, the Congress party raised question mark on the Batala House encounter itself. Senior Congress leader and former Chief Minister of Madhya Pradesh Digvijay Singh was the most vocal on this issue. Digvijay Singh visited Azamgarh and met the family members of terrorists Atif Amin, Mohammad Sajid along with other terrorists who killed in the Batala House encounter. He openly said that the Batala House encounter was fake in which the IM, North India commander Atif Amin and Mohammad Sajid were killed and many other terrorists had fled. In this daring encounter, Delhi Police Inspector Mohan Chand Sharma was martyred, who had been awarded six times by the President of India for his bravery. Digvijay Singh said that Inspector Sharma was not killed by terrorists but in the firing by Delhi Police. Digvijay Singh even said in the meeting with the Ulema Council leaders in Azamgarh that the National Human Right Commission was investigating the case and the NHRC would give the report against Delhi Police soon. After that report, the terrorists who had escaped, would get bail.

On the advice of Digvijay Singh, Ulema Council arranged to transport a large number of Muslims by a special train to hold a protest at Jantar Mantar in Delhi, with the active support of the Congress Party. On 25 July, 2013, IM terrorist Shahzad Ahmad alias Pappu arrested from Azamgarh was jailed for life by Delhi Court. Even after the punishment, Digvijay Singh kept saying the encounter was fake and demanded a judicial inquiry. In 2014, the UPA Government headed by Dr. Manmohan Singh was ousted from power and a majority NDA government headed by Narendra Modi was formed. In 2019, at the time of Lok Sabha election, on the occasion of the 10th anniversary of Batala House encounter, hundreds of Ulema Council activists were brought to Delhi from Azamgarh by '*Kaifiyat Express*' to hold a protest and demanded judicial inquiry in the Batala House case. The Congress Party wanted to keep the Batala

House issue alive with an eye on elections to maintain their hold on the Muslim vote-bank.

Sonia Gandhi cried on looking at visuals of Batala House encounter

Apart from Digvijay Singh, Salman Khurshid, Law Minister in then Congress Government also did not lag behind for the same. In an election rally during Assembly elections in Azamgarh on 10 February, 2012, he said that Sonia Gandhi had burst into tears after looking at the visuals of the Batala House encounter and had asked the Prime Minister to help those who had absconded. He also said that despite it's best efforts, the Congress Party could not succeed in providing justice to Azamgarh boys.

Death penalty to terrorist Ariz alias Junaid in Batala House case an embarrassment for Congress

On 8 March, 2021, the Saket Court of Delhi convicted terrorist Ariz alias Junaid Khan and on 15 March, 2021, gave him the death sentence on the charge of murder of Inspector Mohan Chandra Sharma. Besides, the court also imposed a fine of Rs. 11 lakhs out of which Rs. 10 lakhs were to be given to the family of late Inspector Sharma. The Court declared this case as 'the rarest of rare' case and justified the death sentence. In the same case, on 25 July, 2021, accused Shahzad Ahmad alias Pappu had got life imprisonment.

After the Batala House encounter in Delhi on 19 September, 2008, Ariz alias Junaid Khan fled to Pakistan and after returning from there, settled down in Nepal. The special cell of Delhi Police arrested him in February, 2018. A reward of Rs. 15 lakh was declared on him and the Interpol issued a 'Red Corner' notice against him.

Politics heated up as the death penalty was announced for Ariz alias Junaid Khan. The Budget Session of Parliament was going on and mediapersons kept looking for Rajya Sabha MP Digvijay Singh for his reaction, but he avoided making comments.

Salman Khurshid, who had claimed that Sonia Gandhi had burst into tears after seeing the pictures of the Batala House encounter, was also not able to give any answer. I was present in the Rajya Sabha Session at that time. While coming out of Parliament House, media sought comments from me and the then Union Minister Prakash Javdekar. Both of us said that Digvijay Singh and Salman Khurshid had no answers now. These two leaders had tried their best to prove that the Batala House encounter was fake. The family of martyred Inspector Mohan Chandra Sharma had got justice as death sentence was awarded to the convict. The Delhi Police was also saved from the embarrassment which it faced as the Congress leaders had alleged that Inspector Sharma was killed in firing by Delhi Police. Doordarshan had recorded 15-minute programme in connection to the Batala House encounter and Indian Mujahideen at my residence in Delhi. It was telecast on Doordarshan.

The then Union Minister Ravi Shankar Prasad had called a Press conference after the death sentence was announced to Ariz alias Junaid Khan. He targeted leaders of opposition parties. He referred to the statements of Congress leaders Salman Khurshid, Digvijay Singh and Trinamool Congress president Mamata Banerjee. The Delhi Police had been demoralised because of such statements. He demanded that there must be a probe into the impact on the morale of Delhi Police of such condemnable campaign by opposition leaders. He said, "doubts were expressed on the veracity of the Batala House encounter intentionally to demoralise the Delhi Police and for giving direct support to terrorists and their conspiracies. Why so? Only for the vote-bank politics."

Besides the Congress Party, the leaders of Samajwadi Party and Bahujan Samaj Party also made tremendous efforts to gain the sympathy of Muslims in the Batala House encounter case. Leaders of these parties had turned the villages of the terrorists in Azamgarh into something of a pilgrimage and, meeting with their family members, they were terming the Batala House encounter as fake to gain their support.

How could Mamta Banerjee lag behind? She also reached Jamia Nagar in Delhi on 17 October, 2008. She was accompanied by the then general secretary of Samajwadi Party Amar Singh. These leaders said the Batala House encounter was fake and demanded a judicial inquiry into it. Mamta Banerjee had declared from a public platform that if the Batala House encounter was proved genuine, then she would quit politics. This statement from her had earned a lot of applause.

Amar Singh, a native of Azamgarh, alleged that the BJP and especially L.K. Advani, were opposing the demand of a judicial inquiry and demanded an apology from him. Amar Singh also announced monetary and legal assistance to the families of the terrorists. He added that international media groups, such as BBC and CNN were questioning the veracity of the Batala House encounter.

□

47

Ishrat Jahan encounter and criminal conspiracy of Congress Party

It was 4 a.m. on 15 June, 2004. A team of Ahmedabad Police was chasing a suspicious blue Indica car. The police had information that there were terrorists in this car, armed with AK-56 rifles and explosives, were planning to commit a terrorist act. Joint Police Commissioner P.P. Pandey directed his team to arrest the terrorists before they committed a major attack on that day itself. Firebrand IPS officer D.G. Vanzara, Additional Commissioner, was also engaged in this operation. The police team comprising ACP Dr. Narendra Amin, Girish Singhal, Inspector Jai Singh, Inspector Ibrahim, Inspector Patel and a commando team from Ahmedabad were chasing the suspicious car and surrounded it. The terrorist sitting in the car opened fire on the police with automatic weapons. The AK-56 rifle fired 600 bullets per minute, creating fear in the entire area. People hunkered down in their homes and morning-walkers ran to hide and save themselves. Police officers returned fire and the firing stopped around 5 a.m. When the police searched the site, they found the bodies of a young woman and three men. The girl was 19 to 20-years old, wearing a salwar-kameez. They were identified as Ishrat Jahan from Mumbra, Pranesh Pillai alias Javed Gulam Sheikh from Kerala and two Pakistani terrorists Zeeshan Johar and Salim. One AK-47 rifle, three automatic pistols, explosives and mobile phones were recovered from them. Explosives were kept in the car's boot as IED.

Ishrat Jahan, daughter of Mohammad Shamim Raza

Ishrat Jahan was a second-year student of B.Sc. in Guru Nanak Khalsa College at Mumbai and second among seven brothers and sisters. Her lower middle-class family belonged to Bihar and was living at Rashid Compound in the Muslim-dominated Mumbra area of Thane district. Her father Mohammad Shamim Raza used to run a construction company and had died two years ago while her mother Shamima Kausar worked in a medicine packaging company at Vashi, in Mumbai. Ishrat Jahan gave tuition to children along with her studies to earn some extra money. She also worked as secretary in the company of Javed Sheikh alias Pranesh Pillai and the latter had often sent her out of station in connection with work.

Javed Gulam Sheikh alias Pranesh Pillai

The second terrorist killed in the encounter, Javed Gulam Sheikh alias Pranesh Pillai, son of Gopi Nath Pillai, originally belonged to Nooranad of Kerala. He had converted to Islam and in 1991, got married to a Muslim woman named Sajida, changing his name to Javed Gulam Sheikh. The Gujarat Police recovered two passports from him – one in his original name Pranesh Pillai and the other in his changed name, Javed Gulam Sheikh. He also visited Nashik, Bangalore and Lucknow along with Ishrat Jahan. He had also travelled to Dubai in 2003 and Oman in 2004 and after meeting with extremists there, he started following the path of bloody *jihad*. Four criminal cases were registered against him in Mumbai and Pune. He was also involved in the fake Indian currency racket.

Zeeshan Johar

Zeeshan Johar was also known as Abdul Gani and Janbaz. He was a LeT terrorist and belonged to Gujranwala in Pakistan. In 2003-2004, he entered in India through Bandipore border in Kashmir. At that time, Indian Army and security forces had launched the operation 'Sarp Vinash' and six to seven terrorists of Zeeshan Johar's group were killed in an encounter.

Only Zeeshan Johar and his associate Salim could escape. An identity card with a Pakistan address was recovered from Zeeshan Johar.

Salim alias Amjad Ali Rana

Salim, also known as Amjad Ali Rana, belonged to Haveli Diwan village in Bhalwal *tehsil* of Pakistan. He had met Javed Gulam Sheikh alias Pranesh Pillai in Oman. After coming to India, he met Ishrat Jahan through Javed and introduced Ishrat Jahan to Zeeshan Johar.

Police investigations revealed that all of them were members of Pakistani terrorist organisation LeT. The duo had received training at Lashkar headquarters in Muzaffarabad. LeT chief Hafiz Sayeed had sent them to India through border infiltration to execute terror activities in India. **The then Gujarat Chief Minister and Home Minister Amit Shah were on their target. They included Javed Gulam Sheikh and Ishrat Jahan in their team after coming to India. This group had conducted a recce of Chief Minister's residence and the Akshardham Temple in Ahmedabad many times.** They had found that police vigilance was a little lax in the morning as there was a change of duty and some were preoccupied with washing or bathing, etc. **The terrorists had chosen this time for the attack on Chief Minister's residence and Akshardham Temple, so that they would face least resistance from the police and thus achieve their target.**

Politics on the deaths of terrorists in the police encounter

Lok Sabha elections had taken place in April-May, 2004. At that time, the ruling NDA (National Democratic Alliance) led by BJP had won 181 seats and the UPA (United Progressive Alliance) led by Congress had got 218 seats. UPA formed the Government and Dr. Manmohan Singh became the Prime Minister. Shivaraj Patil of Congress became the Home Minister of India from 22 May, 2004 to 30 November, 2008, followed by P. Chidambaram from 30 November, 2008 to 31 July, 2012.

On 7 October, 2001, Narendra Modi became Chief Minister of Gujarat for the first time. By his aggressive working style, he became a role model for not only Gujarat, but the whole country. Since then, top leaders of the Congress Party had started conspiring to remove him from power. On 27 February, 2002, Coach number S-6 of '*Sabarmati Express*' from Ayodhya to Ahmedabad was set on fire by the Muslim extremists at Godhra, in which 59 Ram devotees were killed. As a reaction to the Godhra massacre, riots broke out in many cities of Gujarat in which about 1,000 people were killed. The then Railway Minister in UPA Government, Lalu Prasad Yadav, changed the whole scenario of the Godhra massacre as part of his Muslim appeasement politics. He claimed that the fire was accidental. A campaign was launched to prove that Ishrat Jahan encounter was fake. Besides the Congress Party, the Left parties and their supporters in media also started to promote the false narrative. Their only motive was to oust Chief Minister Narendra Modi from power so that the BJP Government in Gujarat could be toppled. The Congress Party had made the Ishrat Jahan encounter as a political issue. Ishrat Jahan's mother moved Ahmedabad High Court and alleged that Ishrat had been murdered by police officers. In 2011, the Ahmadabad High Court ordered the setting up of a SIT to investigate the case.

Unusual SIT

As per the Ahmedabad High Court order on SIT, one senior IPS officer was to be nominated by the Central Home Ministry. A second IPS officer was to be nominated by Gujarat Government. **The most unusual clause was that the third IPS officer to be included in the SIT was to be nominated only on the basis of the consent given by Ishrat Jahan's mother.**

Satyapal Singh (IPS-1980) of Maharashtra cadre was nominated by Government of India in this SIT, but he later withdrew from it. Later, RR Verma (IPS-1978) of Bihar cadre was nominated, who was at the time on deputation to the Centre. Mohan Jha, IG Police, was nominated by Gujarat Government and Satish Verma, IPS of Gujarat cadre, was nominated only on the basis of the consent given by Ishrat Jahan's mother. This case was also handed over to CBI along with the SIT.

The SIT submitted after the investigation that the police encounter was based on wrong facts. The police also made a statement that Zeeshan Jauhar and Salim were not Pakistanis, but were actually Indians.

Incidentally, no one came forward to claim the bodies of Zeeshan and Salim, whereas if they were indeed Indians, then someone would have come to claim their bodies.

In 2012, the cases of murder, the conspiracy of the murder, etc. were registered against the police officers of Gujarat by R.R. Verma. CBI said that Ishrat Jahan and three others were brutally murdered in a fake police encounter. Cases of murder, conspiracy of murder, etc were registered by CBI against P.P. Pandey, the then Joint Police Commissioner, D.G. Vanzara, Additional Police Commissioner, Dr. Narendra Amin and G.L. Singhal, Assistant Police Commissioner, Tarun Barot, Anaju Choudhary and J.G. Parmar.

Arrests of these police officers started in 2013. P.P. Pandey and D.G. Vanzara were also arrested along with other police officers. If chargesheets are not submitted against the accused in the court within 90 days after their arrest, then they automatically get released on bail. The CBI did not file the chargesheet against G.L. Singhal, Anaju Choudhary and Tarun Barot within 90 days as per a plan, as a result of which they were released on bail. This soft treatment was adopted so that they could later be used against P.P. Pandey, Dr. Narendra Amin, Home Minister Amit Shah and Chief Minister Narendra Modi.

Dr. Narendra Amin was sent to jail in the Sohrabuddin encounter and bail was granted to him on 1 April, 2013.

Due to his poor health, he was admitted to a hospital in Ahmedabad. The CBI arrested him from the hospital bed and he was so brutally tortured by Satish Verma that his muscles were ruptured. He had to be admitted to hospital again. He had gained weight because of prolonged hospitalisation and had difficulty in breathing because of the torture. Dr. Narendra Amin's daughter gave an application in court fearing that the CBI would murder her father and she submitted that if her father died, then the CBI would be responsible.

The CBI arranged a medical check-up of Dr. Narendra Amin and doctors said he was in a critical condition and could die any time. The CBI became frightened, woke him up from sleep at 1 a.m. and took him in custody. His wife, daughter and advocate were not informed about it. The CBI tortured Dr. Narendra Amin and also offered that he could turn approver so that the noose around Chief Minister Narendra Modi and Home Minister Amit Shah could be tightened. Dr. Narendra Amin did not agree to this and came out of jail in 2015 after two years. CBI submitted the chargesheet in Ishrat Jahan encounter, in which prior permission from State Government had not been taken. As a result, cases against PP Pandey, DG Vanzara, GL Singhal, Dr. Narendra Amin, Tarun Barot, Anaju Choudhary along with other police personnel could not proceed. Later the CBI sought the State Government's permission to lodge cases against these officers, but the State Government did not agree, and all officers were acquitted.

Similarly, the CBI also filed chargesheet against Rajendra Kumar, Joint Director, IB, Ahmedabad, along with IB officers Mittal, M.K. Sinha and Rajeev Wankhede by making them accused in Ishrat Jahan encounter case. CBI sought permission from the Government of India to lodge cases against these officers, but the Home Ministry did not allow and they were also not prosecuted.

At that time, the CBI, at the instance of the top leaders of Congress, wanted to establish that the fake encounter of four persons including Ishrat Jahan was done at the orders of

Chief Minister Narendra Modi and Home Minister Amit Shah. On 25 July, 2010, the then Gujarat Home Minister Amit Shah was sent to jail in the Sohrabuddin police encounter case by CBI but was released on bail three months later on 29 October, 2010. In the Sohrabuddin, Tulsiram Prajapati encounter case, Amit Shah was acquitted with honour by the Mumbai Court in December, 2014.

Sohrabuddin, who belonged to Indore, was a terrorist. The police had recovered 40 AK-47 rifles, about 100 hand grenades and 1 lakh cartridges from his home. About 40 criminal cases were registered against him and his reign of terror spread in five states. Congress leaders described this dreaded terrorist as a petty criminal. In Sohrabuddin encounter case, D.G. Vanzara, Rajkumar Pandiyan, Abhay Chudasama, M.N. Dinesh along with other police officers were sent to jail and in the same case Amit Shah was also sent to jail as per a conspiracy hatched by the Congress.

Revelation by terrorist David Coleman Headley (Daud Sayed Gilani)

David Coleman Headley was an American terrorist of Pakistani origin. He was sentenced to 35 years in jail in the United States of America after being convicted of 12 charges of international terrorism. Headley was born in 1960 as Daud Sayed Gilani, son of Sayed Salim Gilani and Alice Cyril Headley in Washington, DC. After his birth, his family had shifted from the US to Lahore in Pakistan. His mother could not adapt to Pakistani culture and returned to the US and got a divorce. Daud Sayed Gilani was brought in an environment of Pakistani nationalism and Islamic fundamentalism. After a dispute with his stepmother at the age of 17, he returned to the US and settled down with his mother Alice Cyril Headley. He also changed his name to David Coleman Headley. He was involved in drug smuggling while living in the US and later became an informer with the US Drugs Enforcement Administration (US DEA).

He visited Pakistan frequently. During a Lahore visit, Headley was introduced to the terrorist organisation Lashkar-e-Tayyaba and he directly connected with its chief Hafiz Sayeed. He had involved himself in terror activities against India and he also got into contact with Pakistan's ISI. On the one hand, he worked as informer with a US government agency, and on the other, he raised money for LeT and recruited new members.

Thus, Headley became a double agent. He was on the radar of the FBI in the US. In 2002, the US DEA removed him as an informer. In February, 2002, Headley came to and joined the LeT training camp in Pakistan and became a terrorist. By 2005, Headley had become a fully trained terrorist. He wanted to fight in Kashmir but Hafiz Sayeed sent him to Sajid Mir who recruited foreigners into LeT. It was on Sajid Mir's suggestion that he went to the US and officially changed his name to David Coleman Headley by adopting his mother's surname. His white appearance and American name made it easy for him to hide his Pakistani identity and establish himself as an American. During 2007, Hafiz Sayeed was finalising the conspiracy of the terror attack on Mumbai. Due to his looks, Headley was considered ideal for secret missions. Between 2007 and 2008, he travelled to Mumbai five times and did the recce of those places in Mumbai where terror attack took place on 26 November, 2008 in which 166 persons were killed. His name was connected to the Mumbai terror attack and he had been made an accused as well. The ISI had planned that Ajmal Kasab be portrayed as terrorist connected with Al-Qaeda, instead of Lashkar-e-Tayyaba, so that at international level, the involvement of Pakistan could be hidden. On 14 January, 2013, a US court sentenced him to 35 years in jail for his involvement in Mumbai terror attack. Headley turned an approver and thus managed to avoid the death sentence. He provided a lot of information to US agencies about LeT and its activities.

On 10 December, 2015, he also became the approver in Mumbai terror attack case. Headley was presented in

a Mumbai Court through video conferencing in a case of Mumbai terror attack on 8 February, 2016. The public prosecutor Ujjwal Nikam did the cross-questioning. Headley's statements were recorded by the court. He told the court that before the 26 November, 2008 Mumbai terror attack, LeT had tried unsuccessfully to launch such attacks - once in September, 2008 and next time in October, 2008. Headley also disclosed that Ishrat Jahan, who belonged to Mumbra, Maharashtra, was connected with the terrorist organisation LeT. Along with her accomplices, she had been planning the assassination of the then Gujarat Chief Minister Narendra Modi.

Indian intelligence agencies had also reported to the Home Ministry that Ishrat Jahan was an LeT terrorist planning to assassinate Narendra Modi. After the disclosure of David Coleman Headley, the conspiracy of top Congress leaders got fully exposed, but as a result of their criminal conspiracy, senior IPS officers P.P. Pandey, D.G. Vanzara, Dr. Narendra Amin, G.L. Singhal, Inspector Tarun Barot, Anaju Choudhary and J.P. Parmar had to go through severe torture in jail for a long time. Even the then Gujarat Home Minister Amit Shah had to remain in jail for three months.

The National Investigation Agency (NIA) headed by Shri Lok Nath Behra, the then Inspector General, (Kerala-1986) and his team **interrogated terror suspect David Coleman Headley in USA from June 3 to 9 June, 2010 for 34 hours** in the presence of his counsels, FBI prosecutors and FBI officials. No audio and video recording were allowed.

In his deposition Headley had asserted that Ishrat Jehan was a Lashkar-e-Taiba terrorist. LeT outfit is headed by Hafiz Sayeed of Pakistan.

It will be pertinent here to mention that Shri Lok Nath Behra, who interrogated Headley in USA, on his return gave a statement in the media on the basis of Headley's deposition that Ishrat Jahan was a LeT terrorist. His press

statement was not liked by the then UPA Government in power as UPA had already proclaimed that Ishrat Jahan was an innocent Muslim girl and her encounter was fake. Immediate fall out of Shri Behra's statement was that Shri Sushil Kumar Shinde, the then Home Minister, ordered immediate repatriation of Shri Behra to his home State of Kerala. An upright officer was made a fallen soldier due to his uprightness and honesty.

Headley is currently serving 35 years sentence in the US custody, after pleading guilty to 12 international terrorism charges, including his role in the 26.11.2008 Mumbai terror attack.

Moreover, the Ghazwa Times, the Lahore based LeT mouthpiece had admitted immediately after the encounter of Ishrat Jehan that she was a brave soldier of LeT and had paid rich tribute to her martyrdom.

However, the Indian media, amply supported by the western added NGO and human rights organizations, suppressed such facts and carried out a relentless campaign against the encounter killing of Ishrat Jahan trying to project her as an innocent college going Muslim girl. Even the Ahmedabad Metropolitan Magistrate, S.P. Tamang, in his strange and partisan judgement had declared Ishrat Jehan and the 3 other LeT terrorist, including the 2 Pakistanis killed in the encounter of 15 June, 2004, as innocent Indians.

□

48

Dirty politics by Congress Party on Mumbai terror attack

On 26 November, 2008, 10 trained terrorists of Pakistani terror organisation Lashkar-e-Tayyaba armed with heavy weapons launched attacks at several places and buildings in Mumbai. These attacks continued for four days in which 166 people were killed. In the attacks, Maharashtra ATS IG, Hemant Karkare (IPS-1982), DIG/Additional Police Commissioner, Ashok Kamte (IPS-1989), Inspector, Vijay Salaskar, Inspector, Shashank Shinde, ASI, Om Bale and Constable, Ambadas Ramchandra Pawar were martyred. Major Sandeep Unnikrishnan of NSG and Hawaldar, Gajendra Singh Bisht were also killed in the battle with terrorists.

Out of the 10 attackers, nine terrorists were shot dead by security forces and one of the them – terrorist Ajmal Aamir Kasab – was caught alive in an injured condition. Terrorists had targeted prominent hotels of Mumbai, such as Taj, Oberoi, Trident, Leopold Café and other establishments, such as Cama Hospital, CST railway station, Nariman House (a religious centre of Jews). All terrorists trained by LeT had entered India by the sea route and the entire operation was controlled from Pakistan. As part of a conspiracy, all terrorists had tied *kalawa* (a sacred thread) on their wrists and worn lockets of idols of Hindu gods and goddesses. Pakistan wanted to defame India by claiming that the terrorists were Hindus. But Pakistan did not foresee that Kasab would be caught alive and Hafiz Sayeed and ISI also never wanted any attackers to be caught.

The Congress Party indulged in politics even on this heinous act. Congress general secretary Digvijay Singh tried to float the theory of 'saffron (*bhagwa*) terrorism' and claimed that the ATS IG Hemant Karkare had talked to him (Digvijay) before going into this operation. Digvijay Singh alleged that Hemant Karkare was investigating the Malegaon bomb blast case of 8 September, 2006. According to him, Hindu terrorists were behind that blast and names of some top RSS functionaries were likely to be exposed in this connection; therefore, Hemant Karkare was killed so that the Hindu terrorism would not get exposed.

Now it is established that Pakistan is the source of Islamic terror attacks in India. Since the creation of Bangladesh in 1971, Pakistani leaders have been trying to divide India. Khalistani terrorism in Punjab was also sponsored by Pakistan. Efforts to separate Kashmir from India are also being made by Pakistan since the Partition in 1947. After the failure of Khalistani terrorism in Punjab, Pakistan put all its might into creating trouble in Kashmir and as a result, terrorism was at its peak in Kashmir after 1990. More than 4 lakhs Kashmiri Pandits were forced to flee Kashmir to different parts of India. Kashmiri Pandits were massacred and three options were given to them through announcement from religious places and by correspondence through letters to their homes. These were: first, to accept Islam and live in Kashmir; second, to migrate from Kashmir; and third, be ready to die.

Pakistan knows very well that it cannot win a direct war with India. Therefore, it has been running a proxy war against India through terrorism. To execute its bloody agenda, Pakistan needs local support, which it gets through intellectuals as well as from people who are eager to get involved in its conspiracy. All through this, Pakistan also needs to protect its image at the international level. It is apparent that if some people in India do not get involved in this conspiracy, it will be difficult for

Pakistan to succeed in its intentions. All over the world most of the people are against Islamic terrorism. Pakistan has always tried to disassociate itself from terror attacks happening from time to time in India and keeps on blaming India and the Hindu community for terror attacks in Pakistan.

For short-term political gains, one section of people in India stands up for Pakistan's nefarious plots. Such instances can be seen from time to time. **Aziz Burney, the Editor of an Urdu newspaper, has written a book in Urdu about the 26/11 incident. Titled *RSS ki Sazish – 26/11,* this book was launched by Congress general secretary Digvijay Singh who said on the occasion that RSS was responsible for the death of Hemant Karkare in the Mumbai terror attack.** However, the Congress Party distanced itself from the statement of Digvijay Singh but did not restrain him because of vote-bank politics. Digvijay Singh was very close to Sonia Gandhi, Rahul and Priyanka Gandhi. It is not possible that he had made the allegation against RSS and Hindu organisations without permission from the Gandhi family.

What is more, Aziz Burney tried to vindicate terrorist Kasab, nine dead terrorists and Pakistan of this terror attack. He blamed Indian investigating agencies, Hindu organisations, Americans and Israeli intelligence agencies for the same. According to Burney, Indian Mujahideen was an organisation established by RSS. Burney said Indian Mujahideen was a code word of Bajrang Dal. According to Burney, all terror attacks in India were conducted jointly by the RSS and the Israeli agency Mossad. He alleged that Hemant Karkare was about to expose this fact and that's why he was killed.

At the launch of Burney's book, Rajya Sabha, Deputy Speaker, K. Rahman Khan further said that the RSS conspiracy was not only confined to 26/11 attacks on Mumbai but also showed the mentality which was responsible for the assassination of Mahatma Gandhi. Rahman Khan was a Congress leader from Karnataka and had been Deputy Speaker of Rajya Sabha from

22 July, 2004 to 21 April, 2006 and from 12 May, 2006 to 2 April, 2012.

A Congress leader and former Chief Minister of Maharashtra in 1980, Abdul Rehman Antulay, gave a statement on 17 December, 2008, that the assassination of Maharashtra ATS Chief, Hemant Karkare, was connected with the Malegaon blast investigations. He further added that some Hindu organisations were involved in the Malegaon blast and that Karkare lost his life as he was about to expose some big names from these organisations. According to Antulay, Hemant Karkare was targeted as he was carrying out detailed investigations into the roots of terrorism.

After the 26/11 Mumbai terror attack, I visited Mumbai to attend the marriage of the daughter of Mohammad Hassan, belonging to Siddharth Nagar district of Uttar Pradesh. Senior NCP leader Nawab Malik had also come to attend the wedding. About 10-12 persons from Siddharth Nagar were sitting with me when Nawab Malik also joined us. Soon, 40 to 50 more people joined the gathering. He started speaking about the 26/11 Mumbai terror attack and said it was sponsored by RSS and Bajrang Dal and there was no involvement of Pakistan in it. I could not stop myself and introduced myself as the ADG Law and Order, ATS and STF in U.P. Police officers in every state are in touch with each other and intelligence agencies of Government of India in connection with terror activities. I contradicted his statement and said he was wrong. He realised that there was no scope for his propaganda, so he quietly quit the scene. **He later became a Cabinet Minister in Maharashtra Government and on 23 February, 2022, he was arrested by the ED in a money-laundering case. He was found to be connected to the gang of international terrorist Dawood Ibrahim.**

S.M. Mushrif had retired from the post of IG Police of Maharashtra. He has written a book, *Who Killed Hemant Karkare*, in September, 2009 and his second book was titled,

26/11 ki Janch (*Nyayapalika Kyon Nakam Rahi*). S.M. Mushrif also accused Hindu organisations and Indian intelligence agency IB for the attacks. Mushrif said that there was no involvement of Pakistan in the 26/11 terror attack and it was masterminded by Hindu extremists with IB also playing a role in it.

Not only this, he also filed a petition in the Supreme Court demanding investigation into the death of Hemant Karkare. Mushrif had filed the case as a PIL in Mumbai High Court but it was dismissed. Then he filed the petition in Supreme Court. Lawyer Indira Jaising had represented the case in the Supreme Court from his side. The petition was dismissed by the bench of the Supreme Court headed by Justice S.K. Sikri. He wrote in his judgement that there was no substance in the petition. Kasab, the only terrorist caught alive in Mumbai terror attack, was hanged to death by the order of the Supreme Court. The Supreme Court said that Mumbai attack was a terrorist act which was confirmed by the death sentence given to Kasab. The Supreme Court asked advocate Indira Jaising why she wanted to reopen this case and said it could not be allowed.

Congress leader Rahul Gandhi also equated RSS with SIMI for damaging the society. At the convention of the All-India Congress Committee (AICC), he blamed the RSS and its allied organisations for their involvement in the terror attacks. Digvijay Singh, Abdul Rahman Antulay, Rahul Gandhi, K. Rahman Khan, S.M. Mushrif, Aziz Burney, etc. tried to cover the hideous acts of Islamic terrorism that is sponsored by Pakistan. By doing this, they not only acted against the country, but also assisted Pakistan to fulfil its agenda.

Apology of Aziz Burney, in reference to his book, *RSS ki Sazish 26/11*

Following is the apology tendered by Burney:

"In the serialised article '26/11, the Biggest Terror Aattack of Indian History, written by me in parts, the article had been written after the release of my book titled **Hafiz**

Saeed Hamara Apradhi Hai, Use Hamare Hawale Karo. ***In the article published in*** **Roznama Rashtriya Sahara** ***on 17 December, 2010, I am neither connecting RSS with 26/11 terror attack nor letting down the Indian stand.***

My aim is neither to blame nor hurt the sentiments of anybody through my article. My intention is definitely not to blame anybody. I apologise if the sentiments of the people of India get hurt due to my article and if required, I am ready to change the title of my book. Being an integral citizen of this country, I am ashamed at this lapse committed by me and I will ensure that in future no one's feelings are hurt. Through this article, I am only making an effort to put my views before the readers. I take full responsibility for the inconvenience caused inadvertently to patriots or those who love the country by my views, and seek my heartfelt apology for the same."

The above-mentioned apology of Aziz Burney was published as a two-column box on top of the front page of *Rashtriya Sahara* newspaper on 17 December, 2010.

Revelation by terrorist Jabiuddin Ansari alias Abu Jandal

The Pakistan agenda to claim that the 26/11 Mumbai attacks were allegedly part of an Indian conspiracy was exposed with the arrest of LeT terrorist Jabiuddin Ansari, the mastermind of the Pakistani design behind the Mumbai attacks. Ajmal Aamir Kasab, the lone Pakistani terrorist who survived the Mumbai attacks, was giving a statement on 21 May, 2009 in the court of Justice M.L. Tahiliani inside the Arthur Jail in Mumbai. He suddenly took a name that was very significant. He revealed that a control room had been set up in Karachi for this 60-hour operation, headed by Jabiuddin Ansari alias Abu Jandal. No one in India had heard this name. Many people were startled at this name and the Government Prosecutor Ujjawal Nikam said that it was a misleading information and this was often done in cases like this. Subsequently, Abu Jandal's name was lost in the court files.

Three years later, on 21 June, 2012, a Lashkar-e-Tayyaba terrorist named Syed Jabiuddin was arrested in Saudi Arabia. He was put on an aircraft and flown to New Delhi. This was bad news for Kasab who was lodged in his prison cell in Mumbai. Very soon the links in this complicated conspiracy started becoming clear. Abu Jandal was the missing link in the intricate conspiracy behind the Mumbai attacks. He told the authorities that the plot of Mumbai attacks was hatched by the ISI and Lashkar-e-Tayyaba had executed it. Jabiuddin Ansari alias Abu Jandal was the key perpetrator.

Born in Gavrai village of Beed district in Maharashtra, Ansari had studied up to Class 10 and completed a technical course from ITI to become an electrician. After the 2002 Gujarat riots, he became a strongly anti-Indian fundamentalist and got deeply involved in terrorist activities. He joined the SIMI and later associated with Lashkar-e-Tayyaba. He had come on the police radar in 2006 itself when he had despatched a cache of 43 kg of RDX, 16 AK-47 rifles and 50 hand grenades to Aurangabad in Maharashtra for terrorist attacks. The Maharashtra police had intercepted this consignment well in time. Ansari thought it prudent to leave India and escaped to Pakistan and joined Lashkar-e-Tayyaba. His name came to public knowledge in March, 2007 when the Government of India submitted to Pakistani authorities a list of 50 terrorists who had gone from India and sought shelter in Pakistan.

Abu Jandal had made himself quite useful for LeT. He knew the Mumbai city very well and came in handy when he planned terrorist activities. On 26 November, 2008, during the attacks in Mumbai, Jabiuddin Ansari was sitting in the Karachi control room and giving directions on every step.

Arrest of Fahim Ansari

The U.P. ATS had arrested LeT terrorist Fahim Ansari of Goregaon in February, 2008. He had gone to Mumbai at the directions of Shabauddin (from Madhubani, Bihar), the India commander of Lashkar, and drawn the maps of those places where attacks were launched on 26 November, 2008. He had obtained a driving licence, computer training certificate, etc. in the name of Sahil Pavaskar. I was at that time, the ADG (Law and Order) and also in charge of U.P. STF and U.P. ATS. I had myself interrogated him and the map recovered from his possession showed those places that were to be attacked on 26 November, 2008. This map was to be sent to the Lashkar chief, Hafiz Sayeed through the Pakistani Embassy in Kathmandu, Nepal. This hand-drawn map depicted Haji Ali, Mantralaya, CST Railway Station, Taj Mahal Hotel, etc. The map also mentioned how much time it would take in going from one place to other by foot or by a vehicle. He had revealed during interrogation that during his training by Lashkar, he had been showed all these places on Google and he had done a recce of all these places after coming to India. He went to these places in a taxi and noted the time taken in the drive. He had worked hard to draw the entire map.

Fahim Ansari was arrested along with the India commander Shabauddin. The latter had come from Madhubani to Aligarh Muslim University for studies and from there, he came in contact with ISI and went to Pakistan. He had got initial training (*daura-e-aam*) and advanced training (*daura-e-khaas*) at the LeT headquarters at Muzaffarabad in PoK. Shabauddin had attacked the scientists during the Indian Science Congress Seminar on 28 December, 2005 at the Indian Institute of Science (Bangalore). In this attack, Prof. M.C. Puri was killed and half a dozen scientists were injured. He had carried out this attack along with Pakistani terrorist Abu Hamza, who came to India via Dhaka from Karachi. After this attack, Hafiz Sayeed appointed him as LeT's India commander and he directed terror activities against India from Kathmandu. A Thuraya satellite phone was recovered from him through which he made contacts with LeT headquarters. He was the mastermind behind the terror attack on CRPF Group Centre in Rampur at 1 a.m. on 31 December, 2007/1 January, 2008. In this terror attack, seven CRPF soldiers were killed. Pakistani suicide attackers, Imran Shahzad and Mohammad Farukh, were also arrested in connection with this attack. Local residents of Rampur, Mohammad Sharif alias Sohail Ansari and Jang Bahadur Khan of Moradabad were also arrested. The UP Police had filed the chargesheet against all these terrorists but it had been withdrawn by the then U.P., Chief Minister, Akhilesh Yadav as part of his Muslim appeasement politics. Along with this, 14 more chargesheets in connection with terror attacks were also withdrawn. The Allahabad High Court had declared this decision of U.P. Government as illegal. This case was heard in the Sessions Court of Rampur. The India commander Shabauddin, Mohammad Sharif alias Sohail Ansari and both Pakistani *fidayeen* Imran Shahzad and Mohammad Farukh were given death sentences by the Court of A.D.J. Sanjay Kumar Singh. Jang Bahadur Khan got life imprisonment and Fahim Ansari got 10 years' jail in this case.

In February, 2008, UP Police had visited Mumbai along with Fahim Ansari under its custody, but the Mumbai Police had taken no action against him. After 26/11 Mumbai attack, Fahim Ansari and Shabauddin had been taken under its custody by Mumbai Police and booked for the terror attack in Mumbai. But due to the lack of evidence against them, they were acquitted by the court. If Mumbai police had taken the arrest of Fahim Ansari seriously, Mumbai terror attack could have been averted. After the arrest of Fahim Ansari, LeT gave the responsibility to Jabiuddin Ansari alias Abu Jandal for creating a map of the places targeted in the Mumbai terror attack. On 26 November, 2008, Ansari was executing the entire Mumbai terror attack operation by sitting in the control room at Karachi.

□

49

Conspiracy of Teesta Setalvad and Ahmed Patel to falsely implicate Narendra Modi in Gujarat riot case

On the morning of 27 February, 2002, the '*Sabarmati Express*', returning from Ayodhya to Ahmedabad, stopped near the Godhra railway station. The passengers were pilgrims returning from Ayodhya. The 2002 Gujarat riots, also known as the 2002 Gujarat violence, was a three-day period of communal violence in the State of Gujarat. The burning of Coach No. 6 of '*Sabarmati Express*' at Godhra caused the death of 59 Hindu pilgrims and *karsevaks* returning from Ayodhya. In retaliation, riots broke out in which 790 Muslims and 254 Hindus were killed and 2,500 injured.

In the affidavit filed in the Session Court of Ahmedabad on challenging Teesta Setalvad's bail plea, the SIT cited statements of a witness and said that the conspiracy was hatched at the behest of Congress leader Ahmed Patel. The SIT said that Teesta Setalvad received 30 lakh rupees from Ahmed Patel to destabilise the then Gujarat BJP Government headed by Chief Minister Narendra Modi.

Teesta Setalvad is the Secretary of 'Citizens for Justice and Peace' (CJP), an organisation formed on 1 April, 2002 to advocate for the victims of 2002 Gujarat riots. **The said amount of Rs. 30 lakhs were supposed to be meant for the welfare of the victims of 2002 Gujarat riots. Unfortunately,**

The said ill-gotten money was diverted and used for committing forgery, fabricating evidences and alluring people to give false affidavits. She was arrested on 26 June, 2022, on charges of forgery and fabricating evidence in the riot case and Foreign Contribution Regulation Act (FCRA) violations. **Teesta Setalvad was awarded Padma Shri as a reward by Congress Government in 2007 to destabilise the then Gujarat BJP Government and maligning the image of Narendra Modi, the then Chief Minister of Gujarat.** Teesta Setalvad is the wife of Javed Anand, a civil rights activist who founded the Mumbai-based Sabrang Communications in 1993. Activist Teesta Setalvad was enacting a larger conspiracy to destabilise an elected Gujarat Government soon after the Godhra incident of 27 February, 2002.

The Special Investigation Team (SIT) was formed to probe Setalvad along with R.B. Sreekumar, then ADGP, Armed Unit, for criminal conspiracy and forgery. The SIT cited statements of a witness and said that the conspiracy was hatched at the behest of Congress leader Ahmed Patel, the then Member of Parliament from Rajya Sabha and Political Advisor to the President of the Indian National Congress, Sonia Gandhi.

Whatever Teesta Setalvad did to destabilise Gujarat Government and implicate Narendra Modi, the then Chief Minister of Gujarat, was at the behest of the Congress top brass and with a clear political agenda. Initially Rs. 30 lakhs were paid to Teesta by the Congress. Setalvad held meetings with Ahmed Patel and received Rs. 5 lakhs as the first instalment. She received Rs. 25 lakhs more two days later, again by Patel. Patel succumbed to Covid-19 on 25 November, 2020. The cash money given to Teesta was not a part of any relief-related corpus but to purchase witnesses to implicate Narendra Modi and destabilise the State Government.

Rais Khan Pathan, a former aide of activist Teesta Setalvad, disclosed to SIT that all the activities undertaken by Teesta during the 2002 Gujarat riots were politically sponsored by the Congress Party and her only motive was to target the then CM, Narendra Modi and topple his government. In 2002, Patel came to Circuit House, Shahibaug in Ahmedabad. Teesta Setalvad accompanied by Khan had gone to meet Patel and told him that she was short of funds to execute the plan. Patel then called a person named Narendra Brahmbhatt, who was Chairman of the Hotel Association, and directed him to provide sufficient funds to Teesta.

Khan also stated that the affidavits filed on behalf of the witnesses in connection with the riots were scripted by Teesta Setalwad and the witnesses had no idea about what was written in the affidavits. Teesta didn't ask anybody before drafting the affidavits; nobody knew what was written in it. Even Madina Pathan, one of the witnesses, didn't knew what was written in the affidavit filed in her name.

Setalvad was arrested by the Gujarat Police on 26 June, 2022, in connection with a case related to alleged fabrication of evidence in the 2002 Gujarat riots. She was also accused of conspiring to fabricate false evidences, documents, tutor witnesses and abuse the process of law by fabricating false evidence to frame people, based on the submissions made before the SIT constituted by Supreme Court to investigate the 2002 Gujarat riot cases and before the Justice Nanavati-Shah Commission of Inquiry.

Teesta Setalvad and her, NGO were co-petitioner with Zakia Zafri in the petition filed against CM Narendra Modi and others in Supreme Court. Jafri's husband and former Congress MP Ehsan Jafri was killed during the riots at Gulbarga Society on 28 February, 2002.

The Crime Branch had arrested former Gujarat DGP R.B. Sreekumar (IPS-1971 Gujarat Cadre) on 25 June, 2022, in connection with a case registered against him for forgery and criminal conspiracy. Sanjiv Bhatt, another accused in this case, was already in jail undergoing life imprisonment for murder in police custody.

The FIR was lodged against Teesta Setalwad, R.B. Sreekumar and Sanjiv Bhatt after the Supreme Court in its observation said, **"As a matter of fact, all these involved in such abuse of process, need to be in the dock and proceed as per law."** In another case, Sanjiv Bhatt had been also charged with planting half a kg of narcotic substance to frame a lawyer.

The FIR was lodged against Sanjiv Bhatt U/S Section 468, 471 (Forgery), Section 194 (giving or fabricating false evidence with an intent to procure conviction), Section 211 (institute criminal proceedings to cause injury), Section 218 (Public servant framing, incorrect record or writing with intent to save a person from punishment or forfeiture of property) and Section 120-B (criminal conspiracy) of Indian Penal Code.

Teesta Setalvad, R.B. Sreeskumar and Sanjiv Bhatt have been accused of having conspired "to abuse the process of law by fabricating false evidence to make several persons to having committed an offence that is punishable with capital punishment".

Sanjiv Bhatt (IPS-1988-Gujarat) had sparked a controversy when he claimed that Narendra Modi, the then Chief Minister of Gujarat, had told senior police officials at his Gandhinagar residence on the night of 27 February, 2002, that people should be allowed to vent their anger against Muslims to avenge the Godhra incident. Bhatt, the then Deputy Commissioner in charge of Internal Security at the State Intelligence Bureau, had given evidences in courts and commissions regarding Gujarat riot cases. Sanjiv Bhatt tried to prove inaction of the State Government of Gujarat, saying it all happened with instructions of the top brass. He was also included as a key witness in Zakia Jafri's complaint in 2006. According to Bhatt, he was one of the first officers to report that the Godhra coach burning incident in February, 2002 could trigger retaliatory violence, which led to the deaths of almost 1,000 people. Sanjiv Bhatt was arrested by the Crime Branch of Gujarat Police for embezzlement of funds and forging documents. **Sanjiv Bhatt has been convicted to life sentence (30 years) in a custodial murder case. He had**

been removed from Government service for his misdeeds. The Leftist ecosystem always rallied behind the disgraced cop and overlooked his misdeeds since he was targeting Narendra Modi.

In 2012, Narendra Modi was cleared of alleged complicity in the violence by SIT appointed by the Supreme Court of India. The SIT also rejected claims that the State Government had not done enough to prevent the riots. In December, 2013, the court upheld the earlier SIT report and rejected a petition seeking Narendra Modi's prosecution. In April, 2014, the Supreme Court expressed satisfaction over the SIT's investigations in nine cases related to the violence and rejected a plea contesting the SIT report as baseless.

The Supreme Court on 24 June, 2022, gave a clean chit to then Gujarat Chief Minister Narendra Modi and 63 others in the 2002 riots in the State and dismissed a petition of Zakia Jafri, wife of slain Congress leader Ehsan Jafri's. Zakia had challenged the SIT's clean chit to 64 people including Modi who was Gujarat Chief Minister in 2002. A three Judge Bench, headed by Justice A.M. Khanwilkar upheld the Magistrate's order rejecting Zakia Jafri's protest petition against the closure report filed by the SIT in 2012.

□

Source index

1. Interrogation report of the terrorists of Indian Mujahideen—
   - Mohammad Ahmad Siddhi Bappa alias Yasin Bhatkal, Bhatkal Karnataka.
   - Bashir Hassan alias Talha alias Maulvi Saheb alias Master Saheb, son of Abrar Husain, Karbala Maidan, Barabanki, U.P.
   - Shahzad Ahmad alias Pappu alias Siraj Ahmad, son of Saiyad Rahmani, Manzil Mohalla Jalandhari, Kotwali, Azamgarh, U.P.
   - Salman Ahmad alias Fahad Ansari, son of Mohammad Shakeel, Sanjarpur, Azamgarh, U.P.
   - Irfan Ahmad alias Pappu alias Mohammad Yunus, son of Mohammad Farukh Bagbani, Nasirpura near Kasaiwali Masjid city Kotwali, Bahraich.
   - Mohammad Sadiq Sheikh alias Yasir aka Imran, son of Israr Ahmad, Para Phulpur, Azamgarh, U.P. and flat no. C/I/19, Cheeta Camp, Trombay, Mumbai.
   - Mohammad Saif alias Kariyan, son of Shadab Ahmad aka Mister, Sanjarpur, Azamgarh, U.P.
   - Syed Abdul Kareem alias Tunda alias Abdul Quddus (in Pakistan) alias Maulvi alias Anwar (in Bangladesh) alias Baba (in Lashkar-e-Taiba) alias Hakimji, son of Mohammad Abdullah, Chhatta Lal Miyan, Dariya Ganj, Delhi, and Bazar Khurd,

Railway Road, Pilkhuwa, Ghaziabad, U.P.

- Mohammad Sarwar, son of Mohammad Hanif, Village Chand Patti, Thana Raunapar, Azamgarh, U.P.

2. Police records of terror activities in Uttar Pradesh, Gujarat, Mumbai, Delhi, Bihar, Madhya Pradesh and Rajasthan.
3. The judgements given by different Courts against the terrorist activities.
4. Personal experiences of the writer while posted as ADG Police/Special DG Police, U.P. STF, ATS, Crime and Law & Order for four-and-a-half years from 2007 to 2011. Later, I was posted as DGP, U.P. This was the time when most of the terror activities were exposed and the terrorists were punished by the Courts. During this period, our close co-ordination with other State agencies in the country I have been able to collect a lot of vital information which helped in tracking and elimination of terrorist activities.